IN SEARCH OF
ELVIS

4-9-97

IN SEARCH OF ELVIS

Music, Race, Art, Religion

edited by
Vernon Chadwick

WestviewPress
A Division of HarperCollins*Publishers*

Cover illustration, *Happy 200th Anniversary Tennessee,* Howard Finster, 1995. Reproduced by permission of Gallery 721, Ft. Lauderdale, Florida, in conjunction with the Tennessee State Museum, Nashville.

Published in 1997 in the United States of America by Westview Press, 5500 Central Avenue, Boulder, Colorado 80301-2877, and in the United Kingdom by Westview Press, 12 Hid's Copse Road, Cumnor Hill, Oxford OX2 9JJ

A CIP catalog record for this book is available from the Library of Congress. ISBN 0-8133-2986-8.   ISBN 0-8133-2987-6 (pbk.)

The paper used in this publication meets the requirements of the American National Standard for Permanence of Paper for Printed Library Materials Z39.48-1984.

10   9   8   7   6   5   4   3   2   1

Contents

PART FOUR
RELIGION

PART FIVE
EPILOGUE

Acknowledgments

The editor takes pleasure in thanking the many friends, colleagues, and supporters who contributed generously of their time, talent, and good will to the Elvis conference and this book. I want in particular to express my gratitude to Bill Ferris, director of the Center for the Study of Southern Culture at the University of Mississippi, for his unstinting and courageous effort to "Tell about the South," the real South, all "white lies" notwithstanding; Colby Kullman, a loving and creative voice within the Ole Miss English Department, who instantly welcomed Elvis to the head of the class; and Larry Clemons, president of Gallery 721, Ft. Lauderdale, Florida, who shares the artistic and pedagogical vision of this book in every way.

My thanks also go to Ger Rijff for generously contributing rare photographs from his world-class Elvis archives; Trent Booker for reading the introduction in an early version and making many valuable suggestions; Anita Bryan for her help with securing photographs from the good folks in Tupelo; Larry Arnett of Light of Day Publishing for inspirational brainstorming and editorial advice; Earl White and Queen Elizabeth Weeden for being Soul Parents Number One; Peter Paul of DigIcon Media Group for his networking skills and entrepreneurial genius; Patricia Chadwick Lamar, my sister, for floating the letters E-L-V-I-S in red carnations in her swimming pool; and Milly Moorhead of Southside Gallery for opening her enlightened space on the Oxford Square to El Vez, Black Elvis, and Man of Visions.

This book and the labor that went into it I dedicate to my parents and their generation of old-style southerners, especially to my father, Dr. Vernon D. Chadwick, Sr., who saw Elvis perform at the 1956 Mississippi-Alabama Fair and Dairy Show in Tupelo while inspecting the animals for the Mississippi Livestock Sanitary Board.

Vernon Chadwick

Introduction

Ole Massa's Dead, Long Live the King of Rock 'n' Roll

VERNON CHADWICK

This book makes available the proceedings of the first annual International Conference on Elvis Presley—one of the most publicized and controversial academic conferences on record.[1] A six-day festival of learning that attracted participants from across America and around the world, the conference was held August 6–11, 1995, at the University of Mississippi in Oxford. A small southern town better known for William Faulkner than Elvis Presley, Oxford is located just forty-five miles west of Elvis's birthplace in Tupelo and seventy-five miles southeast of his home in Memphis, Graceland.[2] This area of north Mississippi and west Tennessee, extending southwest to Clarksdale in the heart of the Mississippi Delta, demarcates a "fertile crescent" of American civilization—the cradle of the blues, gospel, country, R&B, soul, and rock 'n' roll—as original and world-shaping as any before it. Call it Elvis Country.[3]

On the Road to the Elvis Conference

In 1990, when I returned to Mississippi, my native state, after an education that took me to Dartmouth, Oxford, the University of Freiburg (Germany), and Yale, where I received my Ph.D. in comparative literature, I was ready to put my learning to work. I wanted to break new ground for higher education, to open new fields and strike out on new paths. I was filled with many intuitions about what I felt needed to be done. I wanted to test, not merely apply, my training in methods of interpretation with forbidding names like hermeneutics, phenomenology, and ontology, methods well advanced in Europe but fledgling, or nonexistent, in the United States, especially in the humanities.

Elvis, both the historical figure and the discourse surrounding him, attracted me instantly. Apart from the intrinsic merits I saw in the topic of Elvis for serious discussion and analysis, here was a power, through sheer name recognition, that could attract interest to some of the neglected questions of higher education. In the first instance, Elvis names a class (poor, white, blue-collar), an experience (Depression-era), and an outlook (evangelical) to which little attention has been paid by mainstream scholars.[4]

I then looked north to Memphis. Graceland attracts 700,000 annual visitors who come from all parts of the United States and every country in the world. Only the White House boasts more visitors among private residences. Surely this popularity could be tapped not just for tourism and commerce but also for education.

In the spring of 1992, I taught one of the first university courses on Elvis in the country: "Blue Hawaii: The Polynesian Novels and Hawaiian Movies of Melville and Elvis." This course was designed to open the American canon to Elvis and vice versa. Read from the perspective of Elvis's Hawaiian oeuvre (*Blue Hawaii; Girls! Girls! Girls!; Paradise, Hawaiian Style*), Melville's Polynesian novels were Hollywood-style screenplays from a precinematic era. Viewed from the perspective of Melville's Polynesian oeuvre (*Typee, Omoo, Mardi*), Elvis in his Hawaiian roles was a Melville-style hero who transgressed boundaries of race, culture, and society.[5]

Soon after this and other successful experiments with Elvis in the classroom, I began planning an international Elvis conference. The conference would cross the same boundaries Elvis crossed in his music and movie roles. It would welcome scholars, artists, musicians, and ordinary people to join a new coalition of learning. Like Elvis's own national television debut on the Dorsey brothers' show in 1956, the Elvis conference would be no academic business as usual. No, it would be a wake-up call to America and the American university— "Get outta that kitchen and rattle those pots and pans." Elvis was about to come into his own as a rebellious, radicalizing force of democracy, equal opportunity, and free expression.

The Elvis Text:
Desegregating Higher Education

The Elvis conference and this groundbreaking book mark the beginning of the first comprehensive attempt to study the locality and life-world of "Elvis" and its diverse cultures. Assembled here is creative new thinking by interdisciplinary and independent scholars in music, history, sociology, cultural studies, and the "school of life," who employ "Elvis" as a gateway into issues of race, class, sex, religion, and everyday existence. This new scholarship surpasses what was once known as the study of "popular culture"[6] and represents an attempt to formulate a richer, more encompassing, and truer text of the American experience—the Elvis text[7]—beyond the narrow prejudices of high culture and even higher education. In this expanded textual sense, "Elvis" names not only the poor white kid from Tupelo, Mississippi, who rose to unprecedented stardom in the music and entertainment worlds of the latter half of the twentieth century, but also the unjustly neglected and maligned cultures of the poor, white, rural South. "Elvis" names civil rights, the musical and cultural integration that *preceded* legal desegregation in the South and throughout America. "Elvis" names the cultural liberation of Europe that followed the political liberation of World War II (see Jørgensen and Rijff in this volume). "Elvis" names the age of television and mass media in which a single name, stripped of all personal, familial, and regional identity, can live a life of its own as a global icon like any other multinational trademark. In short, the "Elvis" of this book is the thinker's Elvis who changes everything we thought we already knew.[8]

Just as Elvis Presley rebelled against the taboos of a segregated society in the 1950s, so too does the new Elvis scholarship marshaled in this book—which embodies the spirit of Elvis—*dissent* significantly from the academic status quo in the 1990s.[9] The reader will encounter no disembodied, professorial talking heads in these essays but rather real people, with personal histories and human voices, conversing, conferring among their peers. In keeping with his spirit of inclusion and rainbow coalition of musical styles, a conference devoted to Elvis Presley would have to cross the same lines of race, class, gender, and ethnicity in order to remain true to its namesake. Such is the scholarship of the Elvis conference and this book, such is their art of polyphony.

With its rich bricolage of photographs, artwork, and memorabilia, *In Search of Elvis* also breaks the mold of the classically unified academic book and suggests other forms of composition that the scholar-ship of the future may take. It incorporates both traditional and avant-garde elements into a new synthesis—at once academic, aesthetic, and personal—that reproduces a heterogeneous and diffuse social consti-tution of knowledge and reality. The resulting volume can be read on a variety of discursive levels: as *home companion* (a book that combines essays, art, reportage, and practical advice for lonely Americans on the frontier);[10] as *surrealist collage* (a polygeneric composition that ad-vances concepts of multidimensionality);[11] as *polyphonic novel* (a liter-ary construction consisting of the new arts of "radical divestment," "novelistic counterpoint," and the "specifically novelistic essay");[12] and as *discursive network* (a kaleidoscopic field of theory, data, and practice exemplified in the texts of Michel Foucault).[13]

The Elvis Conference: Toward an Insurgent Pedagogy

As an event staged at the University of Mississippi and, by extension, within the American university system, *In Search of Elvis* announces a new pedagogy that challenges traditional models of academic method and authority rooted in nineteenth-century conditions of so-ciety, knowledge, and information.[14] Elvis, the deep-rooted south-erner *and* free-floating Hollywood icon, solicits from his scholars both regional and global studies. Elvis, the personification of contem-porary media culture and the new societies and organizing principles arising from mass media and technology, solicits a new critical media literacy that recognizes the powerful cultural pedagogy constituted by information and entertainment.

The Elvis conference inaugurated its insurgent pedagogy—which opens up the university to multicultural, oppositional voices and inter-ests—by inviting two groups normally excluded from the academic conference: grassroots artisans (Elvis impersonators) and the general public (via the news media). The conference opened with a gala con-cert, hosted by Memphis bluesman Arnold "Gatemouth" Moore, and featured not one but *five* Elvis impersonators: young and old; white, black, and Mexican (see Chapter 15). While some were embarrassed by the "media circus" created by this unprecedented expansion of the arena of academic work and complained that such a hubbub of life was "beneath the dignity of the university," others recognized the multiper-spectival character of the conference's inaugural event, which exploded traditional divisions and privileges by which scholars arrogate authority to themselves and their work.[15] Who were the teachers and who the students at this conference? Who the performers and who the spectators? Who the kings and who the subjects? In the midst of this exhilarating misrule, I realized what the Russian literary theorist Mikhail Bakhtin was getting at with his notion of the "carnivalesque symposium" as opposed to the "classic symposium." Commenting on the famous "Palaver of the Potulent" episode in Rabelais, Bakhtin observes:

> This is a carnivalesque symposium. It has no external logical continuity, no unifying abstract idea or problem (as in a classic symposium). But the "Palaver of the Potulent" has a deep internal unity. It is one grotesque play of debasement carefully organized up to the minutest detail. Nearly every replica contains a formula from the higher level— ecclesiastical, liturgical, philosophical, or juridical—or some words of the scriptures applied to eating and drinking.[16]

Like Thoreau's Chanticleer or Whitman's barbaric yawp, the Elvis conference sounded a wake-up call to university apparatchiks that a new breed of educators is demanding historical, racial, class, community, and environmental accountability in the free exercise of their creative labors.[17] The Elvis conference launched a new commitment to regional, contextual, "worldly" studies that directly address the *ground* of the university and its shaping forces and claims.[18] The most obvious way that the Elvis conference addressed the historical ground of its institutional arena—the University of Mississippi—was by desegregating its academic work across divisions not only of race but of socioeconomic class and the concomitant social norms governing departmentalized disciplines.[19]

It was the Reverend Howard Finster, the visionary preacher and self-taught artist from the hills of west Georgia, who perhaps made the most eloquent case for the importance of the educational outreach represented by the Elvis conference and its democratic pedagogy. In his magnificent "Sermon on Alvis," Finster confessed to the conference:

> And they call me a folk artist. I got to teachin' and I only finished the sixth grade. Man, I never got no education. I'm still an unfinished student. I never even finished high school. And I felt like God sent me here for somethin', but I didn't know what it was. I couldn't figure out nothin' for myself because I felt down sorta, uneducated, only one man of his kind. No chance for me. I couldn't get inside of a schoolhouse door. I'll never even be invited to go and look over a university and see what they look like.[20]

For thousands of Americans, among them many southerners like Howard Finster who had to leave school at an early age to help their parents on the farm, the Elvis conference opened the door of educational opportunity where even an "unfinished student" is qualified to teach.

This book thinks Elvis in relation to the university. It is my hope that through classroom adoption it will return to the university, its ground, to continue the desegregating, democratizing cultural pedagogy of its conference original. The unsettling presence of Elvis on campus, reported in countless newspaper and magazine articles with such alarmist titles as "Presley Conference Causes Stir" (*Montgomery Advertiser*), "Mississippi Town All Shook Up About Presley Seminar" (*Vail Daily*), and "College No Place for Elvis" (*Idaho Statesman*), challenged the politics of exclusion still determining the popular image, if not also the institutional practice, of higher education in America. With its popular stereotypes of the "absent-minded professor" immersed in the "life of the mind," with its sentimental images of quiet tree-lined boulevards and bespectacled scholars cycling to the safety of library or laboratory, it's no surprise that Elvis and the kind of university he inspires, with all the noise and confusion and messiness of the world beyond, threatens the traditional identity of the cloistered academic.

The Names of Elvis

If Elvis offended, in addition to etiquette and good taste, American proprieties of region, race, class, gender, and sexuality during his twenty-three-year career as a controversial stage performer and unsettling cultural presence, the "Elvis" of the Elvis conference also offended proprieties of the proper name. In the analytical and interpretive discourses generated by the Elvis conference and recorded for the first time in this book, the name "Elvis" was used "improperly" in the sense that serious academic sentences addressing serious academic subjects were formulated in a serious academic place using the allegedly nonserious and academically illegitimate, even scandalous, name of "Elvis."[21]

This book examines "Elvis" within a variety of social, historical, cultural, and institutional contexts.[22] The historical Elvis himself was already many different personae and sobriquets: The Hillbilly Cat, The Memphis Flash, The King of Western Bop, The First Atomic-Powered Singer, and of course The King of Rock 'n' Roll. This Elvis, as Peter Nazareth (in this volume) has meticulously demonstrated, was the master of a wide and diverse range of vocal stylings and ventriloquistic effects, from the clear tenor of his country-western heroes (Roy Acuff, Eddy Arnold, Jimmie Rodgers) to the exaggerated vibrato of the gospel singers he loved (Jake Hess, Jim Wetherington, J. D. Sumner). Or take the movies, which comprise an accelerated series of reincarnations of Elvis in thirty-one feature films made in just thirteen years. In a dizzying mathematical sublime Kant would have admired, Elvis was Clint Reno (*Love Me Tender*), Deke Rivers (*Loving You*), Vince Everett (*Jailhouse Rock*), Danny Fisher (*King Creole*), Tulsa MacLean (*G.I. Blues*), Pacer Burton (*Flaming Star*), etc., etc., down to Dr. John Carpenter (*Change of Habit*), an alias Elvis would continue to use post-Hollywood for hotel registrations, airline flights, and hospital stays. Indeed Elvis seldom even looks the same in the tens of thousands of photographs taken during his lifetime and thereafter obsessively reproduced in magazines and books, including this one. This constantly changing look of Elvis, however, was not just self-studied. Rather, it emanated from sources more profound, enigmatic, and certainly worth investigating.

The protean and polysemic being of the historical Elvis is thus only compounded by the multiplicity of posthumous lives that the name "Elvis" enjoys in every culture and media market throughout the world today. As the frequency and variety of his name evoked in these and numerous other contexts suggests, "Elvis" names sheer naming power—a kind of "semantic manna." The inability or unwillingness to read the name of Elvis and the texts it produces, especially by the professional readers of the academic and media sectors of American society, testifies to a disturbing illiteracy that impoverishes our national discourse.

In Search of Elvis can be regarded as a kind of postmodern primer that opens up the book of American education to new ways of reading the heterogeneous texts in which our *real* existence (beyond all illusions and clichés of formal education and standardized literacy) is inscribed. To this end, it may be useful here to summarize a dozen or so of the discourses named in the text of "Elvis."

- *Elvis names musical integration and, by extension, racial and cultural integration.*

This is by far Elvis's best known and most enduring achievement.[23] Before Elvis, as Bill Malone, Stephen Tucker, and Jon Michael Spencer (in this volume) point out, there were notable examples of white singers experimenting with black vocal stylings (Jimmie Rodgers, Gene Autry, Red Foley, Bill Haley, Hank Williams, among others). But none had communicated a *feeling* and *being* as "black" as Elvis's total performance in song, dance, dress, and demeanor—or so his predominantly white audience of the fifties believed (and most feared). Since, in addition to black southern culture, there were sources of this ontological feeling in the spiritual comportment of Elvis's own white, Pentecostal southern upbringing (see Finster in this volume), to dismiss this integration as mere "imitation" and "minstrelsy," as nonsouthern critics frequently do, raises urgent questions about the role that racial and regional politics have played in the history of Elvis's reception in America. The Presleys lived perhaps as close to black life as was possible for a white family in the segregated South.[24] Inhabiting the margins between the two most marginalized subcultures of the Depression-era South—poor whites and poor blacks—Elvis opened white country and gospel to black blues and R&B to disclose a genuinely new sound and thereby cultural attunement.[25]

In future histories of the American civil rights movement, Elvis's achievement will figure more prominently than in current accounts.[26] Not only will this require a new method of analysis capable of reading social transformation in the texts of popular art forms like rock 'n' roll; it will also require serious reexamination of the racial and regional politics shaped by the climate of receptivity of the 1950s that continues to deny to poor white southerners any rights to racial enlightenment (see Campbell in this volume).[27] Elvis performed in song what Martin Luther King Jr. proclaimed in sermon. Both song and sermon, with their similar accents and gestures of racial and regional authenticity, were about feeling, a *moral* feeling that runs deeper than intellectualized prescriptions of law and legislation. Clearly, both kings appealed persuasively to a sentimentality prevalent in southern character and culture.[28]

Recognizing Elvis's contribution to civil rights in America (and it follows from this logic that an Elvis concert of the 1950s *should* be as socially disruptive as the marches and sit-ins of that same era) is doubly important because Elvis names an overlooked source of racial and cultural enlightenment in American social history—the poor, rural, working-class southerner, white and black. Elvis Presley gives a name and personal history to a window of opportunity that opened in the early 1950s and helped break the stalemate of segregation in the South and later in the United States as a whole (see Smith in this volume). It is crucial to recognize that the source of this social transformation did not originate with the political, religious, and educational establishments of the day. Rather, Elvis names a source of social reform that defies conventional models of leadership and the leadership classes as offered in official accounts.[29] Elvis defies the Kennedy model, for example, predicated on wealth, privilege, and formal education.[30] On the contrary, Elvis names the unlikely source, the genius "from nowhere," the possibility that, despite the best-laid plans of social engineers, something incalculable can arise and defy the odds. This is Elvis the "outsider artist," an inspiration to all disenfranchised, marginalized peoples around the world (see Paul and Elvis MacLeod in this volume).

- *Elvis names the spiritual bonds of regional community formed and sustained by grassroots southern music.*

Whether the conversation is about ragtime, blues, jazz, rockabilly, Cajun, gospel, R&B, rock, or soul, all these southern musics can be fruitfully addressed under the symbolic banner of "Elvis," the South's most famous champion of the people's music. Despite the reputation of southern literature as the hallmark of southern culture, despite heavy ideological and corporate investment by southern universities in southern literary icons like William Faulkner, it is music, rather than literature, that remains the South's most characteristic and enduring achievement.[31]

Without ownership of land or control over the means of production, poor white and black southerners strengthened ties of community and ethnic heritage through a rich and evolving array of folk and popular music, including ballads, bluegrass, blues, gospel, and old-time country. As Bill Malone demonstrates (in this volume), such traditional musical forms that nourished Elvis's early rock 'n' roll are also forces of social formation active in the maintenance of local and regional communities. Southern vernacular music evolved in a contradictory social context that combined the region's ills of poverty, slavery, disease, suffering, and deprivation with the solaces of religious fundamentalism and the miracles of faith. Elvis names the spiritual wealth of such poor southern communities sustained by musical fellowship. Although the rock culture Elvis helped to create eventually contributed to the dissolution of the communal bonds formed wherever grassroots music was traditionally played and heard—at home, church, school, country dance, or county fair—one source of Elvis's enduring appeal resides in the call-and-response bond of fellowship preserved in memories of legendary performances and still felt by fans in the recorded music. Elvis names the "soul" of the South.

- *Elvis names the politics of representation that works to secure dominant modes of authority through constructions of history and identity.*

By evoking the images and experiences of a different social narrative of southern history—that of the poor, rural, working-class South—Elvis not only unearths hidden histories worthy of attention but demystifies the act of representing itself. As Linda Ray Pratt's notion of the "Elvis South" suggests, southern history and identity are not objective, universal forms of social and political life but rather the results of relations of power sustained by such factors as race, class, gender, textual authority, and institutional structure:

> Elvis's South is not the old cotton South of poor but genteel aristocrats. His Mississippi is not that of Natchez. Elvis is the Mississippi of pulpwood, sharecroppers, small merchants. His Memphis had nothing to do with riverboats or the fabled Beale Street. Elvis's Memphis was the post–World War II city of urban sprawl, racial antagonism, industrial blight, slums, Humes High. He walked the real Beale Street. Despite Graceland, and "Dixie" in Madison Square Garden, Elvis was the antithesis of the Rhett and Scarlett South. But no one living in the South today ever knew the Rhett and Scarlett South. Southerners themselves go to Natchez as to a tourist attraction. Elvis's South was the one that most Southerners really experience, the South where not even the interstate can conceal the poverty, where industrial affluence threatens the land and air which have been so much a part of our lives, where racial violence touches deep inside the home, where even our successes cannot overcome the long reputation of our failures. Even Graceland is not really beautiful. Squeezed in on all sides by the sprawl of gas stations, banks, shopping plazas, and funeral homes, Elvis's beloved home is an image of the South that has been "new" now for over fifty years.[32]

Pratt's observation that "Elvis's South [is] the one that most Southerners really experience" reminds us of the hegemonic power of representational regimes that construct "reality" with an overlay of superior orders of experience maintained by such cultural practices as entertainment, education, religion, and tourism. The dominant forms of cultural self-representation enshrined in romantic fictions like *Gone With the Wind* thus demonstrate how such systems of representation legitimate strategies of inclusion and exclusion through their depiction of those who make history on the one hand and those who merely serve the makers of history on the other.[33] For his part, John Shelton Reed (in this volume) begins the work of a critical pedagogy of representation inspired by the Elvis South.[34] By juxtaposing a Presley family photograph in 1938, which features the three-year-old Elvis in floppy hat and overalls, with those sharecropping families portrayed by Agee and Evans in *Let Us Now Praise Famous Men*, Reed takes these historical images out of the realm of sentimentality and kitsch and restores them to their social and material conditions.

- *Elvis names the art and education of self-taught peoples outside the boundaries of mainstream culture.*

As art historians and cultural critics are beginning to recognize (see Herndon in this volume), the image of Elvis is one of the most creative sources of contemporary art.[35] Yet just as vital (and perhaps more) is the example and practice of Elvis as artist. Elvis, who had no formal training, was a *bricoleur*, someone who makes the most of his situation with whatever materials at hand.[36] As Roger Manley beautifully explains (in this volume), such artistic bricoleurs are usually working-class people who adapt their manual skills and familiarity with tools and materials to the free play of the imagination and the solution of problems. "Elvis," before any projection by the media, was already the greatest work of art of Elvis Presley. As early as his junior year in high school, Elvis, who could have easily become a third-generation sharecropper or common laborer like his dad, began reinventing himself and his future: His now infamous fifties proto-punk "look" was no mere costume but a "practice of everyday life," a calculated strategy that involved recontextualizing working-class clothes (the uniforms of carhops and truck drivers) together with the exotic duds of the artist outsiders he admired (Beale Street pimps, rhinestone cowboys, and flamboyant quartet singers).[37]

Of all the many thousands of artworks inspired by this famous image and name, Elvis Country has found its definitive map and scripture in Howard Finster's *Happy 200th Anniversary Tennessee* created for the 1996 Tennessee State Bicentennial Celebration (see the cover of this book). In this work, Elvis's guitar, which forms the central support of a Gothic window, holds open a music-enchanted region ("Sun Records All Ways Shines in Memphis") whose being the artist evokes in divine facts of place at once homely and momentous. Here, an Elvisian bricolage of aesthetics, spirituality, and small-time southern doings is gloriously *at work* disclosing the world and region of the Elvis South.[38] The very board on which this ontological disclosure of Elvis Country appears, as Finster reminds us, "Was Cut From A Window-Hole Cut From Paradise Garden."[39] Microphone in hand, guitar thrust between earth and sky, "King of Rock and Roll Elvis Presley" presides at the very axis of this opening of vision around and through which Finster's world-granting artistic play unfolds.

Inspired by Elvis the bricoleur, the self-taught, self-invented artist of everyday life, Joni Mabe, Paul and Elvis MacLeod, Howard Finster, and the other southern outsider artists profiled by Roger Manley (all in this volume) celebrate through their respective works their liberation from the race- and class-bound chains of southern hegemony. Elvis, the quintessentially modern working-class hero, inspires world-shaking cultural transformation not with pitchforks but with blue suede shoes.

- *Elvis names the contested line between the politically correct and the politically incorrect—how and by whom it is drawn.*

Some of the most heinous names in American English have been invented about the people of the Elvis South. As Will Campbell (in this volume) argues, names like redneck, white trash, trailer trash, cracker, Snopes are the last publicly permissible N-words in modern American usage. By recontextualizing the name "Elvis," using it as a legitimate tool of scholarly, even high-cultural analysis, the Elvis conference not only scandalized academic propriety but exposed the fact that such propriety is based not only on objective claims and interests but on the tacit acceptance of a world carved up by racial, regional, ethnic, and sexual slurs.[40]

The Elvis conference's valorization of the word "Elvis," which amounted to a linguistic act of human rights, is analogous to recent reappropriations and recontextualizations of the word "queer" in gay and lesbian studies.[41] Occupying the place of other in the symbolic order of polarized discourses, "Elvis" names a free-floating signifier available for multiple inscription: "Elvis" is code for "nigger," "queer," "Jew," "white trash," and so on. The new critical weapon called "Elvis" fashioned by the Ole Miss conference cuts through the stagecraft of such coded usage and exposes the hypocrisies of political correctness that blindly sanctions—wherever and whenever convenient and rhetorically necessary—the very linguistic bigotry its correctness professes to denounce.

- *Elvis names the South as "other" to the United States, the conflicted site of the "American Dream" in southern culture.*

The very fact that Elvis's phenomenal success story, unparalleled in American or world history, requires such lengthy, convoluted qualification (as this introduction and volume well attest) suggests something crucial for the study of Elvis and southern culture: The "American Dream" does not come easily to the South, and if it does come at all it is not maintained or enjoyed without the special burdens and contradictions that shape the region and its history:

> The inability of Elvis to transcend his lack of reputability despite a history-making success story confirms the Southern sense that the world outside thinks Southerners are freaks, illiterates, Snopeses, sexual perverts, and lynchers. I cannot call this sense a Southern "paranoia" because ten years outside the South has all too often confirmed the frequency with which non-Southerners express such views. Not even the presidency would free LBJ and Jimmy Carter from such ridicule. At the very moment in which Southerners proclaim most vehemently the specialness of Elvis, the greatness of his success, they understand it to mean that no Southern success story can ever be sufficient to satisfy a suspicious America.[42]

Pratt wrote this in 1979 during the first wave of public tribute to Elvis after his death. The same observation could be made about Elvis's reception in America nearly twenty years later, especially with regard to the firestorm of controversy ignited by the Elvis conference—that reincarnation and reassertion of his disturbing cultural presence in academic form. Yet there are also telling differences that need pointing out between the two periods of reception. In the mid-1990s not only was the origin of the view of Elvis's "lack of reputability" (personal or academic) predictably nonsouthern, as Pratt's analysis suggests; it also included a curiously strident, vociferous group of "new southerners," old and young, for whom Elvis can represent nothing of value for the South.[43] The new anti-Elvis southern consciousness, which cannot be simply equated with the moral denunciations of the fifties, suggests the extent to which the cultural, political, and economic colonization of the South has progressed since the late seventies.[44]

• *Elvis names the dynamics of religious formation.*

For those who can approach the phenomena of Elvis adoration with both objectivity and erudition, surely two decades after the singer's death all signs point to an emerging "Elvis religion"—as Gottdiener argues and Finster preaches (in this volume)—that both incorporates and parodies mainstream practices: Fan clubs are churches, impersonators are priests, song lyrics are scripture, souvenirs are relics, sightings are Second Comings, and of course Graceland and Memphis are the holy land for fans throughout the world who visit Elvis's tomb not as tourists but as pilgrims.⁴⁵ As matters of faith, there is nothing intrinsically more real or authentic (or holy, for that matter) about a vial of Elvis sweat treasured by an adoring fan than any other sacred object revered by orthodox religions (see Mabe in this volume).

Latin *religio* (obligation, bond) defines religion not in terms of the truth of dogma but the strength of communal bonds formed by shared belief. The most obvious expression of religious community is found in rites of worship in which a congregation publicly proclaims and preserves its relationship with the divine. Yet an even greater proportion of religious activity is devoted to sacred objects and sites (like Howard Finster's Paradise Garden) whose care and maintenance easily become ends in themselves, independent of explicitly defined and defended articles of belief.⁴⁶ Under late modern and postmodern social conditions, the old divisions of sacred and secular are breaking down around a new experience of that point of transcendence the ancient Greeks called *charisma,* or "divine gift." Elvis's world-shaking charisma, which was made manifest in numinous qualities of voice, face, and demeanor, is an example of a postmodern condition that finds more credible sources of faith in popular music, entertainment, and sports than in the dead metaphors of traditional forms of worship.⁴⁷

Taking the religion of Elvis seriously, then, has the salutary effect of disabusing us of notions we might otherwise harbor about the lofty origins of religious formation. Why not trust the processes of religious formation in our own midst as an indicator of past formations? Elvis here names the risks we take in exposing ourselves to the possibility of such truths. Struck by the religious character of the events surrounding Elvis Week in Memphis, which includes the famous Candlelight Vigil on the eve of Elvis's death, *New York Times Magazine* writer Ron Rosenbaum asked the pertinent question: "Is this the way it was when Christianity was formed?"⁴⁸

- *Elvis names a mechanism of group identity formation.*

No other figure in contemporary America functions as widely in the constitution of social groups, positively or negatively, as Elvis. It is not merely the case that most everyone has an opinion about Elvis. Rather, their opinions involve strong ideas and feelings about region, race, class, religion, morality, gender, and sexuality that supply the materials out of which identity is constructed. In the work of cultural studies, feminists, postcolonial critics, and critics of race, theories of identity formation involve various notions of difference and otherness. From these critical perspectives, identity is not derived from natural origins or the uniqueness of individuality but is rather *produced* through structured representations of difference and the other.[49] Identity construction based on "Elvis," pro and con, extends well beyond stereotypes of the "Elvis fan" and "Elvis fan club" and includes, in one way or another, the whole of modern media culture and its systems of representation.[50]

Witness the recent Elvis stamp election in which more Americans voted than in the 1992 presidential primaries. The choice between the young, thin Elvis and the old, fat Elvis involved more than the public's ideal perception of Elvis. Although the American public jokes mercilessly about "fat Elvis" (as he has been codified), it *identifies* with the eternally young one. Together, these acts of joking identification (which Freud has taught us to relate to the unconscious)[51] reveal something significant about the popular American psyche: Even as America knows that it is old, fat, bored, mean, and addicted—voicing its fears in jokes and other psychopathologies of everyday life—it still flatters itself in the image of the young Elvis—lean, energetic, rebellious, good-humored, and optimistic. The Elvis stamp election, easily derided by conservative critics as a meaningless but profitable publicity stunt, was in fact a revealing theater of national identity formation.

- *Elvis names the conflicted site of regional being in transition to modernity.*

Elvis at Graceland was a stranded Hillbilly Cat, but his tragedy was no mere personal failing. While the South changed, and in large part due to the social and cultural changes that Elvis himself helped to introduce, Elvis remained dependent on traditional forms of the maintenance of southern being. He surrounded himself with an extended family of friends, cousins, and trusted confidants. When he could no longer move freely in public, he rented amusement parks and movie houses in a vain attempt to re-create the lost communal life of his childhood and adolescence. In his later years—bored, depressed, and strung out—he regressed to food, not just to his infamous cheeseburgers (that symbol of modern America) but to the "soul food," prepared by his black cook and longtime friend Mary Jenkins, through which he communed with his rural Mississippi roots.

It was not just fame that isolated Elvis from the traditional support of friends, neighbors, and the intimate customs of small-town life on which he was raised. Rather, the period between 1957, when Elvis purchased Graceland, and 1977, when he died, was one of rapid modernization in the South that violently rent the social fabric of a belated, closed society. Industrialization, urbanization, civil rights, the sexual revolution, and the growing multicultural character of American life all contributed to these sweeping social changes that turned Elvis's southern mansion into a lonely outpost on a hill. "Squeezed in on all sides by the sprawl of gas stations, banks, shopping plazas, and funeral homes," writes Pratt, "Elvis's beloved home is an image of the South that has been 'new' now for over fifty years."[52]

Elvis names the South's painful transition to modernity. Though Elvis created modern forms of expression and behavior, he himself was made out of premodern stuff. Elvis names a generation of rural southerners who failed to cope with the challenges of the modern world.[53]

- *Elvis names a fateful intersection of the regional and the global in American culture.*

As the work of Malone, Nazareth, Reed, Gottdiener, and Neal and Janice Gregory (in this volume) demonstrates, the extremes of re-

The essays, photographs, artwork, and scholarship in this collection—"in search of Elvis"—make the music of funk, whereby music, race, art, and religion meet at the X of a cultural collaboration that has only just begun in America. Eyd Kazery. The Funky Flag. 1992. Collage photo, 8" x 10". Courtesy of the artist.

gionalism and globalism meet in the text of Elvis. Elvis studies offer a unique opportunity for scholars—whose questions are positioned *between* the modern and the postmodern, the local and the planetary—to explore a more subtle dynamic of human possibilities for the twenty-first century than either of these period concepts offers in isolation. As the first full-fledged creation of modern media, Elvis names the new forms of social and political life and the new modes of cultural production brought about by technologies of radio, recorded music, television, cinema, and more recently computers.[54]

- *Elvis names the funky intersection of music, race, art, and religion, which subtitles this book and its multicultural pedagogy.*

Several years ago I announced a new pedagogical imperative—"Make it funky!"[55] Rather than abolish the controversial symbols and traditions of the South's tragic past in the name of a dubious concept of progress, I proposed a new "work on myth"[56] that employs a certain strategy of recontextualization, counterpoint, and surrealist collage James Brown calls "funk." The Brownian imperative "Make it funky!" involves a peculiar "turnaround" that confronts the down side of life (literally *funk*) head on and through a miracle of musical transformation makes it "funky":

> Like the word from which it stole the name (meaning a stench stemming from sex), *funk* betokened a turn-around about what was "polite" in black society. The impulse which could turn an impolite adjective into the ultimate term of approbation presaged a re-evaluation of roots—one which led to the '60s slogan "Black is beautiful." Further down the line, that same transformation would inspire the battle against a "Eurocentric" concept of culture.[57]

The essays, photographs, artwork, and scholarship in this collection—"in search of Elvis"—make the music of funk, whereby music, race, art, and religion meet at the X of a cultural collaboration that has only just begun in America. Here, at this crossracial, crosscultural, crossregional divide, identity is not the corporate merger of forced homogeneity but the outcome of a permanent state of *difference* that embraces rather than evades the creative jabs and jostles between races, histories, and cultures. Elvis, the Great Integrator, ultimately names the very dynamic of the American social experiment.

Sometime in the mid-1960s, at the height of the civil rights crisis in the South, a historic meeting occurred between Elvis Presley and James Brown. As America's radios alternately crooned and blared their current hits—"Crying in the Chapel" and "Papa's Got a Brand New Bag"—these two sons of the South, the hardest-working men in show business, holed up together in a motel room in Los Angeles, singing gospel tunes late into the night: "The two Southern giants shut the door, shut out the world, and harmonized together on familiar chestnuts like 'Old Blind Barnabas,' jointly invoking a poor, rural South where the communal aspiration was somehow to ascend."[58]

This book is dedicated to the "funky flag"—black-and-white "stars 'n' bars" against a field of green—woven that night.

PART ONE
MUSIC

The Hillbilly Cat. *Love Me Tender*, 1956. Collection of Ger Rijff.

1 Country Elvis

BILL MALONE

Sometime in late 1955, during my second year as a student at the University of Texas, I attended a country music concert at the old municipal auditorium on the southern edge of Austin. I went to see my current musical hero, Hank Snow, and was bitterly disappointed when his portion of the show was cut short in order to bring out the evening's headliner, and to make way for a hastily scheduled second show. I do not know now which shocked me most, the physical gyrations of the young singer who dominated the stage that afternoon, or the screaming response of the young women who rushed the stage. After all, neither singer nor audience were acting like they were *supposed* to act— male country singers did not permit physical mannerisms to overwhelm or detract from the lyrics of a song, and neither they, nor country women, were permitted to exhibit sensual feelings in public.

I have long thought that, unlike many others who have given almost religious testimonies,[1] I clearly was not transformed by the experience of seeing Elvis Presley perform for the first time. My passion for music was strong, and as the product of a southern, poor-white, Pentecostal home, I shared a history of social and cultural experiences with Elvis far closer than most of my contemporaries who were swept away by his music. If anything, my search for traditional forms of country music became more intense, especially after 1957 when the rockabilly surge began to reach its peak. Bluegrass music, for example, became a refuge for me and many other "traditionalists" who saw the old styles of music disappearing from the radio and jukebox.

In retrospect, although I did not take up the guitar and become a rockabilly, Elvis's Austin concert did serve as a kind of transforming experience. For me, it was a barometer marking both the beginning of a revolution in American music and my own loss of innocence. I actually had become familiar with Elvis earlier, in the summer of 1954 when his first Sun releases were played on Tom Perryman's radio disc jockey show out of Gladewater, only thirty miles or so from my home in Tyler. I probably sensed then, well before the Austin concert, that the stirrings of a musical revolution were under way, and that southern boys and girls were already ripe for transformation. Rhythm-and-blues songs had begun to dominate the jukebox in the student center at Tyler Junior College before Elvis's first records were released, and my classmates had already discovered the joys of "Dirty Bop" and the suggestive lyrics of such songs as "Fever" and "Work with Me Annie." Nevertheless, until that afternoon in Austin, when the upstart Elvis upstaged the veteran Hank Snow, the physical dimensions of the musical change had not been clearly displayed to me, nor had I actually witnessed the stirrings of feminine revolt, as young women tentatively recognized and openly displayed their own sexual feelings.

Country music had seemed economically strong and stylistically pure in 1954, and had dramatically fulfilled the prophecy made in 1944 by the entertainment trade journal *Billboard*, which asserted that after the war was over, country music would be the "field to watch."[2] Powerful radio stations transmitted the music to all parts of the nation, and scores of smaller ones played both live country acts and country records periodically during their broadcasting hours. An estimated 400,000 jukeboxes contributed mightily to the burgeoning of a rejuvenated recording industry, and approximately 600 record labels introduced the nation's grassroots styles to a public that was eager to savor the prosperity that had been denied to them during the war.[3]

The man who had stood at the center of country music's postwar surge, Hank Williams, had died in 1953, but his records still played often on local radio and jukeboxes. While traditional sounds prevailed in the music of people like Hank Snow, Kitty Wells, and Webb Pierce, one could even hear some really old-timey sounds in the music of such entertainers as Bill Monroe, the Stanley Brothers, and the Louvin Brothers. Country disc jockeys still affected hayseed sounds and demeanors, and they actually played records requested by listeners. Furthermore, when a record started to play, the faithful country music fan could tell who the singer was, because Lefty, Hank, Kitty, and the others used their own musicians on recording sessions. Although stylistic differences certainly existed among country musicians, and terms like "bluegrass" and "western swing" were beginning to be attached to country subgenres by the middle of the fifties, most fans made no distinctions and could easily bestow their affections upon performers who were radically different from each other. All of the substylings seemed grounded in grassroots tradition, and most spoke with a southern accent.

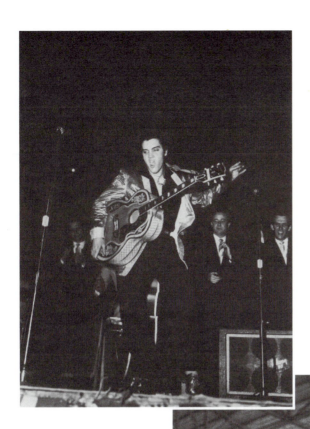

I do not know now which shocked me most, the physical gyrations of the young singer who dominated the stage that afternoon, or the scream-ing response of the young women who rushed the stage. Collection of Ger Rijff.

The social demographics of the era, however, tell a more interesting story. And they explain both the expansion of country music and other grassroots forms, as well as the emergence of Elvis and the Youth Culture that nourished him and the rockabilly phenomenon. Although the contours of change were already present in the rural South before the coming of the great conflict, World War II unleashed a social revolution in the region. Massive population shifts within the South, from agriculture to industry and from farms to cities, and to cities in the industrial Midwest and on the West Coast, promoted economic improvement, altered lifestyles, and new attitudes. Change, though, did not occur instantly, and the habits and assumptions of the rural past receded slowly. Millions of rural southerners changed their residences and occupations, but they found that folkways, values, or expectations could not change as rapidly. Most people approached the postwar period with hope and measured optimism,[4] but they remained cautious about the future. This sense of caution was apparent among our older brothers and sisters who had fought the war, and among my generation, which was born amid the scarcity of the Great Depression. Scarcity, though, slowly gave way to abundance, and our nieces and nephews—the famous baby boomers—grew up in an atmosphere of boundless expectations.[5]

For those of us who grew up in working-class households, our parents still thought in terms of limits and perceived the world through a fatalistic lens. They reminded us often of the Great Depression, and warned that another might surely come. Talk of a third world war was not uncommon during the early years of the Cold War, and the presence of the Atomic Bomb meant that such a conflict would be catastrophic (unless, of course, the United States made a preemptive strike on the Soviet Union).

With a folk wisdom born of experience and nourished by tradition, they told us to be cautious in our choices and not to expect too much from life. I will never forget what my father said to me when he left me off at Tyler Junior College on the first day of freshman registration in 1952: "Don't sign up for anything big like lawyer." And, at first, we *were* cautious. The Consumer Society did not immediately seduce us, but with its promises of clothes, cars, sexual fulfillment, and culture—pop culture—it gradually built a loyal and passionately committed following among the young people of the nation.

While postwar society might be more economically secure, few people before 1954 questioned the assumption that the traditional and "comfortable" hierarchy of relationships among men and women, blacks and whites, and young and old would be preserved.[6] Few of us realized just how strongly those relationships had been undermined by the war. Displaced country people responded to postwar society in a variety of ways, and with varying degrees of receptivity to urban life. In a world still marked by economic flux and shifting gender relationships, most men clung to the vision of patriarchal authority.[7] Many of them sought the comradeship of other men in situations that reaffirmed their masculine dominance. For some men (and an increasing number of women), the honky-tonk provided diversion and escape. In this institution that both eased and mirrored the transition from country to urban life, country music was being preserved and redefined.[8]

Although the honky-tonk won the allegiance of many displaced rural folk, it could not sever the cherished link that many of them maintained with the church. Even the honky-tonk singers, and their audiences, found it difficult to forget or ignore the moral injunctions generated by religious instruction. Consequently, honky-tonk songs were often laced with the themes of guilt and moral ambiguity. The "old-time religion" did bring sustenance to rural folk who were trying to preserve identity and make sense of the sometimes bewildering changes wrought by urban life, but the older forms of faith were changing just as subtly as the people who subscribed to them. As religion moved to town, initially into store-front churches, the tents of the charismatic healing evangelists, or the broadcasts of the radio evangelists, it changed in subtle ways.[9] It waged war with the world while simultaneously embracing many of its innovations—sophisticated advertising, radio, sound recording, and television. As wealth became more available to working-class southerners, the church's response to prosperity became increasingly ambivalent. Visions of "little log cabins" tucked away in "the corner of Glory Land" gradually gave way to promises of mansions in Heaven *and* here on earth.[10] Gospel music, the musical offspring of southern evangelical Christianity, exhibited a similar fusion of otherworldly concern and contemporary awareness. Most dramatically represented by the quartets that had originally emerged from the shape-note singing school tradition, gospel music experienced accelerated growth in the decade after World War II. Appearing often on radio broadcasts and at well-publicized all-night singings, the high-powered gospel quartets enjoyed a symbiotic relationship with country music, and their performances were readily available to southerners of all age groups.[11]

Radio, jukeboxes, the movies, the automobile, and television brought the nation's popular culture into the lives of all southern working people. Not only did these innovations integrate working folk more firmly into the socioeconomic processes of the nation, they also contributed to the making of a self-conscious youth culture. Like young people elsewhere in the nation, southern youth experienced the moods of confusion and uncertainty that gave rise to the famous "rebels without a cause." But southern working-class youths were undergoing additional stresses. Sharing uncertain economic futures, torn between the values of their parents and those promoted by popular culture, Elvis and his blue-collar generation were at once hostile to and envious of middle-class culture. Shut out of the mainstream, they nevertheless longed to enter it. On most levels, then, they were not rebelling at all.

Elvis and his generation were the first southerners to be so strongly molded by popular culture. Like most youth of his era, he was part of everything he heard. Well before his family moved to Memphis in 1948, he had begun to absorb a wide variety of musical sounds in his hometown of Tupelo, Mississippi. But in the big city, with its movies, radio stations, television, automobiles, and more readily available wealth, Elvis was presented with a smorgasbord of influences. Every form of southern music was available to him—the country music loved by his parents; the newer bluegrass style that thrilled him with its energy and speed; gospel music, above all, with its flamboyant singers who dressed smartly and sang with incredible power and vocal range; and rhythm and blues, which was attracting white youth everywhere with its freedom and spontaneity. Mainstream pop music, which sometimes borrowed from these forms, was, of course, constantly available too. And it is no wonder that Elvis admired people like Dean Martin and Perry Como, because they enjoyed a prestige far beyond that of grassroots musicians, and were dominant on the major television shows of the day (country musicians, in contrast, were still sitting on hay bales in the television series that featured them).[12]

By 1954 none of the southern grassroots musical forms were totally distinct from each other, and each had changed in certain ways as their performing contexts became more urban and national. Country, rhythm and blues, gospel, Cajun, and other "rural" southern styles, in fact, drew their vitality and strength from their contacts with the cities. Hundreds of small record labels introduced grassroots musical styles to America after the war, and, in a few cases, recording entrepreneurs consciously tried to fuse the styles of black and white performers. A few "racial liberals," in fact, like Sydney Nathan of King Records in Cincinnati and Sam Phillips of Sun Records in Memphis, tried to break down racial barriers by making black music available to white youth. We are generally aware of the "covers" of black music being made in the early fifties by such white singers as Pat Boone and Georgia Gibbs, but we need to be reminded that white country musicians had been borrowing from black sources since the beginnings of their music's commercialization in the 1920s.[13] Such singers as Jimmy Tarlton, Dick Justice, Frank Hutchison, and, of course, Jimmie

Elvis and his generation were the first southerners to be so strongly molded by popular culture. Courtesy of Tupelo Museum.

Rodgers recorded black-derived material in the twenties, while in the 1930s Cliff Carlisle, Jimmie Davis (who even made some early recordings with black musicians), Buddy Jones, the Allen Brothers, Gene Autry, Milton Brown, and Bob Wills dipped often into the recorded Afro-American songbag.[14] More immediately in his own youth, in the forties and early fifties, Elvis would have heard the covers of black material, both religious and secular, performed by such singers as the Delmore Brothers, Red Foley, Molly O'Day, Martha Carson, the Maddox Brothers and Rose, Hardrock Gunter, Bill Haley, and Hank Williams. The country boogie craze of that era exhibited its influence directly in the lead guitar playing and antic, slapped-bass styles of Elvis's first accompanying musicians, Scotty Moore and Bill Black.

Country musicians had always been fascinated with black rhythms and inflections, as had their "folk" forebears before them. Beginning as early as the ubiquitous black fiddlers, juba dancers, and spiritual singers of the nineteenth-century South, and extending through the early-twentieth-century emergence of ragtime pianists and blues performers, African-Americans had offered white musicians a means of getting off the beat, syncopating it, sliding notes together, and otherwise experimenting with rhythms in ways that had not been emphasized in European-derived styles.[15] Above all, they provided a musical forum for challenging old orthodoxies, rebelling against inherited

He found a way to distinguish himself in the hairstyles of the method actors, and in the loud and flamboyant clothing merchandized by Lansky Brothers on Beale Street.
Collection of Ger Rijff.

standards, and shocking people—presenting a way of being naughty and yet still conveying the feeling that someone else's culture was being utilized. Black culture was presumed to be hedonistic, and the white person who sampled it (whether he be Jimmie Davis, Gene Autry, or Elvis Presley) could always go back to his own, safe way of life after the experimentation.

Elvis's experiments with black music, then, had abundant precedents in the white country tradition. He was even preceded in the 1950s by Bill Haley, of "Shake, Rattle, and Roll" fame, who also toured with Hank Snow several months before Elvis teamed with the great country singer. No one in his right mind, though, would argue that Elvis and Haley were comparable in their treatment of black material or that Elvis was just one more country singer dipping into the Afro-American musical tradition. Elvis was indeed different, and the difference lay in the style of presentation. His country predecessors had performed material that was often sexier than that performed by Elvis; there is nothing in his repertoire, for example, comparable to Cliff Carlisle's "Tom Cat and Pussy Blues," Jimmie Davis's "Red Night Gown Blues," or the Light Crust Doughboys' "Pussy, Pussy." Nor does one find any single performance by Elvis that is as "black" in style or sound as songs performed earlier by, say, Jimmy Tarlton, the Allen Brothers, or Bob Wills.[16] Elvis always sounded like what he was, a white boy from the Deep South experimenting with black music, but his performances released a sexual energy, in both himself and his fans, that had never earlier appeared in "white" music.

If "revolution" accurately describes the changes that occurred in American music in the wake of Elvis's emergence, never was a "revolution" more innocently undertaken. When Elvis launched his recording career in July 1954,[17] he sought neither to defy nor break social conventions, and he certainly intended no defiance of his parents' culture. Like many southern working-class youth of his generation, he may have harbored some resentments against the middle-class culture that denigrated his people, their lifestyles, and their religion (on more than one occasion, Elvis defended his Pentecostal upbringing against the charges of holy-roller excess, and denied that his musical style was rooted in that church). He found a way to distinguish himself in the hairstyles of the method actors, and in the loud and flamboyant clothing merchandized by Lansky Brothers on Beale Street. Elvis was a "hillbilly cat" long before he unleashed his frenetic musical style upon a receptive world. Ultimately, though, he longed for mainstream acceptance.

Elvis's open display of sexuality, however, set him apart from all other white performers who had come before him. His fusion of boyish vulnerability and sexual daring did not simply appeal to women of all ages; it also brought to the surface the contending urges that lay at the core of southern masculine culture, the contest between piety and hedonism.[18] His discovery of his own sexual power came slowly, step-by-step, during the first several months of his career as he ventured out before the public. That recognition was paralleled and in fact preceded by a similar awakening among his fans. The shaking of his leg and the grinding of his pelvis, moves that Elvis liked to describe as nothing more than nervous energy, produced a similarly "nervous" response among his young female fans. Neither singer nor fans initially recognized the full sexual dimensions of this relationship. As these aspects became increasingly apparent to Elvis and to both his detractors and supporters, he consciously exploited his newfound power with each successive appearance. He seemed genuinely surprised and delighted with each awakening. When asked by *Louisiana Hayride* announcer Horace Logan how he came to rhythm and blues, Elvis gave a revealing answer that seems equally applicable to his discovery of his sexual charisma: "To be honest about it, we just kind of stumbled upon it."[19]

Elvis's rapid ascent as a pop-culture icon should not obscure the fact that his early years as an entertainer were spent within the boundaries of country music. Although he pushed those boundaries

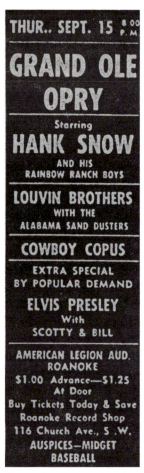

THUR.. SEPT. 15 8:00 P.M

GRAND OLE OPRY

Starring

HANK SNOW

AND HIS
RAINBOW RANCH BOYS

LOUVIN BROTHERS

WITH THE
ALABAMA SAND DUSTERS

COWBOY COPUS

EXTRA SPECIAL
BY POPULAR DEMAND

ELVIS PRESLEY

With
SCOTTY & BILL

AMERICAN LEGION AUD.
ROANOKE

$1.00 Advance—$1.25
At Door

Buy Tickets Today & Save
Roanoke Record Shop
116 Church Ave., S .W.

AUSPICES—MIDGET
BASEBALL

Except for the occasional national television engagement, most of Elvis's early professional appearances occurred at country venues, and usually with other country performers like Faron Young, Slim Whitman, and Hank Snow.

farther than anyone had ever taken them before, Elvis, in a sense, never strayed very far from the sensibilities of the little ten-year-old boy who sang "Old Shep" at the Mississippi-Alabama Fair and Dairy Show in Tupelo. As an adult performer, Elvis often sang this Red Foley classic, about an aging and dying dog, and never burlesqued nor made fun of it. He offered, instead, one of his most sincere and unaffected performances.[20]

Except for the occasional national television engagement, most of Elvis's early professional appearances occurred at country venues, and usually with other country performers like Faron Young, Slim Whitman, and Hank Snow. Despite the initial exposure given to "That's All Right, Mama" on Dewey Phillips's Memphis rhythm-and-blues show in July 1954, his other recordings generally played on country disc jockey programs. The publicity won over country radio, in turn, generated public appearances in areas blanketed by the stations' transmitters. Elvis was particularly popular in the region reached by the powerful transmission of KWKH and *Louisiana Hayride*—east and west Texas, western Louisiana, and Arkansas. And it was there that he exerted his most immediate and dramatic influence, when other young country boys with guitars, like Buddy Holly, Roy Orbison, Bob Luman, and Johnny Cash, abandoned the traditional styles of country music (or so it seemed) and embraced the musically and socially liberating sounds popularized by the Hillbilly Cat.[21]

Television introduced Elvis to America. Steve Allen's and Ed Sullivan's efforts to tame the young singer merely made him more fascinating and irresistible to millions of Americans. He turned increasingly toward the pop music that had always appealed to him, and he won an audience that lay far beyond the bounds of his native South. He never severed his connections with country music, however.

Nashville replaced Memphis as his chief locus of recording, and the vocal backing of gospel quartets and the instrumental support of Floyd Cramer, Chet Atkins, and other session musicians became indispensable and permanent ingredients of his performances. The sound heard on Elvis's recordings, in fact, closely approximated the country-pop compromise that Chet Atkins, ironically, fashioned to preserve country music's viability after the upsurge of rock and roll had sapped its strength.[22]

Elvis's impact on country music was obviously profound, but clearly not as shattering as the effects wrought on mainstream popular music. The pop music that Elvis admired so strongly—the music of Dean Martin, Perry Como, and Nat "King" Cole—virtually disappeared from public consciousness. Youth culture and its commercial allies took commanding control of popular music, and successfully insisted that their defining dictates be followed. Country music was similarly affected, but in ways that cannot easily be measured. By 1957 country recordings had virtually abandoned fiddles and steel guitars, and some great Nashville fiddlers, like Tommy Jackson, had to turn their interests toward the making of square dance records in order to survive. Out in the hinterlands, however—in the honky-tonks of Texas and in the country schoolhouse circuit where bluegrass bands performed—fiddles and other traditional instruments endured. Everywhere, one saw a search for new Elvises, or a demand that mainline performers add some ingredient of rock and roll to their performing style or repertoire. Consequently, performers as varied and as hard-core country as the honky-tonker George Jones or the bluegrass duo the Stanley Brothers included rocking sounds in some of their performances. The most immediate tribute to Elvis, however, came with the proliferation of rockabillies, the young men and women who did not abandon the country music of their parents but instead combined it with the rocking beat of rhythm and blues. For a brief period, they invaded the pop-music charts—the furthest intrusion ever of the blue-collar South into the mainstream of American popular culture.[23]

Nashville's response, the country-pop compromise engineered by Chet Atkins and other record producers, did contribute to the survival and expansion of country music by making it palatable to a large group of listeners who liked neither rock and roll nor the rural or honky-tonk connotations of traditional country music. While the compromise did result in some great music, such as that of Jim Reeves and Patsy Cline, it too often produced a product that lacked both soul and clear definition. Even its chief architect, Chet Atkins, eventually admitted that the compromise had gone too far, and that country music was losing its identity.[24]

Ironically, the neotraditionalist movements that have occasionally surfaced in country music in the last two or three decades have been directed not against the rockabilly style that seemed so scandalous in the mid-fifties, but against the country-pop phenomenon. Only a few singers, such as Ricky Skaggs and Dwight Yoakam, have consciously articulated protests against the pop impulse, but a much larger number have revived or updated styles that derive from country music's past.[25] Usually these are sounds and songs that the singers absorbed while growing up, either from commercial sources or from their parents. And these sounds include rockabilly. As this Memphis-born phenomenon faded from the popular music scene, it left its marks on the music of mainstream country musicians.

Many young people who were first attracted to music through the performances of Elvis and the other rockabillies later drifted into country music, sometimes becoming disc jockeys when all-country radio stations proliferated in the sixties, or more often becoming singers or instrumentalists. Fender electric guitars and basses became the proud possessions of country musicians everywhere, and instrumental licks born in rock and roll moved into the music of most country bands and even into the "pure" acoustic domain of bluegrass music. Even the pedal steel guitar—one of the defining sounds of modern country music—won a new lease on life as well as a new audience in the playing of musicians who served their apprenticeship while playing with such country-rock musicians as Ricky Nelson and the Flying Burrito Brothers. Later, country music became a retreat for aging rockabillies, like Conway Twitty, Jerry Lee Lewis, and Bob Luman, who adjusted beautifully to hard country styles, and a haven for newer singers such as Gary Stewart and Billy "Crash" Craddock who were attracted to the rockabilly idiom. Stewart built a style that suggested no real incompatibility between rockabilly and hard country. Veering between the rollicking, hedonistic sound of rockabilly, and the earnest, cry-in-your-beer lament of honky-tonk, he in fact demonstrated that the two styles came from the same source—the divided psyche of southern working-class culture. Yet some of the newer singers, like Craddock and Ronnie McDowell, even affected the look and style of the later Elvis, complete with sequined jumpsuits, swept-back hair, and swaggering demeanor. In country music as a whole, aggressive sexual energy and a sensuousness of style, in both presentation and song, became more apparent in the days following Elvis's emergence.

Most modern country singers have incorporated elements of Elvis and the rockabillies into their performances, not as a conscious imitation but merely as part of a synthesis of sound drawn from all of the musical forms that have been available to them. Like Elvis, they are a part of all they have heard. Most of these musicians would probably be surprised to hear that controversy once swirled around the rockabilly genre, not merely because Elvis's music seems so innocent today, but because his style has been so thoroughly integrated into today's country music. The influence of the later Elvis, with the patterned and highly choreographed Las Vegas style, can be seen and heard in a host of modern country performers, ranging from Tanya Tucker to Sawyer Brown, Billy Ray Cyrus, and the Oak Ridge Boys. But, ironically, it is the early Elvis—the one who seemed to be destroying traditional country music—that remains most attractive to today's young country singers. Buck Owens, for example, along with his indispensable electric guitarist, Don Rich, were hailed in the 1960s as saviors of traditional country music, even though their hard-edged honky-tonk sound received its punch and vigor from an infusion of rockabilly. Owens's most ardent disciple, Dwight Yoakam, has fashioned a similar fusion of sounds, along with an array of sinuous and sexy stage movements, while becoming one of the most successful and outspoken neotraditionalists of our own time. To singers like Yoakam, Marty Stuart, and Travis Tritt, rockabilly is a vital *traditional* country style that merits preservation.[26]

Forty years have passed since that afternoon in Austin when Elvis walked across the stage of the coliseum and instantly forced me to reassess my illusions of country music purity and my confidence in the stability of the southern rural society that nurtured me—even though my leaving home to enter the University of Texas had done far more to shake the bedrock of those foundations. I'm sure that I still hold my share of illusions, but I like to think that time, reflection, and study have given me a more mature understanding of what I only vaguely sensed in 1955. Country music, for example, would have changed dramatically without Elvis's intervention. As an organic expression of a working-class culture that was itself undergoing profound change, country music had no choice but to change, or to find itself becoming a relic known only by a few uncompromising traditionalists. Of course, I thought of myself as a traditionalist at that time (and still do), but I did not fully understand then that "tradition" is a relative term, or that traditional expressions of music must incorporate elements of both the past and present in order to be authentic representations of an evolving culture. Above all, I could not have foreseen in the mid-fifties that rebirths of "tradition" would periodically occur in country music, and that they would in some cases receive their most vital reinvigorations from entertainers like Gary Stewart, Dwight Yoakam, and Marty Stuart who grew up under the rockabilly influence unleashed by the young man from Tupelo.

Country music's fate, though, was not the only matter that troubled me in the mid-fifties, nor was it the only concern that I carried away from Elvis's performance. Why was I troubled by the music of a young man whose age was almost the same as mine, and whose social and cultural background was remarkably similar? Personal prudishness, of course, helps to explain the queasiness I felt when Elvis's pelvic thrust evoked screams of delight from the Austin girls; then again it may have been jealousy that aroused my disquietude. Beyond that, I think I may have also sensed the crumbling of a familiar world while feeling no small measure of guilt at my own personal role in the abandonment of that world through departure from my family's circumscribed culture and through my enrollment at the University of Texas. I was not yet mature enough to know that many aspects of that world needed to disintegrate. Music was not the only domain where "country" was becoming a blurred entity. A similar vagueness had insinuated itself into every aspect of life, as a new working-class synthesis—forged in urban settings throughout the South, and built out of a mixture of tradition and innovation—replaced the rural consciousness of the past. Most working people I knew eagerly embraced the material fruits of this new society, but few people adapted immediately or easily.[27] Elvis's personal synthesis—conscious and unconscious—wrought profoundly revolutionary consequences for American popular culture.

The entire scheme of relationships through which I was taught to view the world and my place within it was collapsing. Whether viewed as a liberator, a synthesizer, or nothing more than a cultural barbarian, Elvis acted as a dynamic agent of change who forced Americans to reassess their cultural priorities and definitions. His critics and detractors understood far better than I did what his ascendancy meant, and, whether speaking with the moral outrage of a fundamentalist preacher, the hauteur of an establishment art critic, or merely the condescending contempt of a Steve Allen, they set out to ridicule, restrain, or tame him. Elvis certainly did not single-handedly unleash the changes that swept across America in the two decades following his emergence, but to a remarkable degree he became emblematic of America's social transformation. Elvis was perceived as a threat in the fifties because he and his music fundamentally endangered the consensual social order of generational, gender, racial, class, and even regional relationships. Elvis and his music represented the emerging dominance of youth culture, the growing importance and sexual self-awareness of women, the attractiveness of black culture, the assertiveness of working-class culture, and movement of the southern version of that culture into the national mainstream. Elvis, in short, challenged the very idea of culture that had been supreme in the United States.

Elvis should be remembered and valued for many reasons, not the least being his role in the redefinition of culture in our country. Because of him we may have inched a bit closer toward an appreciation of the varied strands and multicolored hues that brighten our cultural tapestry. And we may have come closer to an understanding that our popular culture is not a national embarrassment, but one of America's great contributions to the world. I would like to think that he also contributed to the dissipation of one of America's most enduring prejudices, that directed against the southern-white working class. He and the other rockabillies introduced their versions of culture, and their "good time" vision of life, to a receptive world at a time when only bigots and racists seemed to dominate the mental landscape of the South. Along with Fats Domino, Little Richard, and other southern exponents of rhythm and blues, they not only enriched the music of the world, they also reminded us, at a time of growing racial polarities, of the affinities of southern-white and -black culture.

Elvis, of course, now belongs to the world. It is fitting that proper emphasis should be devoted to his enormous cultural impact, but I am pleased that the organizers of the first international Elvis Presley conference have not forgotten his roots as a southerner and a country singer. We need to remember that not only did the southern and country Elvis precede the international one, but that those roots always endured as defining traits of both the man and his music. I once despaired of the threat that Elvis Presley supposedly posed for country music, and in a modest way my scholarship may have contributed to the perception that he otherwise stood totally apart from that music's development.[28] In an act motivated by both admiration and contrition, I speak now, as an older and I hope wiser man, to reaffirm

Elvis's crucial role in country music history and to complain that he has never been named to the Country Music Hall of Fame. My concluding way of recalling and commemorating the country Elvis, while also proudly linking my own cultural history with his, is to remind you of that fine old country song that meant a lot to both myself and Elvis Presley, and to many kids who grew up in the years following World War II: "Old Shep."[29] I wish to recall the song in the way that Elvis treated it, not as a piece of kitsch, but as a loving recollection of that sincere and sentimental culture that produced us both. Elvis first publicly sang this song at the Mississippi-Alabama Fair and Dairy Show when he was ten years old; he was still singing and recording it many years later as an adult. As you know, Elvis used several different styles or voices when he performed his songs. When he sang "Old Shep" he sang in a perfectly straight manner, with no sensuousness or exaggerated vibrato. This, I think, was his paean to the way of life in which he was rooted, and from which he rose as an unwitting revolutionizer of American culture.

2 Rethinking Elvis and the Rockabilly Moment

STEPHEN TUCKER

Many years ago, in an early attempt to assess Elvis Presley as a cultural phenomenon, I closed an essay by musing that each of us has our own vision of Elvis.[1] Although somewhat less than profound, the statement stands true today, especially after a review of much of the literature devoted to explaining Elvis in the ensuing years and in light of the impressive and varied approaches taken during this most stimulating conference. Fundamentally, all of this is recognition and tribute to the truly protean talent of the young man from Tupelo.

But if it is true that there seems to be an unending procession of views of Elvis, it is equally true that one image occupies center stage and remains dominant, that of a young, guitar-wielding, hyperkinetic dervish—in a phrase, "Rockabilly Elvis." It is the Elvis of the U.S. Postal Service, Sam Phillips, Sun Records, *Louisiana Hayride*, Memphis, and Gladys, in contrast to the Elvis of Colonel Parker, RCA, Las Vegas, "Aloha from Hawaii," and Priscilla. It is Elvis the Hillbilly Cat, the King of Western Bop, the Tupelo Flash, the World's First Atomic-Powered Singer, the Boy Who Dared to Rock, and so forth. It is the Elvis poised forever in time in the fullness of what Greil Marcus called "the Rockabilly Moment."[2]

It is an image of relative purity, innocence, and possibility and thus one that appeals most directly to Elvis scholars—that vanguard of observers, pundits, and commentators represented so well here and now at this university. So it is an image freighted with meaning and heavily larded with prose that has ranged from the profound to the simplistic. Perhaps it is appropriate to reexamine Elvis in the context of the rockabilly moment and to reexplore the many dimensions of the music, particularly as we recognize its venerability.

The First Atomic-Powered Singer. Tampa, July 1955. Collection of Ger Rijff.

It all seems so fresh, even at a removal of four decades and who knows how many generations. Elvis, Scotty Moore, Bill Black, and Sam Phillips somehow created rockabilly music in Memphis in 1954. It was a genuinely synthetic concoction that surged across musical categories and leaped cultural barricades, emerging from the cramped confines of that tiny studio at 706 Union Avenue. It borrowed from white gospel, bluegrass, hillbilly boogie, black gospel, country blues, and rhythm and blues. It echoed not just the Grand Ole Opry and the Apollo Theatre but also minstrelsy, vaudeville, and Tin Pan Alley. Here Arthur Crudup met Bill Monroe in the shadows of Al Jolson, Louis Jordan, the Maddox Brothers and Rose, Tennessee Ernie Ford, Red Foley, Roy Brown, Hank Williams, and Dean Martin. Here Sam Phillips first began to realize his long-held dream of a crossracial sound, a sound that he had envisioned but never really heard. His struggle had yielded only near misses: Harmonica Frank Floyd, Doug Poindexter, and Charlie Feathers, who joined the noble but flawed efforts of more famous musicians of the era: Johnny Ray, the Crew Cuts, Billy Haley, and Pat Boone.

It all changed at once. "Before Elvis, there was nothing," John Lennon once said.[3] Journalist and native Memphian Michael Bane put it this way in his book *White Boy Singin' the Blues*: "It is seldom that history and fate conspire to give us a single point that we can look back on and say, 'There. It changed then.'"[4]

Of course, those who create also inspire. And so the rockabilly moment lingered. And still lingers. Depending on one's critical flexibility and semantic resilience, rockabilly music flourished a good four or six years. Its heyday was unquestionably 1954 to 1958, arguably 1954 to 1960. Such minor distinctions aside, the far more important point remains clear: Just as many claimed to have played rockabilly before Elvis, many more have continued to perform in his style.

As Peter Guralnick has argued, rockabilly was, in one sense at least, largely an act of homage to Elvis, as scores of young men and women emerged from places like Bemis, Tennessee; Ferriday, Louisiana; Wink, Texas; Tin Town, Missouri; Pocahontas, Arkansas; West Point, Mississippi; Norfolk, Virginia; and dozens of locations in between and far beyond, including eventually Minnesota, New Jersey, California, and Canada.[5] Before the moment passed, rockabillies emerged among Louisiana Cajuns and Chicanos from south Texas. Rockabilly music encompassed the enduringly great—Carl Perkins, Jerry Lee Lewis, Johnny Cash, Roy Orbison, Buddy Holly—and the fleetingly creative—Jimmy Lloyd ("Rocket in My Pocket"), Hank Mizell

("Jungle Rock"), Joe Penny ("Bip a Little, Bop a Lot"), Skeets Mc-
Donald ("You Oughta See Grandma Rock"). Sun Records alone
yielded such exemplars as Billy Lee Riley, Sonny Burgess, Carl Mann,
Hayden Thompson, Warren Smith, Conway Twitty, and Charlie
Feathers. Rockabilly embraced the febrile savagery of Memphis's
own Rock 'n Roll Trio (Dorsey and Johnny Burnette and Paul Burli-
son), the sublimity of the Everly Brothers, the slick pop of Tommy
Sands. It ranged from those near the country mainstream—Johnny
Horton, Marty Robbins, and even Webb Pierce—to Hollywood and
Ricky Nelson. It included the fiercely talented Gene Vincent and the
immensely gifted Eddie Cochran. Rockabilly generated numerous female artists: Janis Martin, Maggie Lewis, JoAnne Campbell, Lorrie
Collins (in tandem with her prepubescent guitarist brother, Larry),
the magnificent Wanda Jackson, the frighteningly precocious Brenda
Lee. It gave us Dale Hawkins, Boogie Boy Perkins, Sonny Fisher,
Benny Joy, Al Ferrier, Ersel Hickey, Sleepy LaBeef. The rockabilly
realm included a king and many commoners, a few giants and many
dwarves, all of whom at one time or another made—to my ears at
least—the most joyous, exuberant, exhilarating, aggressive, and bois-
terous music of the age.

Rockabilly was a music that was readily identifiable but difficult to
define.[6] It was chiefly a subgenre of country music, the overwhelming
majority of whose purveyors were white southerners. They sang
most often with a strong southern accent complemented by a gaggle
of vocal gymnastics—hiccuping, gliding into a lower register, swoop-
ing up to a falsetto, growling, howling, and stuttering. The classic
rockabilly lineup was an acoustic rhythm guitar, an electric lead guitar, and an acoustic stand-up bass. Over time, drums, electric rhythm
guitar, electric bass, piano, saxophone, steel guitar, and fiddle made
appearances. "The beat, the beat, the beat," Reverend Jimmy Rodgers
Snow (himself a type of lapsed rockabilly) stridently sermonized, was
at the heart of the rockabilly moment.[7] It was insistent and infectious
but seldom heavy and never ponderous; rockabilly rhythm echoed
freedom, buoyancy, and youth, with only occasional gestures toward
the darker side of human nature. It was tough, bold, sexy, and wild.

Sociologically, rockabilly represented the emergence of a teen-oriented consumer subculture. Increased leisure time and a spreading affluence, along with patterns of suburbanization, reinforced the new
subculture. Postwar adolescents found themselves relatively free
from the pressures of poverty and war with four years of high school
to be experienced in relative isolation from parental oversight and

with unprecedented personal freedom, symbolized by the motorcycle and the automobile, the drag strip and the drive-in. They acquired almost by default a generational outlook and mind-set with specialized tastes in food, clothing, transportation, and entertainment, especially music. Rockabilly was an early salvo from the South, heralding a new cultural civil war, this time more generational than geographic, the authentic aural complement to Brando's sullen defiance and James Dean's inarticulate but tormented dissent.

Economically, rockabilly was a product of the decentralization of the record industry, exemplified by the emergence of independent companies, each catering to specialized tastes. Such was Sun, a business that reflected both the experimental temperament of its owner and the largely untapped riches of Memphis's music culture. Sun was deliberately and conspicuously dedicated to individualism, nonconformity, originality, even eccentricity. "All of 'em were totally nuts," said publicist Bill Williams about the Sun artists. "They were free spirits, they were all uniques. I think every one of them must have come in on the midnight train from nowhere. I mean, it was like they came from outer space."[8] The rockabilly moment, then, was a testimony to the entrepreneurial and the artistic spirit. As always, Elvis served as a paragon and exemplar.

Rockabilly inevitably brought questions of race to the surface as it emerged almost simultaneously with the modern civil rights movement. Although it may be difficult to agree that the early Elvis sounds particularly black, it was not so obvious in the Deep South of 1954. We recall Dewey Phillips's anecdote (first told to Stanley Booth) about adducing Elvis's all-white school affiliation so as to reassure radio listeners of his race, even as we remember Phillips's own indiscriminate use of black patois.[9] We instantly recognize the sentiment behind the characterization of rockabilly by a spokesman for the Alabama White Citizens Council as "animalistic rock 'n roll nigger bop," a judgment that echoed sharply across the South for years.[10] Much of the basis of the Nashville country music establishment's antipathy towards its bastard child from Memphis was clearly racial. Paul Ackerman, the *Billboard* editor who championed the new style, received heavy criticism in Nashville for this very reason. One could hardly mistake the thrust of country disc jockey Randy Blake's editorial broadside, published in *Downbeat* in 1955: "Country music is country music, period. Rhythm and blues is a field unto itself."[11] A recent historian has put the matter succinctly: "Clearly the grid had been taken out of the ice cube tray."[12] With Montgomery, Little

Rock, Selma, Albany, Birmingham, and ultimately Memphis ahead, rockabilly served its own notice of a new day.

Lyrically and thematically, rockabilly expressed the black influence in imaginative terms. "Ubangi Stomp" and "Jungle Rock" were only two such attempts. Other themes also emerged: the medicinal property of the new sound in the Rock 'n Roll Trio's "Rock Therapy"; generational division in "You Oughta See Grandma Rock"; generational malaise in Eddie Cochran's "Nervous Breakdown" and "Summertime Blues"; and an entire gallery of tributes to teen heroines, as in Johnny Cash's "Teenage Queen," Cochran's "Jenny, Jenny," Jerry Lee Lewis's "Milkshake Mademoiselle," Warren Smith's "Rock 'n Roll Ruby," and Gene Vincent's "Teenage Partner." Dancing often served as a metaphor for freedom, as in the Rock 'n Roll Trio's eponymous "Rockabilly Boogie," Gene Vincent's "Blue Jean Bop," and Carl Perkins's "Dixie Fried." Teen consumerism found sublime expression in Cochran's "Somethin' Else." As always, Elvis had gotten there first with the most—his "Good Rockin' Tonight," "I Wanna Play House," and "Milkcow Blues Boogie" were nothing if not anthems of the new style and attitude, suggestive in the extreme. It was he who gave us the Pink Cadillac as the material touchstone of the moment.

It is the spirit of rockabilly music, however, as Nick Tosches has stated, that sets it apart, a spirit that "bordered on mania."[13] We owe to Tosches and other astute commentators, especially Guralnick, Marcus, Dave Marsh, and Robert Palmer, our growing appreciation of the literary context of rockabilly music. We are now free to see Elvis as the fulfillment of Whitman's hopes for a vulgar domestic cultural awakening, to hear at last the culmination of his prophetic call in *Democratic Vistas* for a measure of "Tennessee repartee." In Elvis we can now see Billy Budd, Natty Bumpo, the Marble Faun, and Huck Finn himself, questing for interracial understanding in the midst of savage inequalities. Elvis suggests so many literary connections, high and low—Roy Hobbs, Danny Fisher, Stag Preston, Conrad Birdie, John Milner, and Leroy Kirby, to name just a few.

Most of all, we recognize Elvis and his rockabilly cohorts most clearly in W. J. Cash's splendid portrait of the "Man at the Center" in his *Mind of the South.* The romantic hedonist personified the essence of the southern character in Cash's construction, which was written over a decade before the rockabilly moment. Let us again immerse ourselves in Cash's swelling prose. "Inevitably then, the dominant trait was an intense individualism" that exhibited a "tendency to violence" coupled with romantic hedonism:

Most of all, we recognize Elvis and his rockabilly cohorts most clearly in W. J. Cash's splendid portrait of the "Man at the Center" in his Mind of the South. *The romantic hedonist personified the essence of the southern character in Cash's construction, which was written over a decade before the rockabilly moment.* Collection of Ger Rijff.

He stands before us . . . as a romantic and a hedonist . . . he is inevitably back upon imagination . . . his world construction is bound to be mainly a product of fantasy . . . his credibility is limited only by his capacity for conjuring up the unbelievable . . . he is the child-man, that primitive stuff of humanity lies very close to the surface in him . . . he likes naively to play, to expand his ego, his senses, his emotions . . . he will accept what pleases him and reject what does not . . . in general he will prefer the extravagant, the flashing, and the brightly colored.[14]

What of the influence of black culture? "Negro entered into white man as profoundly as white man entered into Negro," Cash wrote, "subtly influencing every gesture, every word, every emotion and idea, every attitude."[15]

Cash also emphasized the southerner's "fondness for rhetoric" that, combined with the black influence, produced a "tendency to seize on lovely words, to roll them in his throat, to heap them in redundant profusion one upon another until meaning vanishes and there is nothing left but the sweet, canorous drunkenness of sound, nothing but the play of primitive rhythm upon the secret springs of emotion."[16] And, finally, Cash incisively described the effect of "orgiastic religion" with its "jazzily febrile" hymnody on his man at the center, the very force, in the form of Pentecostalism, that animated and catalyzed rockabilly music.[17] In sum, Cash's portrait was as accurate, albeit unintended, a depiction of the rockabilly generation as it was of those earlier young southerners who manned Stonewall Jackson's army. It explains the strange alchemy of "Mystery Train," "Great Balls of Fire," "Get Rhythm," and "Dixie Fried" as effectively as it does Pickett's Charge.[18]

Rockabilly flourished only briefly, though like other pop phenomena it has recurred often in subsequent years. It informed much southern-based rock 'n' roll and rock music in the 1960s and 1970s—one hears echoes in many of Johnny Rivers's hits as well as in such successes as Gene Simmons's memorable "Haunted House" (1964) and Bobby Fuller's masterpiece "I Fought the Law" (1965). It was foundational for the early Beatles. The first song that John Lennon and Paul McCartney played together was Eddie Cochran's "Twenty-Flight Rock."[19] Rockabilly remained a vital ingredient in the music of numerous country stars: Gary Stewart, Bob Luman, Merle Kilgore, Joe Stampley, Narvel Felts, Crash Craddock, and many others. Both an Elvis-clone like Orion and also a fine neorockabilly artist such as Billy Swan reminded audiences of the potency of the form. A full-scale rockabilly revival began in the late 1970s and peaked in the 1980s with the popularity of the Stray Cats and included such talented new artists as Tav Falco's Panther Burns, Matchbox, the Leroi Brothers, Billy Hancock, Robert Gorden, and most appropriately Johnny and Dorsey Burnette's sons, Rocky and Billy. The revival rejuvenated the careers of the obscure and half-forgotten: Sleepy LaBeef, Ray Campi, Joe Clay, the Everly Brothers, and Ricky Nelson. Today, the music of Billy Ray Cyrus, Travis Tritt, Tanya Tucker, Marty Stuart, and Dwight Yoakam, to mention only a few current stars, bears eloquent tribute to the viability of rockabilly. Perhaps the most talented contemporary heir to Elvis's legacy is Chris Isaak. Even Bob Dylan has recently used a rockabilly arrangement to great effect in the recreation of one of his own classic rock numbers, "Tombstone Blues."

Mostly we reclaim rockabilly by reexperiencing it. The echo we most enjoy is the original one, conjured up those many years ago, which has the power to burst asunder even now in a crazy riot of attitude, imagery, and sound. We listen to the voice of the young Hillbilly Cat; we again ride that Mystery Train; once more we get "real, real gone," and when we do, somehow a moment seems like forever.

The band that rocked America in 1955. Elvis Presley, Scotty Moore, and Bill Black. Collection of Ger Rijff.

3 From Denmark to RCA

On the Road with Elvis, Scotty, and Bill

ERNST JØRGENSEN

I was born November 19, 1950, in a suburb of Copenhagen, the capital of Denmark. The country was then, and is now, one of the safest and wealthiest places in the world. I never knew hard times, and everything seemed to prosper in our country.

The Danish people survived World War II with only minor scars. Led by a social democratic policy, a welfare system was quickly established in what would become an open-minded and tolerant society. So when rock 'n' roll finally hit us in the early sixties, it was without the drama of its American debut. Although the older generations did not necessarily like it (my mother did), it was hardly anything to get upset about. My parents were middle-class, but coming from broken working-class homes they always tried to steer me toward a safe life. "Work hard and don't be too ambitious," they would tell me. Apparently I didn't pay much attention.

My parents had a record player, but it was very seldom used. A collection of classic music on 78s and a few others were all we had. In the fifties and sixties Denmark had one radio station for the whole country, and there was no American rock 'n' roll played until the early sixties. There was hardly even a show that would play German-influenced oompah pop music or local covers of the top tunes of the day, including Tommy Steele (the British pop sensation). Elvis Presley's record company, RCA Records, did not have a Danish affiliate or licensee until late 1959, and the few who owned an Elvis record had either imported it from the United States or taken a ferry to Sweden where his records were available.

None of this I knew at the time. My first recollection of pop music was from my mother's sister, who had a nice collection of singles and EPs. I must have been eleven, and I remember that she was a big Pat Boone fan. She had Elvis records too, but didn't play them as much as Boone's. However, the image of one of the record sleeves, a single of "Surrender," still sticks in my mind. It wasn't a hip picture at all (a publicity shot, made for the movie *Flaming Star,* of a cowboy-style Elvis with acoustic guitar), but he still looked different from anybody I had ever seen. The name "Elvis Presley" seemed to hold a mystery all its own. I had never heard of anybody with the name Elvis, nor Presley for that matter.

The first conscious, music-related observation I have is of the day in 1962 when I heard "Little Sister" on the radio. I was excited. It sounded like nothing I had ever heard, and I vividly remember the sleeve. By this time Danish radio had established a weekly, thirty-minute pop show, and they started to play Elvis records and a lot of British and American pop and rock 'n' roll. However, like most

The *"Hound Dog"* session at RCA's New York City Studios, July 2, 1956. Left to right: Hoyt Hawkins at the piano, Bill Black, Neal Matthews, Hugh Jarrett, Elvis, Gordon Stoker, and Scotty Moore. Courtesy of Larry Brooks Arnett.

Danes, I was exposed to the post–rock 'n' roll Elvis. His records started to sell like nothing the country had ever experienced, but his fame was built on such hits as "It's Now or Never," "Are You Lonesome Tonight," "Surrender," "His Latest Flame," "Good Luck Charm"—not "Heartbreak Hotel" and "Hound Dog." The music was received without much understanding of where it came from and with no real controversy. We were also ignorant and indifferent to the color of the artist, and to most of us teenagers the lyrics had very little significance. How could we know what "a one-eyed cat peeping through a seafood store" ("Shake, Rattle, and Roll") meant when even RCA didn't know? We often understood the words, but rarely what they were really about.

My own personal situation at the age of thirteen or fourteen was that Elvis was my hero. To choose Elvis as your hero was perfectly acceptable at the time, and I spent almost all my money buying his records. It was like being a kid in a candy shop, as you started delving into not only his new records but also dreaming of all his original fifties recordings you might buy someday—a dream shared by thousands of young Danes. The triumph was in 1963 when "Devil in Disguise" occupied the top spot on the newly established Danish singles chart for thirteen consecutive weeks. Danish radio proudly announced that because of the enormous success of "Devil in Disguise" Denmark would be the first country to release the follow-up, "Bossa Nova Baby."

Although Presley's real breakthrough in Denmark was in the early sixties, there was nothing to stop the British Invasion from happening. As the sixties progressed and Elvis's output consisted mainly of inferior movie soundtracks, new artists rose to fame and most of Elvis's fans started finding other favorites. I loved the Rolling Stones and later such groups as the Doors, the Beach Boys, Jefferson Airplane, and, of course, Bob Dylan. In school, history was my favorite subject, and detective novels were also an endless fascination. Maybe that's why, combining the two interests, I eventually had to *understand* the decline of Elvis's recording career.

Throughout the sixties it became increasingly difficult to defend Elvis with my friends. But sporadic greatness, as shown in the gospel album *How Great Thou Art* (my friends didn't understand it) and in singles like "Big Boss Man," "Guitar Man," and "U.S. Male," made me still consider Elvis as an artist. I knew that he could still do it, and I decided to find out the mechanism behind the erratic nature of Elvis's recording career.

With the comeback special in late 1968 and the subsequent recordings from Memphis, "In the Ghetto," "Suspicious Minds," and the mind-blowing *From Elvis in Memphis* album, I felt I was proven right. By 1970 I had started history studies at the University of Copenhagen. At the same time I discovered the Official Danish Elvis Presley Fan Club (a somewhat less intellectual pursuit, I thought). Much to my surprise, the two main people behind the club, Johnny Mikkelsen and Erik Rasmussen, were as obsessed as I was about *understanding* Elvis.

Simultaneously, but independently, we had all collected pieces of information relating to Elvis's music. Although the club had to publish a monthly fan club magazine, the three of us soon started spending a lot of time piecing together information about Elvis's recordings and movies. I had discovered that Elvis's singles had what is called "matrix numbers" on the labels. If you just understood the system you could figure out which year the recording was made (this is a simplistic explanation) and suddenly a pattern did emerge. The important thing, though, was that we suddenly had tools to understand things that were not known, basically not supposed to be known, about Elvis's record releases. We found out that a lot of the mid-sixties singles were actually leftover recordings from earlier RCA sessions because Elvis didn't deliver any new recordings for them to release other than the movie soundtracks.

Over the next seven years we wrote hundreds of letters to musicians, producers, the staff at RCA Records, and anybody we thought might have relevant information. Not surprisingly a lot of people chose not to respond, but to our delight quite a few did. The overall reaction from the responses was surprise—surprise that anybody would care about this. What surprised us the most was the fact that nobody in the United States was even attempting to do what we were doing. After all, many fans lived next door to a lot of the information we had such difficulty gathering thousands of miles across the Atlantic.

Biannually, we released updated versions of a little book we called *Recording Sessions*. By 1980 the information included in our books had reached a stage where not only Elvis fans but also the music media started to take notice. To our dismay, an American Elvis fan and writer took the liberty of using, without permission or acknowledgment, the information from our books and included it in his own Elvis book, which was published by a well-established New York publisher. We got quite mad at this piracy and, since one of our Elvis fan club members happened to be a young, successful lawyer, we started legal proceedings. The outcome was a settlement that for the first time enabled us to travel to the U.S. and complete our research, with the goal of writing *the* book about Elvis's music.

By 1977 I had left the university and started a career in the recording business at the local division of Polygram Records. During these years I learned a lot about the record business, information that proved very useful in understanding the whys and wherefores of RCA's decisions over the years. In 1984 we were ready with our new book, *Reconsider Baby* (released in the U.S. by Pieran Press in 1986), and much to our delight it soon established itself as the "definitive Elvis sessionography" (it was also the only one). I don't think we were ever as proud as the day Joyce Triplett of RCA's Asheville office ordered ten copies of our book for in-house use. The triumph, as we saw it, was: "We know more than they do."

In late 1988 I had talks with BMG, the new owner of Elvis Presley's record label, RCA, and I was offered the position of managing director, with the assignment to build their Danish company from scratch. At that time very few at BMG knew that I had done all this research on Elvis Presley, but shortly after my employment the rumor started to spread. When BMG had taken over RCA in 1986, my ambition was to find a way to present Elvis Presley's catalog in an honorable way. Here was my chance, once and for all, to get rid of RCA's image of decades-long misrepresentation of Elvis's repertoire.

By 1990 a committee was established with the full support of Priscilla Presley and the Elvis Presley estate. Key players from the estate, Jack Soden and Jerry Schilling, were as determined as the German top executives at BMG to start a fresh relationship after years of counterproductive fights between the old RCA company and the estate. The committee was put together on a worldwide basis, as opposed to being run by the U.S. company, and I was fortunate enough to become a key member—the music expert within the group.

After three years at BMG Denmark, I was offered the opportunity to work exclusively with Elvis's repertoire, and by 1992 the first major result of what all parties had been working toward came out, *The King of Rock 'n' Roll*, a five-CD box set of Elvis's fifties masters. It had been a complicated pregnancy. Bob Buziak was the president of RCA when we started to get involved, and he didn't seem to care one bit about the Elvis repertoire. The German parent company had put my colleague Roger Semon and myself in charge of the box set, but in principle it was an RCA project. With Buziak's departure and the entrance of Joe Galante and Randy Goodman, we were left alone to do basically what we wanted. I still remember when the first finished sets became available to us. Joe Galante congratulated me and said how proud RCA was of what we had accomplished. I was soon informed that the people in marketing had raised their estimate of potential sales to 40,000.

Several months later, however, after ecstatic reviews, three Grammy nominations, and sales that topped 500,000, we had surpassed even the wildest dreams of anybody involved in the project. Yes, out there were serious fans—call them even connoisseurs—who wanted to know more about the history of the music Elvis made and to study it in its historical and cultural context. This was exactly the encouragement we needed. It was immediately decided that all of Elvis's repertoire, irrespective of commercial potential, should be released in the best possible audio quality, with historically correct notes and appropriate packaging. Over the next three years two additional box sets have appeared in similar, meticulously researched and produced editions—*From Nashville to Memphis* and *Walk a Mile in My Shoes*.

The sixties box set was a much more difficult task because of the sheer volume of Elvis's recordings during that decade. We wanted to show that Elvis had a recording career that ran parallel to his movie career and soundtracks. *From Nashville to Memphis* included all his studio masters recorded at RCA's Studio B in Nashville and at Chips Moman's American Studios in Memphis. Our point was that in addition to the Elvis of the movies, over which he had very little artistic influence or input, there remained the Elvis of the recording studio in full control of his glorious art.

With the seventies box, *Walk a Mile in My Shoes*, the record label wanted us to create a "best-of" package, primarily to overcome the unjust ridicule that posthumously was attached to this period of Elvis's career. It was a compromise to which the purists among the fans will probably object, but we felt that this was the only way to restore historically the music Elvis made during these years. With Dave Marsh's persuasive and intelligent liner notes and through the repertoire choices, we felt that indeed we could get a look at the career from a different angle—Elvis's point of view. It is true that by eliminating the weaker performances and the most average songs, we introduced an element of distortion into the total picture, but doing box sets like this is as much a statement of editorial intentions as it is a slavish record of the times. In the seventies, according to the critics, Elvis was fat, forty, and falling apart. Our collection does not buy into this myth. Rather, it insistently proclaims that Elvis made music of high artistic and commercial significance during this decade. A lot of people will get the message, and we sincerely apologize to the completists who anyway can't be pleased with anything less than everything.

We now found ourselves in a climate in which we could gain support for a very thorough production strategy. It was agreed to make all the movie soundtracks available on a series called *Double Features* (two or more soundtracks on one disc). Both a Christmas CD, *If Every Day Was Like Christmas*, and a two-CD gospel set, *Amazing Grace*, also have been released.

Working for RCA opened other doors. With the credibility earned by the first box set, it became a lot easier for me to establish contact with important people to interview. Likewise, I was more visible to those people who wanted to collaborate with me on various research projects. What was originally a boy's teenage dream had become a reality—to explore my curiosity and ambition to the fullest, to open new doors only to find more wonderful opportunities awaiting. Nothing has been as fascinating as traveling the South—and Mississippi more so than anywhere—in search of the young Elvis. I visit local libraries, interview interesting old-timers, uncover long-buried photographs, and roam from small town to small town just as Elvis, Scotty, and Bill did, traveling thousands of miles and forty years back in time to a world that a young Danish boy could only dream of.

Joni Mabe. *The Elvis Playpen with Einstein and Jesus Walking on the Water.* 1984.
Mixed media. 6' x 10'. Photo by Dennis O'Kain. Courtesy of the artist.

4 Elvis as Anthology

PETER NAZARETH

Music possesses such solidity one may hold it in one's mind, sculpt it into a mysterious flute, a flute that is akin to a spiral or a curious ladder that runs into space.

—**Wilson Harris,** *The Four Banks in the River of Space*[1]

Anancy spin a web and drop into Africa. And you know what happen? As he land up foot on the West side, the first thing is that he meet up with Anancy. Yes. Truth. Anancy meet up with Anancy self, him proper old Africa self. / You should see how them facing one image in two body! The old Anancy chuckling like shak-shak seed, as he stand up watching the newness of the new Anancy from over the water.

—**Andrew Salkey,** *Anancy, Traveller*[2]

The first rock 'n' roll song I heard was Bill Haley's "Rock Around the Clock" in the movie *The Blackboard Jungle*. I had grown up on country-western music in Uganda. I listened to and sang songs by Jimmie Rodgers, Roy Rogers, Gene Autry, Montana Slim, and later Slim Whitman. But I tended to like music with a beat, so my favorite song, next to "St. Louis Blues"—which I first heard by Paul Robeson—was "In the Mood," the version by Joe Loss, which I realized was based on a boogie, so I took to "Rock Around the Clock." Later, I asked my cousin Anthony D'Mello, who played clarinet and saxophone with Nobby and His Band, what they were going to play for the next function. "Rock 'n' roll," he said. What was this? Was there more than "Rock Around the Clock"?

I had grown up on country-western music in Uganda. I listened to and sang songs by Jimmie Rodgers, Roy Rogers, Gene Autry, Montana Slim, and later Slim Whitman. Peter Nazareth playing clarinet in Uganda, circa 1958. Courtesy of Peter Nazareth.

Shortly after that, I took my Overseas School Certificate exams and went from Kampala to Entebbe, the town I had grown up in, where I met Henry Rodrigues, who used to play bass with Nobby. Henry produced an American rock 'n' roll magazine; on the cover was a photo not of Bill Haley but of someone with the strange name "Elvis Presley." Henry took me to visit Nobby, who triumphantly produced a 78 by Elvis that he said his cousin had just brought from England. "You cannot get any Elvis records in Uganda!" he said. He played it. It was the slowest song I had ever heard, and it had no beat, no drums! The song was "Love Me Tender" and I did not like it. The other side was not much better, although sung with more energy: It was a ballad called "Any Way You Want Me."

The next day, I went back to Kampala. I was walking past Assanand & Sons when I saw a square photo in the window called *Elvis Presley*, mouth wide open. I had never seen an LP before. Some impulse took hold of me. "We'll never get an Elvis record here again!" I thought. I persuaded my aunt to give me money to buy the record, although I did not have a record player for 33s and 45s. So I had to play the LP at the houses of friends when I went back to Entebbe.

Except for Henry and Nobby, they all hated it. But since I had bought it, I was determined to discover what there was in it. After repeated playings, I began to get hooked on Elvis—but not right away. I kept on trying the various Elvis records that came to Assanand's or the rival store, Shankardass. I bought Elvis's "Heartbreak Hotel," seeking completion to the version by one Stan Freberg, whose record I had tried first in innocence. It is strange to hear a parody before you have heard the original; Freberg's was hilarious as long as I played the original first. (I also bought Lonnie Donegan's "Rock Island Line" because of the parody on the flip side of Freberg's record.) On the whole, there

were few Elvis songs I heard in 1957 that I liked right away, except "All Shook Up" and "Teddy Bear," which I heard on the radio before they came to the record stores. (Sergio Coelho, who was teaching in the same school as I was before going to university, told me he had heard Elvis's new song, "Shaggy Bear.") Psychocyberneticians say when one has made a decision, one makes further decisions to reinforce the first one; maybe it is because I had bought the LP, which was very expensive in Uganda (seven times the price of an LP in the U.S.) that I kept listening to Elvis over and over again in order to get my (aunt's) money's worth. But it is equally possible that since I had to work at liking what Elvis did, I got to appreciate it more profoundly.

I will never forget the time I tried Elvis's "My Baby Left Me." An Englishman in the store reacted as though he had been shot. "What's that?" he asked Surinder Assanand. "It's the most horrible thing I have ever heard!" Today, I believe what horrified the Englishman was an African-American *and* African quality in the music that Elvis brought in from the original 1950 version by Arthur "Big Boy" Crudup, the quality that was being denied aesthetic and political validity under the Manichaean world of colonialism in which the colonizer appropriates to himself all values while attributing to the colonized the negation of values. While Elvis's rock 'n' roll records of the time had a backbeat, that is, the second and fourth beats were emphasized, "My Baby Left Me" had polyrhythms, just as the original by Crudup did, and so was really rhythm and blues.

The most amazing thing to me was that each song I tried by "Elvis Presley" seemed to be by a different person from the one I had heard before: There seemed to be twenty or thirty people, all called "Elvis Presley." (I understand from my daughter Monique, a David Bowie fan, that this was the feature of Elvis that fascinated the young Davy Jones, who went on to develop his different personalities.) For example, when I heard "When My Blue Moon Turns to Gold Again," I wondered if this could be by the same man who sang "Blue Suede Shoes." Both had a backbeat—which I believe was a way of counteracting the emphasized first and third beats of the Western march—but the voice in the former was more "open" and plaintive, although when compared to the version by Slim Whitman popular in Uganda, it had a rock 'n' roll energy. (When I played it in class, Mary Gravitt said it also had a gospel sound.) Even the covers of the LPs, entitled *Elvis Presley* and *Elvis*, looked different. On the first, the man looked square-jawed, masculine, looked as he sounded on tracks like "I Got A Woman" and "One-Sided Love Affair"—raucous, demanding, menacing, masculine. On *Elvis*, the face was round and soft, feminine, the pose stereotypically that of a female "waiting to be bitten by a vampire," according to Beryl Fletcher, the novelist from New Zealand, and he was wearing a pink-striped shirt that looked like a blouse. (In England, HMV issued the second LP with another cover photo: Elvis wearing what looked like a black leather jacket and a mean look, thus reinforcing the image of the masculine rebel.)

I was taking in many Elvis songs very quickly because three years of his music came to us over a few months, out of chronological sequence, chiefly from England, although the *Elvis Presley* LP was pressed in South Africa. I would read about new Elvis records in *New Musical Express*, the British paper Assanand's subscribed to, or *Melody Maker*, the British paper ordered by Shankardass; I would listen for the songs on radio, asking Norman Remedios to buy the records for me in Mombasa, Kenya, or, in one case, asking Francis Lobo to ask his English colleague at the office to get the records for me from England.

At this point, I should explain that I was born in Uganda of Goan origin, Goa being a portion of India that had been conquered and ruled by the Portuguese from 1510 until India took over in 1961. In East Africa, Goans were not classified as, or considered to be, Indians, although there *was* an Indian connection: On the whole, Goans did not consider themselves to be Indians. The Goan story has been told by me elsewhere.[3] My mother, though Goan, was born in Malaysia, where my grandfather was a professional (Western) classical musician. East had met West in Goans under pressure, thanks to long Portuguese rule. It may be the Portuguese impact on Indian culture in Goans that made us love country-western music. This is what Goans had in common with indigenous East Africans: They too loved country-western music, apparently because, I was told by African-American poet Sarah Fabio, East African and country-western music have similar roots. So I was an African who was not an African, an Indian who was not an Indian, and a Goan who was not a Goan in that while other Goan parents talked to their children about Goa, my father talked about Goa and my mother about Malaysia. "From our researches into you, you as well live among cultures, a traveller between worlds," said Israel Segal, interviewing me on TV in Tel Aviv on December 16, 1993. "Is that what drew you to Elvis?"

I had discovered from *Elvis and Gladys* by Elaine Dundy that Elvis's great-great-great-grandmother on his mother's side was a full-blooded Cherokee who died one hundred years before he was born and his grandmother on his mother's side was Jewish (which was known to my Israeli friend, Freddy Tiv, who said that under Jewish law, Elvis was therefore Jewish).[4] I also read of Elvis's Scots-Irish ancestry, behind which lay French ancestry. And could there be more? Elvis indicated to us through the way he sang "King Creole" in the movie of the same name that he was "Creole," a mixture of black and white. No wonder when the narrator of Alice Walker's story "Nineteen Fifty-Five" first sees the Elvis figure, she says he looked like a "Loosianna creole."[5] The stress on "creole" could be as much *choice* on Elvis's part as genes: He was conscious of his Cherokee ancestry, which means he was conscious of having colonizer and colonized in him, as can be seen from his role in his 1960 movie *Flaming Star*, where he plays Pacer, whose father is white and mother Kiowa.[6]

Although I had to work at liking Elvis's music, there were some things I could identify with. On the *Elvis Presley* LP, he did a rock 'n' roll version of "Just Because," which was available in Uganda by Frankie Yankovic and His Yanks as a polka. Elvis broke it up by singing staccato, stuttering "be-because." Bill Black gave the piece a rhythm that Nobby thought came from rubbing two pieces of sandpaper together, which today I hear as a slapping bass; Scotty Moore's guitar solos sounded like responses to the accordion solos of the original. So I could appreciate the Elvis version because I knew the one by Frankie Yankovic; Elvis was breaking up the world of Yankovic in which one had to plead for acceptance.

For some reason, I liked buying two or more versions of a song. That was the time when many recordings of a song would be released in the U.S. and England. For example, Guy Mitchell had a No. 1 hit in England with "Singing the Blues," and so did Tommy Steele with what I realized later was a "cover" (and later still I discovered that Guy Mitchell's version was itself a cover of the country hit by Marty Robbins). Clive D'sa, who played guitar for the band I started at Makerere University College,[7] said to me, "Why do you buy two records of the same song? Why don't you just buy the best?" I didn't know why myself; I only knew that when I played the two versions in juxtaposition, I did not feel that one was better than the other but that both were good, that they responded to each other, that the second bounced off the first: So you had to hear the first because the second implied the first by leaving a space that you, the listener, had to fill, and then the first sounded different when you went back to it.[8]

The original pop versions of "Blue Moon" were well known in Uganda: A friend of mine who used to play piano and sing, Ancy Menezes, was outraged by Elvis's version, from his first LP, which she said sounded like "Blue Horse" (because of the "walking" guitar and because Elvis replaced the chorus with an eerie yodeling moan). On his Christmas album, I wondered why he mangled Bing Crosby's "White Christmas." I loved his version of "Silent Night," but Francis Lobo exclaimed disgustedly, "The piano is playing a downbeat!" When I first heard Elvis's "Blueberry Hill," released on an EP in England, Elvis seemed to be doing a straight copy of Fats Domino, except that his rhythm was slower and more pronounced; I recall a British critic in *New Musical Express* getting totally confused that Elvis, who really could not sing, was now imitating Fats Domino's big hit. "True Love" had just been a big hit by Bing Crosby and Grace Kelly: Joe Pereira was angered by Elvis's version on the *Loving You* LP because you could barely hear the solo voice. "Where's Elvis?" he sneered. I realized in the U.S. that Elvis sang it like gospel music. Bing had in effect criticized Elvis in his previously released duet with Louis Armstrong from *High Society*, "Now You Has Jazz," implying jazz has roots and rock 'n' roll does not; by redoing "True Love" as gospel, with many voices instead of two, Elvis was saying to Bing that their music had the same roots. (Elvis's buddy in *Loving You*, coaxing him to sing his first song, shouted "Go, man, go!" in the same way as Louis Armstrong did when Bing was singing.) "Have I Told You Lately That I Love You" was a country standard thanks to Gene Autry: I loved the way Elvis gave it a beat, singing it low. Clive D'sa was struck by the way Elvis sang, "Have I told-ah," and he was amused by the way Elvis did the same thing in another classic, popularized by Jo Stafford I believe, "(Now and Then There's) A Fool Such As I." In the summer of 1992, in Boston, I found an anthology compiled by Billy Vera containing a version by the Robins, precursors to the Coasters, recorded in 1953. Elvis's version is similar, both being sung in a low register, except that Elvis has added a country rock guitar and a backbeat. (I began to discover that 1953 was an anchoring year for Elvis, the year he made his first test recordings of "My Happiness" and "That's When Your Heartaches Begin": Throughout his life, he kept coming back to and recording music from 1953, for example, in 1975, he recorded Faye Adams's "Shake a Hand," doing it like LaVern Baker's version.) And of course I knew when Elvis sang "Fever" on his first postarmy LP, *Elvis Is Back!*, he was doing Peggy Lee's song: much to the disgust of my classmate at Makerere, John Nagenda, who thought he should have left her song alone. (In Uganda, we did not hear the original by Little Willie John, whose backing Peggy Lee pared down and whose words she changed.)

When Elvis came out of the army and recorded "It's Now or Never," I knew he was doing Mario Lanza. And a year later he was doing Lanza again when he recorded "Torna a Surriento" as "Surrender" (my RCA Italiana record listed both titles). When the news about my Elvis class broke in the *Wall Street Journal*, the Mario Lanza connection was emphasized—while other singers I mentioned such as Jackie Wilson and Clyde McPhatter were left out—because of skepticism that Elvis could be doing "serious" music.[9] "That's opera!" someone in the audience in Memphis gasped when I played Lanza and Elvis during my presentation at the annual meeting of the Tennessee Heritage Alliance on May 8, 1992. Interviewing me for National Public Radio, Lyn Neary thought I had done some clever sleuthing. In fact, there was nothing to it. At Makerere University College, Appolonia Lobo, who loved classical music and opera, was trying to convert me and hence I got to know the two songs Elvis did by Lanza. "Come Back to Sorrento" was one of her favorite songs. She did not like Lanza, though, because she felt he had no control over his voice. I recall reading in 1957 that Lanza praised Elvis, saying he was the only young singer he (Lanza) admired because he had the courage to sing as he (Elvis) felt. And, added Lanza, Elvis said he had been influenced by him (Lanza). This sounded improbable then but not in 1960. "It's Now or Never" was not released in England for several months because of copyright problems: The owners of the copyright allegedly did not like the idea of a rock 'n' roller singing "O Sole Mio." When it was finally released, with all the publicity, it went to No. 1 in the week of release. Elvis himself gave us a clue in one of his last concerts, released on his posthumous *Elvis in Concert*, about how to listen to his music. He says that in 1960 he recorded "It's Now or Never," which was based on the Italian "O Sole Mio"; he was going to ask Sherill Neilson to sing the Italian and then he would sing his version. He asked the audience to listen to the voice.

So I would occasionally discover that Elvis had done somebody else's song—but I thought this was a random happening rather than a pattern. I was excited every time Elvis recorded a song I knew such as "I Gotta Know," which I heard first by Cliff Richard, and "Are You Lonesome Tonight," which I had by the harmonica player Danny Welton. It was in the late eighties that I heard a version of "Are You Lonesome Tonight" by Al Jolson and discovered that Elvis even did Jolson's recitation, except that there was a second section that Elvis omitted. (The hit version in 1927, though, was by Vaughn Deleath.) But I did not know that Carl Perkins was the first to have a hit with

"Blue Suede Shoes": I first heard Perkins's version on radio in Munich in 1973 on my way to the U.S. My not knowing that there were previous versions of many of the songs Elvis recorded emphasized the nagging notion that Elvis was many different singers. He even *looked* different in each of his movies.

When I came to the U.S., I was in a position to find out about and track down the "originals" of the music.[10] In 1958, I had bought the first Elvis LP issued by HMV in England because it had five different Sun tracks from the first Elvis LP issued by South African RCA: This LP had liner notes that stated that Elvis was influenced by one Sister Rosetta Tharpe. When Chris Bury of ABC's *World News Tonight with Peter Jennings* asked me to act out the scene of buying a record from Real Records, I discovered a CD by Sister Rosetta Tharpe and really bought it. I found "That's All Right" by Arthur "Big Boy" Crudup on a cheap LP of sixties and seventies rock performers. (I discovered later that it was not the original recording by Crudup but his response to Elvis's version, recorded on the Fire label in a session paid for by Elvis.) Each time I found an "original," I played it in juxtaposition with Elvis's version: And what I heard was not "rip-off" but a dialogue that made each version alive and complex. Since I heard "That's All Right" by Elvis after I had heard much of his RCA music of 1956, it did not sound to me as though it had energy or a beat: Elvis sang it at a higher pitch than "Blue Suede Shoes," "Heartbreak Hotel," and "Hound Dog." ("He's even singing like a girl!" said Bennet Dias, the other Goan bandleader, when I tried the record in his presence at Assanand's. He had just told me that Pat Boone was a better rock 'n' roll singer than Elvis. "I give Elvis six months!" he said.) So I did not like "That's All Right" until I heard Crudup's version first and Elvis's immediately after. Now I could hear the energy in his version. I could hear what Greil Marcus said in *Mystery Train*: that this was a young man in a hurry, moving on.[11] I now liked Elvis's version—and thanks to him, I found and liked Crudup's. I did not hear Elvis copying Crudup and hoping we would never find the original: I heard what I was later to call "twinning." More about this later.

I kept on my hunt, tracking down originals such as Roy Brown, "Good Rockin' Tonight," Ivory Joe Hunter, "It's a Sin," and one of my key finds, Chuck Willis's "I Feel So Bad," which was an R&B hit in 1953 and a pop and R&B hit for Elvis in 1961. I remember being astonished by Elvis's song when it came out. He had been doing "mainstream" pop songs, which my friends thought were tremendous: When he came out with "It's Now or Never," Adolf Mascarenhas, who had tried in vain, like Appolonia Lobo, to convert me to classical music, said, "I feel I should congratulate you." Then came this strange "I Feel So Bad," which Elvis sang with a different voice and an unusual rhythm. I realized later it was so odd because it was rhythm and blues, *for which I had no frame of reference*. Lavoisier Cardozo thought Elvis had lapsed after becoming a good singer. Actually, the same thing had happened in 1957 with "Milkcow Blues Boogie." Armando Ramos jeered at me when I bought it on an HMV EP and played it at his house in Mombasa: I was embarrassed by its seeming crudeness and mumbled, "It is fascinating." *It seems as though I was surrounded by friends who did not know what Elvis was doing or appreciate that he knew what he was doing—but I am naming each one of them because in my world, they were important music critics who stimulated my thinking.* Rock critics said that Elvis had done a straight copy of Chuck Willis, but I had not heard of, let alone heard, the original at the time.[12] When I found Willis's version in Boston in 1987 and played it, I was very excited. Yes, Elvis was doing a straight copy: And no, it did not sound like rip-off but dialogue, a way of bringing back into existence something that had been eclipsed. "I Feel So Bad" is about the colonial's loss of center, the center that has been taken away by colonialism, so the person knows he feels bad but does not know what to do about it. This is explained, Trickster fashion, in Andrew Salkey's novel, *The Late Emancipation of Jerry Stover*.[13] Thanks to Elvis, I had found Chuck Willis. *Was this not what Elvis had always intended?* Why did Elvis on his first national TV appearance begin not with his new release, "Heartbreak Hotel," but with Bill Haley's big hit of two years earlier, "Shake, Rattle, and Roll"? Why were the words of the last verse different? When we checked, we found that the second part was "Flip, Flop, and Fly," originally done by Big Joe Turner, who did the original version of "Shake, Rattle, and Roll." *Elvis was taking the song back from Haley to Turner.* To emphasize this, when Elvis went into the studio shortly after this television appearance, he sang the first verse of the song from Turner's version and not Haley's. Thus through "twinning" Elvis led us to the overlooked Turner.

I played the "juxtapositions" to friends, and the friend with whom it caught fire (or rather who, according to Margaret Richardson of the University of Iowa Library, must have seen the fire in my eyes) was Jonathan Walton, an African-American colleague who was born in Chicago. Jonathan and I used to talk about rock 'n' roll music because he had seen some of the performers in Chicago. Jonathan was with Lee Cloud at my house when I played some "twins." Both agreed that we were not listening to rip-offs. Lee Cloud, an African-American musicologist, said that the saxophone solo on Elvis's "I Feel So Bad," played by Boots Randolph, reversed the one on Chuck Willis's. "You simply must teach a class on this because nobody in America is listening!" said Jonathan. He told me to write down a course description and I would know what to do. I tried to dodge it, but he came back at me again and again over the next few days. I met Jonathan and George Barlow outside the theater after seeing Spike Lee's *School Daze*. Finding out that George liked Elvis, I asked him whether he would be interested in team-teaching a class on Elvis with me. "No, you must do it yourself!" said Jonathan.

A few months later, during the summer of '88, when I was in Toronto for the first International Goan Convention, my daughter Monique phoned me from Boston to say that Jonathan had died. At the time, I was holding up the ceiling in the basement with my wife and sister Ruth while my brother-in-law Cyril fixed it. I could not hold up the ceiling after the news. My last words to Jonathan before we left Iowa City for Toronto had been, "See you." He had replied, "Will you?"

I could not go to Chicago for the funeral because the Goan Convention was about to begin. In the fall, a memorial service was held in the Old Capitol senate chambers in Iowa City. Many people spoke at the service, people of different ages and sexes and races and occupations and classes. All talked about how Jonathan had done something special for them at a critical point in their life. Jonathan seemed to have been twenty or thirty different people to have played a key part in so many people's lives, to have helped them open the door to their creativity. The spirit moved me. "I will teach the class on Elvis for you, Jonathan," I announced.

The American Studies Program at Iowa under Al Stone was willing to let me teach the class because it had a suitable course on the books, American Popular Arts. Darwin Turner, chair of the African-American World Studies Program, supported the idea of cross-listing the course. But I wasn't ready.

Students came to me to ask when I was going to teach the class. Two summers later, visiting my daughter Kathy in Boston, I received a double-jointed message telling me I was ready. I was rereading Ishmael Reed's eighth novel, *The Terrible Threes*, and came to the section where the Pope is reading the autobiography of Chuck Berry.[14] The next day I came across the autobiography, bought it, read it, and was ready. I had my title: "Elvis as Anthology."[15]

"Imagine a book called ELVIS: Open the book and you find Little Richard, Clyde McPhatter, Jackie Wilson, Mahalia Jackson, LaVern Baker, Mario Lanza, Bing Crosby, Dean Martin, Sister Rosetta Tharpe, Ivory Joe Hunter, Chuck Willis, Jerry Reed," I explained to many interviewers. "Does that mean when you open the book, there is no Elvis?" asked Chris Bury. I had no answer then, but when Voice of America asked me the same question two days later, I did. "I have edited a book," I said, "and I have my name outside as well as inside." There are many chapters in the book.

The book I had in my mind was Bessie Head's *Maru*.[16] In this novel, the leading metaphor is that of a door opening. I drew attention to this metaphor in my course description by using as an epigraph the following statement by Little Richard in his *Rolling Stone* interview: "I thank the Lord for sending Elvis to open that door so I could walk down the road, you understand?"[17] I took "you understand?" to be black code for "take this on a deep level." In Head's novel, set in Botswana, the door for the Masarwa people is opened by Maru, the chief-to-be of the Batswana, who have enslaved the Masarwa. Maru has been delaying his ascent to chieftaincy because he wants to bring down the whole structure of oppression so that he can be free. He has the (inner) kingdom of the moon while his friend, his blood brother Moleka, has the kingdom of the sun. Maru has been looking for a woman who will be his true complement: He finds this woman in Margaret Cadmore Jr., a Masarwa who had been adopted by an Englishwoman because her mother had died just after giving birth to her. Margaret Cadmore, the wife of a missionary, had begun opening the door for Margaret Jr. and the Masarwa people, believing "Environment everything; heredity nothing." Thanks to her, the little girl had a good education and became a teacher, being sent to the village of Dilepe: The bosses there had not known she was a Masarwa because the Masarwa were their slaves, and no Masarwa woman had had an education or the name "Margaret." Moleka "found" Margaret for Maru. Moleka found an old, empty library building for Margaret to live in. When he took her into the room, their hearts went "bang": In a flash, the old, arrogant, sexist Moleka was gone and a new, humble one emerged. Seeing him later, Maru knew that the woman who could do this to Moleka, who could open his inner door, was the woman for him. A series of "twinnings" takes place: Maru/Moleka, Moleka/Margaret, Maru/Margaret. We also see the possibility of a second self emerging from within each person. Margaret opens Moleka's inner door; then as artist, she helps confirm the vision of

Maru's third eye. When she paints pictures in a kind of breakdown, not knowing the paints and materials she had received from her friend Dikeledi had really come from Dikeledi's brother, Maru, many of the paintings reveal the potential of people to give birth to new selves. The paintings speak directly to Maru's heart: He could interpret them, though he could not paint them himself, while she could paint but not interpret them. The artist and interpreter/critic need each other, as we see at the end of Tayeb Salih's novel, *Season of Migration to the North*.[18] At the end of *Maru*, Maru literally opened a door for Margaret, taking her away from the library that had both freed and enslaved her in the sense that before she had only books as companions but now she needs to move from books to life; consequently, an inner door opened for the Masarwa people because they realized that the chief-to-be of their oppressors had given up the throne to marry one of their own and so they had value as people.

Bessie Head drew my attention to her connection with Elvis: When she was in the International Writing Program in Iowa City in 1977, she used to come to my apartment and ask me to play "Heartbreak Hotel" over and over again. I now feel that "Heartbreak Hotel" led Head to *Maru*, published fifteen years after the record: Note the parallel notions of loneliness, being trapped in rooms, and doors opening.

My class showed how Elvis opened the door by "twinning," a term I began using later thanks to a discussion with Marilyn Houlberg of the Chicago Art Institute. She said she had been an Elvis fan in the fifties and then had lost sight of him until she was in Nigeria in the sixties. She was studying Yoruba culture and discovered the Yoruba concept of twins. The Yoruba people believe that each person has a spirit-double in heaven. When twins are born, the double has come down to earth. If a twin dies, a statue must be made of him/her and treated like the twin that is alive because there is a connection between the twins. This discovery drew Houlberg back to Elvis because he was a twin whose brother was born dead. She therefore made a shrine to Elvis and his twin. Shortly after our discussion, I went to Memphis, where I met Joan Nelson, who told me that twins converse in the womb, and Elvis clearly missed his twin. Elaine Dundy was one of the first writers to recognize the importance of Elvis being a twin.[19] Mark Childress develops the notion of twinning in his novel *Tender*: Leroy Kirby, the Elvis figure, talks to his twin in a mirror and twins himself in music to many other singers; by the end, the reader realizes that the novel has given us not Elvis but a twin.[20] Pieces of a jigsaw puzzle were beginning to fit together.

Elvis himself provides us with clues about twins from his very first movie.[21] At the end of *Love Me Tender* (1956), Vince/Elvis is dead but a "ghost" Elvis sings a new verse of "Love Me Tender," the words of which could be interpreted as those of the missing twin expressing undying love and giving strength. In the next movie, *Loving You* (1957), as Rachel Ray pointed out to me, when Elvis is challenged to sing and does "Mean Woman Blues," after which he fights (a scene that was repeated/reversed in *G.I. Blues* [1960]), a "twin" figure gets up and dances just like him and then watches over him as he fights. Later in the movie, when he is singing, twin sisters in the audience clap their hands, one hand from each twin needing the other for completion. In *Jailhouse Rock* (1957), Elvis has twin basset hounds, each like the one he had to sing "Hound Dog" to on *The Steve Allen Show*. Elvis's father in *Follow That Dream* has adopted twin boys. Elvis talks to twin sisters in *Double Trouble* (1967). He plays a doctor, that is, a healer in his last feature film, *Change of Habit* (1969); when he is examining a pregnant woman, she asks whether she is going to have twins. There is also the twinning of names *between* movies. In the first movie, Elvis is Clint and his brother is Vance. The third movie has Elvis named Vince (a near Vance) while the next "Western," *Flaming Star* (1960), has Elvis's brother called Clint. Ann-Margret in *Viva Las Vegas* is "Rusty"; this is the name of Elvis's character in *Girl Happy* (1965). There are even more twins, as we shall hear.

In Uganda, I used to wonder why in "Love Me," on his second LP, Elvis sang the fifth and the tenth words of the first line of each verse a little sharp. I had never heard the song before, but I sensed those words should have been a little flatter—and yet the way Elvis sang them was the charm of the song. I had the answer when, thanks to Thalia Saposhnik, who worked for Leiber and Stoller Inc., I tracked down the original version of the song, which was done two years earlier than Elvis by an African-American duo, Willie and Ruth. When I played their version just before Elvis's, the answer was clear: We could hear Elvis singing the seconds on the words I have noted and implying the first voice. He was not doing two voices: He was doing one voice, but *it contained within itself the second unheard voice*. Joachim-Ernst Berendt says in *The Third Ear*:

> Music does not merely take place within time. It also exalts and surmounts time. It is not just that the present and the past merge. The future is also involved to the extent that in the harmonious progression of music the note sounding "now" anticipates the future note in which it

will be resolved. The note to come is, as it were, contained in the present note, which could not otherwise "summon" it. Anyone musical knows it is hardly possible to break off certain cadences before the final note. The final note is "there" whether it is played or not. It may sound later—or not at all—but viewed in a higher sense it was heard much earlier. [22]

I am not using the lines in quite the way Berendt means them in their context, but the quotation does make my point about one note implying another that is not (yet) heard. Berendt goes on to say later: "*Anahata* and *ahata*, the unplayed and the played note, are two key concepts in Indian music. Both are equally important—and some schools even say that the unplayed is more crucial since it provides the foundation for what is actually played. *The sounds which are played are symbols of the unplayed.*"[23]

My argument is that Elvis constantly and deliberately drew attention to the "unplayed" sounds, namely, the sounds of the versions that predated his and that were waiting to be heard, versions for which he was opening the door so that the people could walk through, versions that he wanted us to hear to complete what he was doing. Since many fans were obsessed with only his music, he provided us early with clues by "twinning" his own music. For example, in the movie *Loving You*, he has two versions of "Got a Lot O' Livin' to Do," one at the beginning when he is innocent and inexperienced and the other at the end, when he has self-knowledge and is before TV cameras. The title song is a rock 'n' roll version of "Loving You," which dovetails into an instrumental. Later, Elvis sings the song as though it is a waltz converted into 4/4 timing, with a guitar and without drums: When he recorded it for single release, the piano played a downbeat and the timing was converted from 3/4 to 4/4. Here is multiple twinning. In *Love Me Tender*, Elvis had two versions of the title song, the second as ghost-figure at the end superimposed on the action, singing a new verse after he was dead; while "Love Me Tender" was No. 1 on the charts, "Love Me" entered the Top Ten on an EP. "Love Me Tender" was sung like a "white hymn," "Love Me" as a "black duet," and then came "Loving You," which changes love *me* to the process of loving *you*.

On the *Loving You* LP, as a studio recording, Elvis released "Don't Leave Me Now"—*before* we saw him sing it in his next movie, *Jailhouse Rock*. The *Jailhouse Rock* EP includes the version that was supposed to be without much feeling in the movie while the one on the earlier album is the bluesy version, the one that, following the suggestion by Judy Tyler, he makes his own by singing with feeling. (He also anticipates the accusation of rip-off by having this version in the movie copied by an established white singer.) Three other songs in *Jailhouse Rock* had different versions on the EP and the single from the ones in the movie: "Jailhouse Rock," "Treat Me Nice," and "I Want to Be Free." The first is one of Elvis's most famous production dance numbers, done before TV cameras: The record, the one the audience would *hear* and *see in their mind's eye*, is a little slower, the guitar sounding like the clanging of the door of the jail cell—Brian Austin-Ward said that the guitar boogie sounded as though it was being played on the bedsprings we were sleeping on at Makerere University College—and the voice desperate. This is no show, the record implies: Deconstruct the movie. "Treat Me Nice" in the movie is an appealing song—Elvis sings it high-pitched and pleading: He wants to be loved. On the record, the boogie is heavy and his voice low and menacing. (Near the end of the record, Elvis throatily "mumbles" the words, parodying Freberg's parody of his mumbling in "Heartbreak Hotel.") "I Want to Be Free" is sung straight and framed in the movie: It is on TV from prison; on the record, the voice is in crisis, breaking on "I want to be free," repeating and dragging out "free" twice. He is singing about the desire to fly to freedom. His passion should not surprise us, given the scene in which he is whipped like a slave. At that time there were people in Memphis whose parents had been slaves—Memphis had twelve slave markets and the Blues Museum in Memphis, opened in 1991, begins with chains and posters for the sale of slaves and for the capture of runaway slaves.

Another example of Elvis twinning his music: "Lover Doll" from *King Creole* was released in two versions, one on LP and the other on EP, the latter being the movie version while the former has a low-voiced member of the Jordanaires punctuating each line with "uh-huh." EP Vol. 1 of *King Creole* had the same photo on the cover of the LP except that one was a mirror image of the other. Yet another case: The version of Willie Dixon's "Doncha Think It's Time" is different on the second gold discs LP from the single release. In *Jailhouse Rock*, Elvis sings more than one version of "Young and Beautiful." Elvis is letting us know through his own "twins" that in order to understand what he is doing, "on listening to the world" (the subtitle of Berendt's book), *we must find the twin/s*. Andy Warhol may have understood this: In 1964 he painted "Elvis I and II"—two panels of Elvis, the left silk screen on acrylic on canvas and the right silk screen on aluminum paint on canvas.

Wilson Harris's well-known novel *Palace of the Peacock* begins as follows:

> A horseman appeared on the road coming at a breakneck stride. A shot rang out suddenly, near and yet far as if the wind had stretched and torn and had started coiling and running in an instant. The horseman stiffened with a devil's smile, and the horse reared, grinning fiendishly and snapping at the reins. The horseman gave a bow to heaven like a hanging man to his executioner, and rolled from his saddle on to the ground.
>
> The shot had pulled me up and stifled my own heart in heaven. I started walking suddenly and approached the man on the ground. His hair lay on his forehead. Someone was watching us from the trees and bushes that clustered the side of the road. Watching me as I bent down and looked at the man whose open eyes stared at the sky and ruled my living sight but the dead man's eye remained open and obstinate and clear.[24]

It turns out that the narrator is having a dream. The third paragraph reads, "I dreamt I awoke with one dead seeing eye and one living closed eye. I put my dreaming feet on the ground in a room that oppressed me as though I stood in an operating theatre, or a maternity ward, or I felt suddenly, the glaring cell of a prisoner who had been sentenced to die." The narrator is literally the dreaming eye. He is fascinated by his brother, "Donne," the doer, while hating the way he (Donne) exploits his Amerindian mistress, Mariella. Donne is a Creole, a descendant of the colonizing Europeans, and like his European antecedents wants the Indians to work "his" land; he decides to go into the interior to fetch the Indians. As he and his boatload of men arrive at the mission (also called Mariella), they are seen by the Indians, for whom time has not changed, as being the same boatload of people who had drowned (in the past) on their colonizing mission. At night, the narrator has another dream, which shows he is a premature rider not yet ready for Mariella, for whom he yearns.

In the morning, the Indians have gone, except for an old woman, from whom the only man who knows the language finds out they have gone into the interior. Donne decides that they can go by boat and head them off at the pass. They capture the old woman and take her along as guide: On the trip, she seems to be twinned to Mariella. As they make their way through all the dangers, the seven-day trip becomes the seven days of creation and the seven stages of the alchemical transformation of base metal into gold. In other words, the base self is being transformed into the higher self. "I saw that Donne was ageing in the most remarkably misty way," says the dreaming I on page 54. Two pages later, it is Donne who says to him in solicitude, "Why you're looking haggard as hell."

The narrative "I" has an incomplete existence by himself. He is literally the dreaming eye and seeks his twin, his brother: that is, seeks integration with his brother, an integration that will transform him into his creative, active, and intuitive self. Compare this to Elvis's movie *Kissin' Cousins*, which was made in 1964, six years after *Palace of the Peacock* was published. In the movie, Elvis plays a dark-haired self who goes with the army into the interior and meets his "twin," his distant cousin, played by himself with blond hair. Observe the way Elvis plays the blond "twin": He not only has a pronounced "interior" southern accent but also seems to be a ghost-like "absence," someone without personality except that he loves women and loves to sing—in fact, the stereotype people have of Elvis in his later movies. The last song in the movie, when the problems have been resolved, is "Kissin' Cousins," a duet Elvis sings with his twin. Compare this to his 1954 version of "Blue Moon," which he sings with such echo that it seems he is singing with his twin, whose voice is coming from another world, emphasized by the eerie way he yodels/moans instead of singing the "pop" chorus, thus displacing the old center and creating a new center to the song.[25] As in *Palace of the Peacock*, Elvis is "seeking his twin," that is, seeking integration with his twin. This was confirmed for me when I was invited to Graceland on May 8, 1992. As I was going down the staircase to the basement, I noticed that the whole wall was a mirror, within and over which were mirrors. If you looked straight at yourself, you could not see yourself: But if you looked at an angle, if you got out of yourself in a manner of speaking, you found an infinite set of twins, an anthology.

As the boat goes into the interior, all the crew members are historically and biologically related to one another: And as each person dies, each self becomes part of the integration. Compare this to the way Elvis "twins" himself to various singers and performers. The *Palace of the Peacock* frame of reference is not irrelevant: I saw large images of twin peacocks on the first floor of Graceland. Steve Marshall told me that Elvis used to keep real peacocks, and if I looked carefully at the jumpsuit he wore in *Elvis—That's the Way It Is* there is a "tail," indicating a peacock. The network on which Elvis did his 1968 TV special has a peacock logo. The colonization of South America began as the search for gold, literally for "El Dorado," the Golden Man, who supposedly took a daily bath in gold dust and lived in the Palace of the Peacock. The second golden discs album has several images of him in a golden suit; he is El Dorado. In Harris's novel, Donne inadvertently reenacts the journey into the interior to exploit the people and the land; the novel turns into a search for the golden man within, within Donne himself—the search for his bigger Self in order to transform the legacy of colonial oppression. Donne himself is the twin of the poet John Donne, whose poems were full of images taken from the dawn of European exploitation of the "new world": as Julie Minkler said to me, in *Palace of the Peacock* the protagonist is undone (a word that has its force in sound). The peacock becomes the rainbow of hope at the end, the multiple "eyes" of the peacock's tail taking the place of the single "I," which is the single "eye" according to Berendt;[26] this is also a multicultural, multiple way of seeing the world, of seeing the possibility of transforming our perception of a colonial history of an implacable opposition between exploiter and exploited.[27]

So Elvis is not a simple, that is, single figure. Jung asked me, "Why are there so many Elvis sightings? Why no Nat 'King' Cole or Bing Crosby sightings?" (I am referring not to Carl but Micky Jung of The Wholearth Natural Foods of Iowa City.) I discussed this question with Marsha Browne in Boston. My explanation was that people were seeing what was in their own heads. She said that just as in the case of ghosts, there are sightings because there is still unfinished business. It is as though we are missing a phantom limb: Elvis cannot be understood and appreciated until we realize there is a phantom limb, until we find the twin. I think this is why Elvis fans keep on buying new releases of Elvis records containing "alternate takes" of previously released songs, which strictly speaking are rehearsal takes as Elvis was working toward what he wanted: The fans are feeling a subconscious imperative to find completion by looking for "Elvis twins." But these are not the "twins" Elvis wanted us to find: They were not released when he was alive. These "twins" can be misleading. For example, some rock critics, obsessed with finding the macho in Elvis, believe he changed the words of Smiley Lewis's "One Night of Sin" when he recorded "One Night" only because he had to make the song less suggestive and therefore acceptable to the pop market. When his version containing the same lyrics as Smiley Lewis's was released in the eighties on one of the Legendary Performers LPs and then on the bluesy *Reconsider Baby*, it was considered by some critics to be the real version, the one Elvis would have wanted to release. Peter Guralnick says, "it was delivered with undiminished, unexpurgated force. Upon his return to the studio a month later to complete various album and single tracks, he re-cut 'One Night' with cleaned-up, more teen-oriented lyrics in a performance which, despite its lyrical compromise, actually matches the intensity of the original."[28] Guralnick is expressing the conventional view when he thinks the lyrics of the released version have been expurgated just to be oriented toward teens, that Elvis compromised. Such an interpretation denies Elvis intelligence in what he was doing in his music. It overlooks the fact that two years earlier, Elvis had taken Bill Haley's toned-down version of "Shake, Rattle, and Roll" some steps toward the more suggestive version by Big Joe Turner, and that two years later, he was to do the very suggestive "Such a Night." I think the released version of "One Night" is what Elvis wanted: Instead of using the piano, he played block chords on the guitar and he made his voice lower, hoarser, and "dirtier," like Little Richard singing "Baby Face." (In 1958, while "One Night" was No. 1 on the charts in England, "Baby Face" was its twin at No. 2.) When I played Smiley Lewis's version and then Elvis's in class, Mary Gravitt said that Elvis had deconstructed Lewis's: Lewis was regretting the one night of sin, which he was now paying for, while Elvis was looking with anticipation to one night "with you," which he was now praying for. Brooks Ammerman observed that if indeed Elvis had been made to clean up the lyrics by some "overseer," he engaged in wordplay and made the song more suggestive, expressing no regret for any wrongdoing, thus outsmarting the overseer. One must be punished for one's sexual transgressions in a Puritan society, which is what is happening in Lewis's version, not Elvis's. Guralnick's conclusion that in spite of the change in lyrics Elvis's version matched the intensity of the original not only contains the obvious meaning, namely, that Guralnick is surprised that the lyrically "compromised" version is as intense as the original, but also a hidden meaning: We need the *original*, the one by Smiley Lewis, to understand the "matching."[29] This is why when Elvis sang "One Night" in his 1968 TV special he sang some of Lewis's lyrics. *The twins Elvis wants us to find are not the alternate takes not released in his lifetime but the versions he responded to, sometimes his own, and more often the original versions of others.*

• • •

The plan of my course "Elvis as Anthology" was comparable to that of Raven the Creator in the mythology of the Northwestern Amerindians who is always creating, not being done with it once and forever. I would plan each class two days before. My idea was to discuss the juxtapositions of the different versions as I have indicated above, then later to reverse the process: in other words, first to play "original"/Elvis, then Elvis/new version. (I blew the class's mind when I played them Elvis's 1967 "Suppose" and John Lennon's "Imagine" of four years later: Both had a heavy piano and both used the conceit of imagining a world of nature dying; but whereas Elvis sings in the chorus that it is impossible to imagine, Lennon starts his song with the imperative to imagine. It is clear then that Lennon is responding to Elvis's song and taking the ideas further.) I made the course more complex by also integrating videos and excerpts from movies, and then even more complex by integrating discussions of books and fiction.

For example, when Chris Bury came to the class on the third day, we began by discussing Alice Walker's story "Nineteen Fifty-Five" from her collection *You Can't Keep a Good Woman Down*. The story is narrated by a woman like Big Mama Thornton, who sang the original version of "Hound Dog." She recorded her version in 1953 and it was No. 1 on the R&B charts in 1954. Elvis recorded his version in 1956 and his version was No. 1 on all three charts in 1956. The narrator in the story is named Gracie Mae Still, like Willie Mae Thornton, and the Elvis figure is named Traynor. This is how she sees him when he is brought to her by his manager: "He's about five feet nine, sort of womanish looking, with real dark white skin and a red pouting mouth. His hair is black and curly and he looks like a Loosianna creole."[30]

In the story, Traynor buys her song and begins to sing it just like her, except that he does not understand it. He keeps asking her about its meaning. He keeps giving her credit for the song, buys her gifts such as cars and a house, and finally arranges to take her on the Johnny Carson show for her to sing her song so the audience can see where the song came from. The audience response is polite; then he sings his version in order to show how good hers is and is disgusted when he still gets the screams. In 1977, he dies, and she says,

> In the morning we heard Traynor was dead. Some said fat, some said heart, some said alcohol, some said drugs. One of the children called from Detroit. Them dumb fans of his is on a crying rampage, she said. You just ought to turn on the t.v.
>
> But I didn't want to see 'em. They was crying and crying and didn't even know what they were crying for. One day this is going to be a pitiful country, I thought (20).

Then I played the class Big Mama Thornton's version of "Hound Dog," followed by Elvis's release of 1956, followed by his live version from the TV special of 1968, followed by his live version from Madison Square Garden in 1972. The class noted that Elvis began his single by growling out the first few words without musical accompaniment just like Big Mama Thornton, but then his version was different and simpler because apparently it was really about a hound dog whereas hers was about a cheating man. His version also had a backbeat. The TV special version, Kathryn Bassman said, inserted a line from Big Mama Thornton that was not in the Elvis single. What did this mean? Kathryn offered two explanations: Big Mama Thornton's version was on Elvis's mind and he went back to it subconsciously, or he was consciously inserting a line from her to draw attention to her, to give her credit the way the Walker story suggests. In the last version, Elvis begins "You ain't nothin'," stops, repeats it, stops again, and says, "You don't know what I'm going to do yet." It is a clue from Elvis that what he is doing is not what we expect him to do—a clue to his die-hard rock 'n' roll fans who believe he sold out by going "mainstream" in the sixties—and then proves his point: He sings "Hound Dog" slowly, with a wah-wah guitar, before speeding it up.

I next played the class two videos of Elvis's performance of "Hound Dog": first from *The Milton Berle Show*, the one in which he danced around and caused a storm nationwide, and second from *The Steve Allen Show*, where Allen had him dressed in tails so he could not dance and performing to a real, live hound dog who seemed to be drugged. I asked the class how they knew that Elvis was distancing himself from the setting, how he was showing that he did not approve. The answer: When he patted the dog, he wiped his hand on his trousers, and later when he patted the dog again, he rubbed his nose. The question the class had to consider was how Elvis was negotiating before the media, a media that had more power than he had. This question was a real one because we had the television media in the class so the class would see how I was "negotiating" with it, although the class would have to wait a few days for the story to appear on *World News Tonight with Peter Jennings* to see how successful the negotiation had been. (Peter Jennings and Chris Bury had the power to make a complete mockery of me and my class—or their bosses at the network did. As it turned out, they did an excellent job and captured the essence of the class in a report of a few minutes—as later, in different ways, did Janet Davies of ABC-TV Chicago and Keith Morrison of NBC's *Today Show*.) In other words, Elvis did not have absolute power: He had to acquire power the way the underdog did by "signifying" (to use the black American term). Should he have performed on *The Steve Allen Show* at all? Yes, said Wade Lookingbill, because when he sang without dancing we saw in our mind's eye the earlier performance when he did dance. There was a strong protest from fans. Elvis went to the studio the next day to record "Hound Dog." The single release was different from his live versions: It was much more menacing. "Who did he address it to?" I asked. The class was unanimous: Steve Allen, and those who stood behind him. So all these years, apparently, Steve Allen has not realized that while he was criticizing Elvis as having little talent, Elvis's hit was aimed at him!

I now asked the class who had written "Hound Dog." John Baskerville knew: It was Leiber and Stoller, the most famous composers (outside of Chuck Berry) of the rock 'n' roll era. The rest of the class had assumed that Big Mama Thornton had written the song. When Tom Dent spoke to the class a few weeks later, he told us he had met Big Mama Thornton at one of her last performances and she was bitter at Elvis getting the credit and the money for her song. But the song was written *for* her by two young, white Jewish men who, according to Baskerville and Mary Gravitt, had written very accurately about the black experience. They had been asked to write for her by her manager, Johnny Otis, who, it was rumored later, was a white man passing for black. And the reason why Elvis did a version with different lyrics from Big Mama Thornton was that in Las Vegas he saw Freddie Bell and the Bellboys doing a comic version of the song, liked it, and decided to incorporate it into his act. (On *Milton Berle*, Elvis sings the first line like Freddie Bell and the Bellboys, who repeat "hound dog" behind the lead singer: Elvis sings "hound dog" and his "second voice" repeats "hound dog." By the third verse, he sings the phrase like Thornton.) I asked the class why it was that, although "Hound Dog" was not written by Big Mama Thornton but by Leiber and Stoller, the Walker story had the narrator say that Traynor had come to buy her song, which she wrote herself. One of the African-Americans in class said this was because lots of African-American composers had been ripped off, their songs being stolen or bought for a pittance. I said that this might be true in general, but there was no evidence that Leiber and Stoller had done this: On the contrary, there was every evidence to support their authorship of "Hound Dog" on the basis of dozens of songs they composed for rhythm-and-blues and rock 'n' roll groups (such as the Coasters and the Drifters) and frequently tailored to particular performers. (The *Jailhouse Rock* and *King Creole* songs they wrote for Elvis could be considered "his" songs, but not his compositions.) A few years ago,

David Letterman asked Leiber what happened to the suit by Freddie Bell for royalties on his modified version of "Hound Dog": Leiber said that Bell lost the case because he had made the changes without permission. Things are shaggy doggish. Johnny Otis initially took co-composing credit for the song and Leiber and Stoller had to sue to get it back.

No, the answer was not rip-off: The answer was that the narrator of Alice Walker's story was not Big Mama Thornton but a fictional character, one into whom were rolled many strong black women singers, women who acted as the mother-figure or *the matrix* to Elvis, who was in training. A few weeks later, I played back-to-back "Twelve Gates" by Sister Rosetta Tharpe (who had a gospel show on WELO in Tupelo that Elvis used to listen to) and Elvis's "I, John," from his 1972 inspirational LP *He Touched Me*; then "Walk to Jerusalem" by Mahalia Jackson and "Joshua Fit the Battle of Jericho" from Elvis's 1960 LP *His Hand in Mine*; then LaVern Baker's 1961 "So High" and Elvis's "So High, So Low" from his 1967 gospel LP, *How Great Thou Art. It was clear that Elvis was "doing" each gospel singer in the lyrics and in the way he articulated, held, and inflected his notes.* It is significant that one of Elvis's earliest live performances was his version of LaVern Baker's "Tweedlee Dee" (the hit that was covered for the pop market by Georgia Gibbs)—a song Elvis never recorded in the studio and from which it is clear *he is in training.* This is emphasized by the fact that he recorded the flip side of her song, "Tomorrow Night," backed only by a guitar: It was first released with additional accompaniment a decade later on *Elvis for Everyone.* Look again at *King Creole*: After the titles, we hear a black woman, Kitty White, calling out/singing "Crawfish," and after she is deep into the piece Elvis leans out of the window and sings along with her. She ends the song. We are being told that the song comes from her— and Elvis is indicating this to us. Elvis later gives credit to black women in his Las Vegas performance of B. J. Thomas's hit, "I Just Can't Help Believing." Thomas sings it like a gospel song: Elvis takes Thomas's arrangement and makes it even more gospel, at the end coaxing the Sweet Inspirations to sing the song—and they take the song over and out. So Elvis takes the song from a pop situation in Las Vegas and hands it to the black women, who of course provided the springboard and the safety net in the first place.

Walker's story is therefore a much more complex dialogue and dialectic than a straightforward suggestion that Elvis ripped off Big Mama Thornton's song: It is the black woman's song the Elvis figure has been learning. Note that despite her initial suspicions, she recognizes that he keeps on trying to give her not only gifts but also credit. True, he at first does not understand the song, but this is not a black-white or fe/male thing: She does not give the song to Bessie Smith because it was not her song. Also, Traynor begins to understand the song as he gets more experience, just as Gracie Mae herself did. On her part, Gracie Mae begins to grow out of her suspicions, which have been instilled by the history of slavery and what followed: She begins to develop a relationship with Traynor such that she can see what is good in him and in what he is trying to do for her while maintaining her own judgment and sense of proportion and the ability to see things within a political context. The story is also redeeming Big Mama Thornton by showing that the historically exploited black woman can understand her history of exploitation and refuse to be trapped in it.

What we are doing here in this essay, as I did in the class, is "spiraling" or "looping."

Let me loop. In class, I played Clyde McPhatter and the Drifters's 1954 R&B hit "Such a Night," followed by Johnnie Ray's pop cover (which was banned in England by the BBC), and next Elvis's 1960 version. Then I played Jackie Wilson's first solo single, his 1957 "Reet Petite," which was posthumously a No. 1 hit in England in 1986. I showed the class that what Elvis had done was go through Johnnie Ray to the original version and then do it like Jackie Wilson, using slurs, glottal stops, swoops, and so on. ("Why is he singing like this?" a puzzled Norman Remedios asked me at Makerere.) To prove that Elvis was deliberately singing like Jackie Wilson, I played the class extracts from *The Million Dollar Quartet*. Elvis was now famous as an RCA star, having just had his huge double-sided hit, "Don't Be Cruel"/"Hound Dog." He dropped in on the Sun Studios on December 4, 1956, where a recording session was taking place with Johnny Cash, Carl Perkins, and Jerry Lee Lewis. Elvis jammed with them; unknown to any of the performers, a tape recorder was turned on, the recording being released after Elvis's death. Elvis later began to talk about the young lead singer he heard with Billy Ward and the Dominoes at Las Vegas. He was fascinated by the singer whose name he did not know at that time. This was Jackie Wilson. Elvis said he did a takeoff of "Don't Be Cruel" and sang it "much better than that record of mine." Elvis comes back to Jackie Wilson's version several times, even agreeing to sing his recently released (on his second LP) "Paralyzed" (cowritten by Otis Blackwell, who wrote "Don't Be Cruel" and later "All Shook Up," "Return to Sender," and "Easy Question") in the style of Jackie Wilson singing "Don't Be Cruel." Armed with this knowledge, we can discover two things. First, Elvis could not quite do it like Jackie Wilson at the time: He lacked some of Wilson's vocal abilities. But spending two years in the army, giving his voice a rest from performing and (so I read) taking voice lessons, he did acquire the weapons to sing like Jackie, and he was out to prove it on his first postarmy LP with "Such a Night." The other point is this: Though he was already famous, Elvis wanted to sing like Jackie; instead of protecting his turf, he did not feel threatened that Jackie was singing his song better than he had done. Elvis appeared on January 6, 1957, on *The Ed Sullivan Show* and was filmed only from the waist up. The unstated agenda was that TV did not want to show Elvis dancing like a black man. So what Elvis did was when singing "Don't Be Cruel," he gave a signal to the band and switched to singing it Jackie Wilson's way. He pulled a fast one on the power structure, implying, "You don't want to see me dancing like a black man? I'll give you a real black man: Jackie Wilson." From his upper-body movement we could imagine the rest.

When Elvis came out of the army and had his first recording sessions, he recorded "It's Now or Never," which, as we have already noted, is him doing Mario Lanza. The month in which he went into the studio to record the song, Jackie Wilson was in the top ten with "Night," a song sung not in his usual style but in the style of Lanza: And he ends the song on the same note Elvis was to hit at the end of "It's Now or Never." We could imagine them meeting offstage and saying, "Let's both do Mario Lanza!" Lanza had died in 1959: Both versions could be tributes—or twins. What is also fascinating is that in 1949, Tony Martin had a No. 2 pop hit with a version of "O Sole Mio" under the title "There's No Tomorrow." Elvis drew our attention to Martin in a still from the recording studio in *Jailhouse Rock*; behind Elvis is a large portrait of Martin such that if we look at the photo two-dimensionally Elvis's face is touching his.[31] Jackie's "Night" begins with the same violin introduction and the same first note as "There's No Tomorrow."

Peter Guralnick makes the Jackie Wilson connection in his liner notes to the video *The Great Performances, Volume 2*. Guralnick says that in his 1962 movie *Girls! Girls! Girls!*, Elvis was doing Jackie visually when he performed what was to become a big hit, "Return to Sender."[32] I played my class both the video of "Return to Sender" and a video of Jackie doing "Baby Workout" on *Shindig*: And it was clear that Elvis was doing Jackie Wilson, though with less energy. What accounts for this? Part of the answer is that Elvis was performing on a very small stage. But there could be a further explanation. When Priscilla Presley hosted *The Great Performances* on TV, she said that Jackie Wilson was on the set of the movie when Elvis performed this song. Therefore Elvis was performing Jackie Wilson before Jackie himself! And perhaps he was seeking Wilson's approval, as a younger brother would of an older brother. Just notice Elvis's hairstyle in the movie, which is like Jackie's. According to Nelson George in *The Death of Rhythm & Blues*, the greasy hairstyle for which Elvis became famous was the result of using the hair dressing black men used to straighten their hair.[33] (Look at the 1956 photo of Elvis and B. B. King taken in 1956 at the WDIA fund-raiser in Louis Cantor's *Wheelin' on Beale*,[34] and a second photo prominently displayed at B. B. King's Blues Bar on Beale Street. Other performances of Elvis where he is visually "doing" Jackie: "Bossa Nova Baby" from the 1963 movie *Fun in Acapulco* and "Viva Las Vegas" from the 1964 movie *Viva Las Vegas,* where Elvis is called "Lucky Jackson."

With *Fun in Acapulco* we come across a surprising twinning: Nat King Cole. In Childress's novel *Tender*, we read: "Nat 'King' Cole was singing 'You Made Me Love You' with a soft velvet intensity. Leroy never sang any song half as well. It comforted him to hear somebody so much better than he would ever be."[35] In the early eighties, RCA released volume 4 of Elvis in its *Legendary Performer Series*, which included a home recording of "Mona Lisa." This recording was apparently made in the fifties, but Elvis does not do the rock 'n' roll version of Carl Mann or Conway Twitty: He does the song Nat King Cole–style, as a slow ballad. Elvis was singing for himself, trying to catch Cole's spirit: The record was not meant for release. So how would Elvis "do" Cole? Obliquely. In *Fun in Acapulco* Elvis ends with the song "Guadalajara," using the same arrangement as Cole did in his version in his second Spanish album. Elvis could do Cole when he (Cole) was stepping out of himself: Although both sang in Spanish, Cole sang it in his inimitable low-key way while Elvis did it Latin-style. And since Elvis loved Cole, I figured he must have paid tribute to him when he (Cole) died in 1965. What was it? It was "Love Letters." Cole recorded it in 4/4 timing in the forties. In 1962, Ketty Lester had a hit with a waltz arrangement of the song. Four years later, a year after Cole died, Elvis released his version of the song, also done waltz-style, but with a low voice close to Cole's. The desire to do Cole could be seen earlier. The first single Elvis re-

The greasy hairstyle for which Elvis became famous was the result of using the hair dressing black men used to straighten their hair. Joni Mabe. *Elvis with Bluesmen.* 1991. Glitter collage. 31" x 32". Courtesy of the artist.

leased when he came out of the army was "Stuck on You," sounding like "All Shook Up" in rhythm, theme, and syllables (thus giving the lie to the notion that he "died" in the army). The release was backed with "Fame and Fortune," a ballad. On the latter, which he performed on *The Sinatra Timex Show*, he sings the low notes like Billy Eckstine and the middle ones like Nat King Cole, particularly the way he holds the notes at the end of each verse (comparable to Cole's way on "Looking Back" of two years earlier, which has the same type of guitar backing as Elvis's "As Long As I Have You" from *King Creole*). And getting even more indirect: The Nat King Cole trio recorded Offenbach's "Barcarolle" as an instrumental in 1945—and Elvis sang it as "Tonight's So Right for Love" in his movie *G.I. Blues* when asked by Juliet Prowse to explain what he meant when he said the music must "ooze."

When I played "Fame and Fortune" the class did not hear Cole but Sam Cooke. "Okay," I said, "I will bring you Elvis doing Sam Cooke." I played the class Bobby Darin's big hit from 1959, "Mack the Knife," then Cooke's hit from 1963, "Frankie and Johnny," and then Elvis's 1964 single "Frankie and Johnny." The class could hear Elvis using Bobby Darin's arrangement and inflecting his voice like Sam Cooke. Mary Gravitt pointed out that Elvis had changed the point of view: Instead of singing as the omniscient narrator, he was singing as Johnny. Since she took the song to be a black song, she said that Elvis had taken on a black persona. Elvis released his single a year after Sam Cooke was shot dead by a woman. The line "Frankie I beg you don't shoot me" then takes on a new significance: Elvis was singing as Sam Cooke and pleading for his life. The fact that the song was from the movie *Frankie and Johnny* actually emphasizes the point since the version released as a single (also included on the LP) was not the arrangement used in the movie, even though the LP was called a soundtrack album.

Let me return to the point I made earlier about Elvis breaking up the words on "Just Because." This was not only because he stuttered. What he was doing was a profound political act: As Wilson Harris says of Conrad in "Heart of Darkness," he was breaking up the imposed colonial worldview, that is, the worldview imposed by the colonialists through their language. Harris says that Conrad does this by using hesitant and hedged adjectives.[36] Elvis was breaking up the inevitability of the language too, "language" including pop structures and idioms. This becomes clear when we hear his version of "White Christmas." Unfortunately for Bing Crosby, because I do not believe this is what Crosby intended, his version of the song was heard worldwide not only as a mainstream pop and seasonal song that everyone sang but also as a way in which the colonialists controlled the mind and the subconscious, the way in which the colonials were made to dream of a white Christmas, to dream of whiteness. Frantz Fanon explores the dreaming of whiteness in *Black Skin, White Masks*.[37] The song, which was a perennial favorite and, according to the *Guinness Book of World Records*, has sold more copies than any other pop record in the world, was therefore being used in colonial mind control. This was recognized very early by a black group called the Ravens (note their name, which is also the name of the main character and poet-storyteller in Ishmael Reed's novel *Flight to*

Canada.)[38] The Ravens did a version of the song in 1948 that signified on Bing Crosby's: A low voice sang it lower than Bing, and then the group took it higher and did all kinds of things with it. A few years later, Clyde McPhatter and the Drifters signified even more intensely, emphasizing the Ravens's version, the high voice of McPhatter becoming sprite-like, a trillingly mocking angel, and then ending with a few lines of that other perennial favorite, "Jingle Bells." When Elvis was recording his first Christmas album, he used the two versions as a guide, singing staccato, slurring the high notes, then combining the two ("I-hi-I-hi-I-hi-I"), ending with the piano playing "Jingle Bells." It was a politically subversive interpretation, smashing up the inevitability of the imposed aesthetic. Elvis was conscious of what he was doing: He reportedly laughed after recording the song and said he wondered what Bing would think of it. To emphasize the subversiveness of the Christmas album, "White Christmas" is the second song: The first is a growling blues (written by Leiber and Stoller) in which Santa Claus is a sugar daddy coming in a big black Cadillac.[39] Later on the same side, we have "Blue Christmas," then "Santa Bring My Baby Back to Me," a rock 'n' roll song that sounds like "Teddy Bear"—or like Jackie Wilson's "Reet Petite," which was in the Top Ten in England at the same time as the Elvis song, released in that country as a single. (I listened to the Top Ten at the time and heard Elvis at No. 7 followed by Jackie at No. 6.) Side two of the Christmas album ends with black gospel blues.

After "White Christmas" I played Bing's "Blue Hawaii," which was from the 1937 movie *Waikiki Wedding,* and then Elvis's version, done for the 1961 movie *Blue Hawaii*: Elvis is doing Bing straight, down to the opening guitar chords. Does this mean that Elvis sold out? The true opposition to a colonizer's (or European's) worldview, as Wole Soyinka suggested, is not reversing the system but having a worldview so broad it takes in the opposite and the thing itself. Brooks Ammerman said that after Elvis had revolutionized the pop boundaries, he was free to interpret and reinterpret the "traditional canon." Bing Crosby's "Blue Hawaii" was so well-known that Elvis wanted us to hear it in his version. It is not that Elvis thought nobody would ever hear Bing so he could get away with ripping Bing off. There is a second explanation: Elvis wanted us to respond subliminally to the notion that we were going to be watching the classic American movie about Hawaii as paradise, that is, a place whose simplicity (and sexual simplicity) the white man longs for—a version of the feudal world in which the lord is served by happy natives. Having established this feeling, Elvis subverts, or rewrites, it. This is emphasized by the last song, which is Elvis's reworking of the Andy Williams hit of two years earlier, "Hawaiian Wedding Song." Elvis wanted us to hear Andy Williams's in his version: but with a difference. In the movie *Blue Hawaii* the song begins with Hawaiians singing in their language. Elvis, dressed like a Hawaiian bridegroom, crosses a bridge to meet his Hawaiian fiancée and marry her. Near the end of the song, he sings in the Hawaiian language. It is not that Elvis is a Hawaiian, though it is remarkable how much like a Hawaiian he looks—it is that Elvis is crossing a bridge, taking back the music to the Hawaiians instead of ripping them off, as so much American music had done. One could say that Elvis was being a "bridgegroom."

When the movie begins, Chad/Elvis is met at the airport by his girl-friend, who is Hawaiian, though her father is French. He sings to her "Almost Always True," which is based on the French "Alouetta." In other words, he is bringing back a song to her from Europe, where he was stationed: Just because he was in the army did not mean he had only done army things. He makes her take him not home to his parents, who run a pineapple plantation and factory, but to the beach, where he can wash off the army experience. When in the water, he sees his (male) Hawaiian friends on a boat. Beginning with the native shell horn, they sing to him in their language, "Aloha Oe." He climbs onto the boat and ends the song with the line about meeting again. Recorded by Bing Crosby in 1936, the song was written in 1878 by Queen Lili'uokalani—who was deposed by the Americans in 1893. As I understand it, the phrase "aloha oe" means much more in the context of Hawaiian culture than the romanticized American usage. Elvis later sings what became one of his most popular songs, "Can't Help Falling in Love." The piece is based on "Plaisir d'Amour" by Giovanni Martini (1741–1816). Elvis sings it to his girlfriend's grand-mother, Mrs. Maneka, for her birthday as she sits on a throne-like chair. He gives her a music box he has brought from Europe and when it plays, he sings. The love song is therefore a tribute to the ma-trix. Elvis is paying respect to a relative of Queen Lili'uokalani, seeking to open a door (his last name is Gates) to correct history.[40]

In the movie *Girls! Girls! Girls!*, Elvis has dinner with a Chinese couple who are like his parents. After dinner, he takes his girlfriend to the balcony, where they see a Chinese lute. She asks him to sing something lutish. Playing a chord, he attempts to sing in a Chinese way, "Oo-oo-oo-oo-oeoooooo." He hears laughter: The two little daughters of the neighbors are laughing at him. Catching them, he asks them what's so funny. They tell him he sings Chinese very funny. Saying everybody wants to be a critic, he tells them to sing. They sing in Chinese and he translates into English. Then singing in Chinese, he dances behind them. Here we are presented with the notion of a bridge, this time with Chinese music. No wonder the working title of the movie was *Gumbo Ya-Ya*, a Creole expression meaning "everyone talk at once." The final title of the movie has been misinterpreted by some critics because it may be a smoke screen: Although "girls" would sound sexy, and even sexist, when many "girls" appear at the end, including the two Chinese girls, and dance to a version of the title song that has new words, they are dancing bridge versions of their own cultural dances while Elvis is adapting to them. The ending is not macho sexuality but stylization: Just as in the case of the Walker story, the "girls" (from whom Elvis is learning) can be seen as matrices of multiculturalism insofar as the little brother of the Chinese girls is playing the lute, which he could do because he had a cultural matrix.

• • •

In Alice Walker's novel *The Temple of My Familiar*, Fanny writes that Ola, the African dramatist, is writing a play about Elvis Presley because he is an Indian and the Americans do not see this. Ola says that in his play Elvis will be a metaphor for something he (Ola) is attempting to point out: "That in him white Americans found a reason to express their longing and appreciation for the repressed Native American and black parts of themselves. Those non-European qualities they have within them and all around them, but which they've been trained from birth to deny."[41] In *The Speaking Tree*, a book about India, Richard Lannoy discusses what he calls "the antipodes," quoting Carl Jung:

> Every Roman was surrounded by slaves. The slave and his psychology flooded ancient Italy, and every Roman became inwardly, and of course unwittingly, a slave. Because living constantly in the atmosphere of slaves, he became infected through the unconscious with their psychology. No one can shield himself from such an influence.[42]

Except for Jung's unfortunate use of the word "infected," which should have been in quotation marks and is clearly meant to be considered as such in Lannoy's book, the observation is an invaluable one. But Elvis was bringing in everyone *consciously*, chief among them those who had been locked out, the colonially oppressed, those who had their labor, their center, and their culture taken away from them.[43] He prepared engrams in our minds that we are in a position to extend, and we *need* to extend them for a sense of completion. In *Psycho-Cybernetics*, Maxwell Maltz says:

> Drs. Eccles and Sherrington tell us that the engrams in the human brain tend to change slightly each time they are "played back." They take on some of the tone and temper of our present mood, thinking and attitudes toward them. Also, each individual neuron may become a part of perhaps one hundred separate and distinct patterns—much as an individual tree in an orchard may form a part of a square, a rectangle, a triangle, or any number of larger squares, etc. The neuron in the original engram, of which it was a part, takes on some of the characteristics of subsequent engrams of which it becomes a part, and in so doing, changes somewhat the original engram. This is not only very interesting, but encouraging. It gives us reason to believe that adverse and unhappy childhood experiences, "traumas," etc. are not as permanent and fatal as some earlier psychologists would have us believe. We now know that not only does the past influence the present but that the present clearly influences the past.[44]

What this means is that when we bring in the singers Elvis was twinning himself with, we change our engrams and recognize and embrace the totality, we correct our misperceptions of the past, we recognize the past in the present, we change the past.

Elvis told us he was "King Creole." And what of the art? Ishmael Reed indicates in *The Last Days of Louisiana Red* that all art is gumbo.[45] Each cook has his or her own recipe, each cook takes the ingredients from elsewhere, and you judge the gumbo by its taste. *King Creole* begins with black street vendors calling/singing their wares in New Orleans, "Turtles, Berries, and Gumbo," and one of the carts has the sign "GUMBO." *Pot Luck* is the title of an Elvis LP.

• • •

According to F. Paul Wilson's short story "The Years the Music Died," Elvis is drafted by the army and sent abroad by the shadowy Commission as part of the plan to keep out the black American values colonialism has always kept out but rock 'n' roll has brought in.[46] In "Heart of Darkness," when Marlow goes to see Kurtz's fiancée after returning from Africa, he is unable to tell her the truth about what Kurtz really stood for as the biggest ivory agent and how he really died. He therefore invents a strategy for telling the story in an indirect way.[47] If so, it is possible Elvis was conscious of this being so, as suggested by *Tender*. So what could Elvis do? He sought a brief deferment to complete *King Creole*. When the Mafia-type boss played by Walter Matthau tells/threatens him to sing, Elvis goes up onto the stage and, backed by an all-black band including a trumpeter who looks like Louis Armstrong, growls out a challenging blues, "Trouble." It is possible that this song, as sung throughout the movie to the bosses who drafted Elvis and the forces behind them, is just as rebellious as his recording of "Hound Dog." This is my army, Elvis is saying. In fact, after the first two verses, the drums give out a tommy-gun roll (as in "Hound Dog"), which makes Elvis turn around; turning back he goes on to confidently sing the chorus. If so, would Elvis not continue the challenge in his movies after the army? The first movie is *G.I. Blues*. While this has been interpreted as a lighthearted Hollywood musical co-opting Elvis, one can read it instead as "signifying" on the army. Most Elvis fans had seen the army's cutting of Elvis's hair as comparable to Samson having his hair shorn off.[48] So what did Elvis do when he came out of the army? His hair was long when he gave his first press conference at Graceland. Then he voluntarily cut his hair short for *G.I. Blues*: This is signifying. The first song he sings with his band is a blues about the army. As the song nears the end, the Jordanaires sing the line "occupation G.I. blues" in the soothing way the Andrews Sisters sang "Boogie Woogie Bugle Boy." This provides a trampoline for Elvis to go low with the line and then bounce up screaming it as a restatement. Notice the double meaning of "occupation"—ostensibly "job" but also "occupation" by a foreign army. The narrator of "The Years the Music Died" thought Elvis was making safe movies, but he was really making "dangerous" movies masquerading as safe ones.[49] *Flaming Star*, in which Elvis is half-white and half-Kiowa, deals with the way land was alienated from the Kiowa people and is therefore a movie about colonialism not dissimilar to Ngugi wa Thiong'o's novel, *A Grain of Wheat*.[50] (I believe Elvis's movie was not released in Kenya in 1960 because the British had just succeeded in defeating the guerrillas who had fought to get back the land: The movie would remind the people that it was not the black man but the white man who had come as an intruder and taken away the land.) In *Stay Away, Joe*, Elvis plays a modern-day Navajo, a Trickster who survives by his wits. The movie is about neocolonialism and the bourgeois dreams of Third World people, dreams that turn out to be risky fantasies.

I talked earlier about "Hound Dog" and looping. In 1955, Bill Haley recorded "Two Hound Dogs," which, according to Joel Whitburn, reached its peak of No. 50 on the charts on July 2.[51] Haley's song begins with the band singing out "Hound Dog." Haley sings about rhythm and blues being the two hound dogs. He also has a line about a white rabbit crossing the road. The song ends with the band howling like dogs, just the way Big Mama Thornton's "Hound Dog" ends. Was not Elvis's version, then, also a response to Haley's, where he reverses the hound dog? Elvis recorded "Hound Dog" on July 2, 1956, over a year after Haley's song. To emphasize the Haley connection: In 1956, Haley's "Hot Dog Buddy Buddy" reached its peak of No. 60 on July 6: Elvis recorded "Hot Dog" for his movie *Loving You* in February 1957. Arnold Shaw assumes that Elvis's "Hound Dog" is a "cover" only of Big Mama Thornton's version. "And it makes no sense when a man sings it," he says. "The hound dog scratching around the door is a horny and unreliable male—and Big Mama's scorn was sharp and biting."[52] But Shaw does not note that there is no rabbit in her version whereas there is in Elvis's, as in Haley's. Catron Grieves, who says she is Cherokee, told me that the "hound dog" in Elvis's version is the bloodhound who tracks down the runaway slave on behalf of the master. The hound dog is no friend of the runaway: But he has never caught the rabbit, that is, the Trickster. (There are some Bugs Bunny cartoons in which the hound dogs try to track him down on behalf of the master.) It is interesting to identify the many hound dogs Elvis implies in different performances of the song. For example, in the version at Madison Square Garden referred to earlier, he suddenly breaks into a march.

In Ishmael Reed's *The Last Days of Louisiana Red*, Ed Yellings has been killed. PaPa LaBas (the U.S. version of LegBa, the Yoruba god of the Crossroads) is trying to track down the killer. He discovers that one stanza of "Minnie the Moocher," the hit song by Cab Calloway, has been tampered with. He believes that if he can find out who tampered with the verse and what the tampered verse is, he can find out who killed Ed Yellings. Taking this as metaphor, we have the notion of the tampered text. Who has tampered with the text and why? Do artists do some of their own tampering in order to get their message through? If so, we the listener/reader have to do some de-tampering instead of expecting the texts to be pure. And if there is tampering of texts, we have need of the Trickster, the Jungian light-bringer. In the novel *Stay Away, Joe* by Dan Cushman, Joe (who is trouble: hence people's name for him, Stay Away) has come back from Korea.[53] In the movie, done fifteen years later, it is not clear where Joe, played by Elvis, has come back from: Could he have come back from Vietnam? There is a stylized scene, where Joe is buying a car, that seems to need background music different from the syrupy music actually used. "Too Much Monkey Business" would fit here. Elvis recorded it just after completing the movie. Chuck Berry's version of twelve years earlier mentioned being from "Yokohama": Elvis changes the word to "Vietnam." The movie was released the same year as the song was released on an album entitled *Singer Presents Elvis Singing Flaming Star and Others*, the album only being available at Singer Sewing Centers in conjunction with (the sponsorship of) the forthcoming TV special. Elvis is being the Trickster in *Stay Away, Joe*, just like Anancy of my epigraph.

• • •

"Philosopher Jean Gebser sees Petrarch's ascent of Mont Ventoux in Provence [in 1336] as a key event in eye dominance in Europe, far beyond what had already been initialed by the Greeks," says Berendt.[54] This eye dominance of Europe paved the way for colonialism, as scholars such as Mary Louise Pratt and David Spur have shown: The eye saw the landscape as empty, ready to be occupied, and either did not see the people who were there or saw them as "the other," inferior. Berendt says that humanity's great spiritual books are full of exhortations to hear: "The ear registers ten octaves and the eye only one," he points out.[55] The thrust of my "Elvis as Anthology" was to hear: I made the class listen to 150 songs by Elvis in juxtaposition with 159 by 116 other performers. (And it had taken me decades to discover this: On the cover of my first Elvis LP, which I chanced upon in a Kampala record shop nearly forty years ago, Elvis's eyes are closed and his mouth is open, inviting us to hear, not merely see, the truth of his message.) Not that we sought to block the eye: We did have some videos and extracts from movies and we read books. But we were seeking balance by listening—which, I came to realize, was why Jonathan Walton had urged me to teach the class. The emphasis on hearing and listening was leading to a holistic way of learning and bringing in the folk who had been locked out. No wonder as the narrator in *Palace of the Peacock* is about to achieve wholeness, he hears "the music of the peacock" and realizes "I am in the music" for "this was the inner music and voice of the peacock I suddenly encountered and echoed and sang as I had never heard myself sing before."[56]

After listening, reading, and seeing, there is the question of interpretation. As I said about *Maru* and *Season of Migration to the North*, the artist needs the interpreter, that is, the critic. Traynor as vocal artist in Walker's story did not succeed in his desire to draw attention through his version to Gracie Mae Still's song. Walker as literary artist identifies what he was doing in an aesthetic form. It requires the critic, with a frame of reference, to complete the task.

Traynor came to see Gracie Mae Still not in a little red Corvette but in a red Thunderbird, which, in the new world, is related to the bird that arises out of its own ashes, the phoenix. One of Elvis's suits on display at the museum at Graceland has a phoenix on it. While the word comes from the Greeks, the bird comes from Egyptian, that is, African mythology: It is the double of Ra, the Sun God.[57] Elvis's first records were on Sun. He then moved on to RCA, that is, Radio Corporation of America. The suit he wore at his last concert had on it the Aztec calendar, at the center of which is the Sun God. One of his favorite horses was named Rising Sun. Elvis's best-selling record was "It's Now or Never," which is "O Sole Mio," which is "Oh My Sun."

PART TWO
RACE

To.
The Tupelo ...
Magdalene Morgan
Elvis Presley
my First Love My
First Boy Friend.

*Ten-year-old Elvis and girlfriend Magdalene Morgan after church service in
Tupelo.* Courtesy of Becky Martin.

5 Elvis as Southerner

JOHN SHELTON REED

Let me start with an appropriately modest summary of my qualifications for this job:

- Elvis and I have the same birthday.
- I, too, was a teenager in Tennessee.
- My grandparents, like his, were cousins.

Somehow I doubt that you're impressed, and you probably shouldn't be. The part of east Tennessee I come from is closer geographically to New York State than it is to Memphis, more Appalachia than Deep South. My January 8 birthday came a crucial seven years after his: I don't remember the Great Depression, FDR, or much of World War II; and I was just a thirteen-year-old paper boy when Elvis played the Civic Auditorium in Kingsport—too young to go hear him, too young even to want to. Which leaves us only with those grandparents, and I don't know what can be made of that.

So I can't speak about Elvis with the kind of authority that impresses southerners. I never even met the man. My knowledge, such as it is, is all second-hand book-learning, not from experience or intuition. And even my book-learning is severely limited. Getting ready for this I checked out what we academic types call "the literature" on Elvis, and I'm here to tell you there's a hunka hunka literature out there. Elvis can't quite match the Civil War (which I'm told has generated an average of a book a day since Appomattox), but since 1968 alone the Library of Congress has catalogued over 300 books about him, in at least nine languages. A magazine-and-journal database includes over 200 articles in just the last seven years with the word "Elvis" in the title.[1] You'll find them in publications ranging from the

Journal of Philately to *Christianity and Crisis, Ladies' Home Journal* to the *UCLA Law Review, Bon Appetit* to *Cultural Studies*. There's an article in *Florists' Review* on how to have an "Elvis wedding," while *Studies in Popular Culture* offers a treatise on "Elvis and the Aesthetics of Post-Modernism." Of course, these databases aren't infallible. One article I turned up had the fascinating title "Surgical Management of Collapsed Elvis in a Jaguar," which sounds like the title of a piece of visionary art. But actually it appeared in the *Journal of the American Veterinary Medical Association* and "Elvis" was just a typo for "Pelvis"—not the first time those two words have been associated.

And when we turn from magazines to newspapers things get *really* out of hand: Since 1989 nearly 1,400 stories in major newspapers have referred to Elvis.[2] A recent example from the *Boston Globe* is "Pocahontas: The Elvis Connection," about Wayne Newton's announcement that he's descended from Pocahontas and his belief that Elvis is reaching out to him from Beyond. And this is the more or less *respectable* press: *Weekly World News* and other purveyors of stories like "Statue of Elvis Found on Mars" aren't indexed.

After all this, I quickly gave up any thoughts I had of mastering what's already been written about Elvis. It probably can't be done. Certainly not if you're going to do anything else. Can anything possibly remain to be said? Clearly the boy has made a name for himself. Long ago Elvis became one of those figures like Scarlett or Sherlock, figures on a first-name basis with the world. (Of course it helped that his first name wasn't, say, Robert.) "Elvis" has even become a common noun, as in one news story I found about a guy known as "the Elvis of Bowling."[3]

How did this happen? The sociology of genius is an interesting study, and every bit as important as the genetics and psychology of it. Elvis had an extraordinary talent, but he also had the great good fortune to be in the right place at the right time for that talent to be recognized and acclaimed. His flower didn't bloom unseen or waste its sweetness very long on the desert air of the First Assembly of God. But whatever the balance of individual genius and social readiness to nurture and to reward it, the combination has clearly made him a figure of unique cultural importance.

So I thought I'd begin with how Elvis was *not* unique—how he was, in many ways, quite ordinary. In most respects, it would interest a sociologist that he was born and raised in an ordinary southern white family, and that he was born and raised in an ordinary southern town. You could even say that the Presleys and Tupelo were extraordinarily ordinary—not just typical but exemplary. The histories of the Presleys and of Tupelo illustrate much broader themes in southern history; one way or another they illustrate important trends from the collapse of cotton tenancy to the rise of Pentecostalism, and implicate high-profile southern institutions from Parchman penitentiary to TVA.

It's worth emphasizing Elvis's ordinariness, I think, because that's part of his fascination and his appeal. Although he became a remarkable cultural phenomenon, his background and first nineteen years were, in broad outline, much the same as those of hundreds of thousands of other southern white boys. To understand how he was unique, we have to start by understanding how he wasn't. To understand him, you have to understand where he came from. You can't *stop* there, but that's where you have to start.

He was born, of course, in 1935, in Tupelo, the son of Vernon Presley and the former Gladys Smith, and, as Elaine Dundy's genealogical research makes clear, even his ancestry was typical for a southern white boy.[4] Elvis's ancestors, like those of most white southerners, were mostly British. The Smiths, his mother's family, were of English descent, moving west from South Carolina after the Civil War, but most of the rest were Celtic rather than Anglo-Saxon. The Presley name came to America with Scots who settled in North Carolina in the eighteenth century, then moved south and west over the years. Most of Elvis's other ancestors were Scotch-*Irish,* part of the great wave of migration from Scotland to Ulster to Pennsylvania, then down the Shenandoah Valley to the southern interior from southwest Virginia to Texas.[5]

The story of Elvis's forebears, like those of many white southerners, was one of restless mobility: settling, then moving on, settling again for a generation or two, then moving on again, escaping problems or seeking opportunity or both, looking for a fresh start somewhere else. Most of them were farmers—after the early 1800s cotton farmers—and most were yeomen of the sort Daniel Hundley described in 1860.[6] "Nearly always poor, at least so far as this world's goods are to be taken into the account," Hundley wrote, their only "inheritance [was] the ability and the will to earn an honest livelihood . . . by the toilsome sweat of their own brows." The southern yeoman wasn't often a slaveholder—he couldn't afford it—but when he was he worked alongside his slaves, and Hundley was amused that he was "not offended when they called him familiarly by his Christian name."

Hundley goes on to add that the yeoman exhibited "a manly independence of character"; that he would not "under any circumstances humiliate himself to curry favor with the rich or those in authority"; that he was courageous, never wounded from behind. But he wasn't all tedious Jeffersonian nobility: Hundley added that he was fond of turkey shoots, frolics, barbecues, and—true to his Scotch-Irish heritage—the drinking of home-brewed spirits. (We'll come back to those spirits in a moment because they figure in Elvis's story.)

Two-thirds of southern white families didn't own slaves in 1860. Most of those were yeomen and so were an appreciable fraction of the slaveholders. Culturally if not politically these people were the backbone of the Old South, as Frank Owsley showed some time ago in his pathbreaking *Plain Folk of the Old South*.[7] They furnished the foot soldiers of the Confederate Army. But not all of them stood up for "Dixie" in 1861. Gladys's father was named Robert Lee Smith— hard to get more Confederate than that—but one of Elvis's great-great-grandfathers appears to have been a Confederate deserter (twice), and a collateral relative was a North Alabama Unionist who named a son "Grant," *after* the Civil War. This record of mixed, or shifting, or nonexistent Confederate loyalties is far more common in southern genealogies than the mythology of the Lost Cause allowed, and probably not many latter-day southerners have ancestry that would stand up to the kind of scrutiny that Elvis's has received.[8]

Recall the "American Trilogy," the medley that Elvis often used for his Las Vegas finale, which mixed up "Dixie" and "The Battle Hymn of the Republic" and threw in the Negro spiritual "All My Trials" for good measure. He came by the mixture of Union and Confederate honestly.[9] It hasn't been established that any of his forebears were African-American, but there was a great-great-great-grandfather who first fought the Indians with Andy Jackson and then married one, a woman named Morning Dove White who gave Elvis the Cherokee great-great-great-grandmother that almost every southerner claims to have. (It's not Pocahontas, but it'll do.)

By the beginning of the twentieth century, many of the South's white yeomen had lost their land and had joined the great majority of southern blacks as sharecroppers and tenant farmers.[10] Half the South's farmers—two-thirds of all cotton farmers—didn't own the land they farmed, and half of the South's tenants and sharecroppers were white. Among them were both of Elvis's grandfathers. Vernon Presley's father, J. D., was one of ten children (by unknown fathers) of a "single mother." She supported her family by farming on shares, and her son

Vernon and Gladys were only a generation ahead of the Hale County, Alabama, families portrayed by James Agee and Walker Evans in Let Us Now Praise Famous Men. *Those families were still sharecropping when Agee and Evans paid their famous visit in the late 1930s.* Three-year-old Elvis with his parents, Gladys Love Presley and Vernon Elvis Presley. Courtesy of Michael Ochs Archive.

followed in her footsteps. Gladys Presley's father, Bob Smith, was a sharecropper, too, but soon after he married his first cousin Doll, she went to bed with the tuberculosis that was endemic in the rural South and spent the rest of her surprisingly lengthy life as that classic southern figure, the "shut-in." Bob Smith found it necessary to augment his family's meager farming income by distilling and selling illegal whiskey.

When Vernon Presley and Gladys Smith moved to East Tupelo, they were among the first of their families to leave the land: Gladys to run a sewing machine in the Tupelo Garment Center for $2 a day; Vernon to pursue a string of odd but definitely urban jobs—milkman, cabinetmaker, lumberyard worker, delivery-truck driver (delivering wholesale groceries and also, it appears, bootleg liquor).

Incidentally, Gladys was not unusual in being a working woman. In this century, southern women have actually been more likely than women elsewhere to work outside their homes. Many of them—and probably most of their men—would have preferred it otherwise, but economic circumstances made it necessary. This was certainly true for the Presleys. Whenever the family could afford it, Gladys left the labor force. But they could seldom afford it. She worked for the garment factory before and during her pregnancy. She picked cotton with the young Elvis sitting on her picking sack. She worked at the Mid-South Laundry. After the family moved to Memphis she found work immediately as a seamstress for Fashion Curtains. Later she worked in a cafeteria, then as a nurse's aide.[11]

When Elvis was born, two-thirds of all southerners lived in the countryside and half the South's labor force were farmers. Howard Finster. *Elvis-At-3.* ca. 1989. Tractor enamel on wood. Collection of Peter Paul.

In moving to Tupelo the Presleys were a small part of a great demographic trend that moved rural southerners into towns, farmers into industrial and service occupations. Vernon and Gladys were only a generation ahead of the Hale County, Alabama, families that were portrayed by James Agee and Walker Evans in *Let Us Now Praise Famous Men.*[12] Those families were still sharecropping when Agee and Evans paid their famous visit in the late 1930s; forty years later their children had made the same transition Vernon and Gladys made:

Both men and women were working in service and industrial occupations—welder, meatpacker, nursing-home attendant, and so forth. Economically, they were still near the bottom, but the bottom wasn't nearly so low as it had been in the 1930s.

When Elvis was born, two-thirds of all southerners lived in the countryside and half the South's labor force were farmers; by the time of his death, two-thirds of southerners were urban and suburban folk; fewer than 5 percent were farmers and the sharecropper was an endangered species.

What kind of place was Tupelo when the young Presley family lived there? It was very different from the town of today. And it was part of a state and a region that were very different from what *they* are today. An Englishman named L. P. Hartley once wrote, "The past is a foreign country; they do things differently there"—and certainly that's true for the American South. In my experience as a teacher, I've found it almost impossible for young people today really to understand what it meant to live in the South of the 1930s. What it meant to live with the day-to-day constraints and indignities of Jim Crow—not just to live with them, but to take them for granted as simply *how things are*. What it meant to live in a region as poor as the South—a region with a per capita income about the same as that of Venezuela's today, about half of what it was elsewhere in the United States. We need to recognize that those among us who once lived in that South—those who, like the Presleys, grew up in that "foreign country" of the past—made a transition in their lifetimes as dramatic and sometimes as wrenching as emigration.

In 1938 Franklin Roosevelt would describe the entire South as "the Nation's No. 1 economic problem"—this with the Depression going on.[13] A government commission had drawn a picture of poverty, dependence, ignorance, disease, malnutrition, inadequate housing, and environmental degradation that closely parallels accounts of life in the Third World today. The researches of Howard Odum and his colleagues at North Carolina, Charles Johnson at Fisk, and other sociologists of the 1930s provided the basis for that report and showed that the South's problems were concentrated in the old Cotton Belt of the Deep South, that long arc from eastern North Carolina to east Texas where the shadow of the plantation still lingered. In this respect, as in many others, Mississippi was the most southern of the southern states. In 1931 H. L. Mencken had put together indicators of health, literacy, economic well-being, and so forth to show readers of the *American Mercury* that what he called "the level of civilization" was lower in the former Confederate states than anywhere else in the country.[14] And by these measures, Mencken announced, "the worst American state" was Mississippi.

In the year of Elvis's birth, Tupelo was home to some 7,000 souls and served another 30,000 residents of Lee County as a market, banking, and shopping center.[15] Two-thirds of the county's residents were white; only a couple dozen were foreign-born. Outside Tupelo, four out of five Lee Countians lived on farms, most of them growing cotton, many—like Elvis's grandparents—as tenants or sharecroppers. Vaughan Grisham calculates that in 1930 the cash income of the average Lee County cotton farmer had fallen to something on the order of $200, *before* paying loan interest, fertilizer bills, and the like. Tupelo was in many respects a typical Cotton Belt county seat, and to the considerable extent that its prosperity was tied up with the cotton economy, the town was in serious trouble—like the South as a whole. But in some ways the town was unusual, certainly for Mississippi. It had hedged its economic bets, and it pointed the way to the South's future.

Tupelo had come into being in 1859 when the Mobile & Ohio Railroad was built to pass near a pond lined with tupelo gum trees. Folks from a nearby village bypassed by the railroad moved to the new settlement, which they first called Gum Pond, then Tupelo. Within a year they had built a railroad station, a store, and two saloons. The new town played a modest role in the Civil War—Forrest and Beauregard both headquartered there at one time or another—but the period that interests us begins in the 1880s. It was then that Tupelo beat out its rivals for the St. Louis–San Francisco Railroad, persuading the railroad to deviate from a more direct route by offering what one historian discreetly calls "liberal inducements"—a practice that would come to full flower fifty years later, and one that isn't unknown even today.

Once it had become the junction point for two railroad lines, Tupelo was set to emerge in the twentieth century as a go-getting, industrial town of a sort more common in northern Alabama, Georgia, or the Carolina piedmont than in Mississippi. In 1938 the three-year-old Elvis lived in what the WPA state guide said was "perhaps Mississippi's best example of what contemporary commentators call the 'New South'—industry rising in the midst of agriculture and agricultural customs."[16] The year Elvis was born, Mississippi elected as its governor Hugh White, who instituted a program he called BAWI—"Balance Agriculture with Industry." Tupelo had been trying for decades, with some success, to do just that.

It's easy to make fun of the kind of relentless New South boosters who could write brochures like this early-twentieth-century one, quoted by Elaine Dundy:

> Wanted! Five thousand enthusiastic, thrifty, loyal people to move to Tupelo and Lee County within the next five years and make this their home. Brilliant opportunities loom for people who come to Lee County which promises to be the greatest and the best county in Mississippi.

A pamphlet from the 1920s called "Tupelo, Premier City of Northeast Mississippi" extolled the city's virtues. Dundy says it was "distributed throughout the South boasting of [the town's] excellent schools, government fish hatchery, Tupelo cotton mills, fertilizer factory, fire and sewage system, its handsome courthouse, its beautiful post office, sixteen passenger trains daily, a beautiful Confederate monument, the annual Mississippi-Alabama State Fair; two railroad systems, a cotton market, a well-organized police station, an ice factory, a creamery, the mills, a hospital, and a Coca-Cola bottling plant." The pamphlet

Elvis returns home to Tupelo and the Mississippi-Alabama State Fair, September 25, 1956. Terry Wood photo.

added: "In the city of 6,000, 5,999 are boosters in every sense of the word." And I wouldn't have cared to be the one who wasn't.

Again, it's easy to make fun of this mentality, and W. J. Cash did it savagely in *The Mind of the South*.[17] But the efforts of Tupelo's boosters had paid off. It's instructive to look at the "points of interest" that 1938 guide lists for Tupelo. There's that fish hatchery, obtained for the town by an influential congressman. And there's a boulder erected by the Colonial Dames to commemorate DeSoto's expedition. Otherwise, however, every single point of interest mentioned was a factory or a mill firmly anchored on the products of local agriculture. One of them, significantly, was *not* based on cotton. Following the lead of the *Progressive Farmer* magazine and papers like the *Memphis Commercial Appeal*, Tupelo's boosters had long been active in the southern campaign for agricultural diversification. The railroads had urged farmers to grow strawberries and tomatoes; the town's newspaper and its forward-looking business community had given away packaged home orchards and held lotteries with Jersey cattle as the prize.

Although diversification was a tricky proposition, by the 1930s the Tupelo area had enough dairy operations that Carnation Milk had found it worthwhile to open a condensing plant in the town. By 1938 it was producing 30 million cans of graham cracker–crust pies that had already become a staple of the southern table. Aside from the condensory, however, all of Tupelo's industry depended on the products of those cotton fields. The Tupelo Cotton Mill, one of the largest in the South, produced "more than 25 miles of cloth a day." The garment plant, where Gladys Presley ran a sewing machine for $2 a day, took that cloth and turned it into shirts. Reed's Manufacturing employed 600 women to make work dresses, smocks, and aprons. Milam Manufacturing used the same cotton fabric to make children's clothes. These plants relied on the surrounding countryside for much of their labor, as well as for their raw materials. Gladys was actually unusual in living in town: 85 percent of the 1,200 women who worked in Tupelo's garment factories lived outside of town and rode special school buses to work.

Mississippi's combination of economic distress and reliable Democratic voting meant that the New Deal was very much a presence in the state. The WPA provided at least two of Vernon's many jobs: one in the 1930s when he worked briefly on the expansion of the Biloxi shipyard, another during the war when he helped to build "Japtown," a POW camp near Como. Right outside of Tupelo was the Tupelo

When Gladys was seven months pregnant Franklin Roosevelt came to town, the most exciting event in Lee County since Machine Gun Kelly robbed the bank in 1932. Courtesy of Tupelo Museum.

Homestead Resettlement Project, built by the Federal Resettlement Administration. But the most significant New Deal program for Tupelo was TVA. Thanks to its longtime congressman, John Elliott Rankin, the chief promoter of low-cost power in Congress, Tupelo was named America's "First TVA City," and when Gladys was seven months' pregnant Franklin Roosevelt came to town, the most exciting event in Lee County since Machine Gun Kelly robbed the bank in 1932. A crowd of 75,000 turned out to greet the president, and thereafter TVA supplied the power for everything from the Carnation condensory to the movie projector at the Strand Theater (which the young Elvis preferred, rats and all, to the Lyric, because it was only a dime).

Even more electrifying than FDR's visit was an event that took place a little over a year after Elvis's birth. At 9:04 on the evening of April 5, 1936, a tornado hit the town. In thirty-three seconds it leveled forty-eight blocks, 900 homes, and scores of other buildings including the Methodist Church across the street from the Presley house. It killed over 200 people—twice as many as Hurricane Camille killed in the entire state in 1969 (for which Elvis gave a benefit concert in Biloxi)—and estimates of the number injured range up to 2,000. This in a town of 7,000 inhabitants! The births of heroes are often marked with signs and portents, but this was something else.

Tupelo had often referred to itself as "the city beautiful." This designation didn't apply to the mill housing of South Tupelo or to East Tupelo, on the "wrong side of the tracks" (where Vernon built the house where Elvis was born), or to black neighborhoods like Shake Rag, next door to where the Presleys moved after East Tupelo. But the town had taken great pride in its broad streets and lofty trees. Vaughan Grisham points out that the tornado's devastation apparently put an end to that proud self-designation. The town bounced back with remarkable resilience, but it never again called itself "the city beautiful."

The next year saw another blow to the town's self-image as the labor unrest that had troubled the South's textile industry elsewhere finally arrived in northeast Mississippi. Gladys's $2-a-day wage at the garment plant was standard. That worked out to about $500 a year, and it may have looked good to a cotton cropper whose last crop paid him $200. But it was pretty far from a comfortable living, and in 1937 workers at the textile mill staged a sit-down strike, demanding a 15 percent raise and a forty-hour rather than forty-six–hour week. Soon after, an organizer from the ILGWU appeared in town and began to talk to Gladys's former coworkers at the garment plant.

Vaughan Grisham reports that the town's newspaper covered the dispute objectively and even sympathetically, but most of Tupelo's business leaders moved quickly to oppose the strike and the unionizing drive. Low wages were, after all, one of southern industry's few competitive advantages. The National Guard engaged in "artillery practice" next to the mill. After two weeks the strike folded, after a rumor circulated that the mill owners planned to burn the mill and blame the strikers. Jimmy Cox, a leader of the strike, was grabbed on the street and taken for a ride. A rope was put around his neck and tied to the car axle, but his abductors finally settled for a savage beating. Twenty women at the garment plant who had joined the ILGWU were fired, and the organizer was threatened and driven from town. As it had been elsewhere in the South, ruthless opposition was effective. No more was heard about unionization, and Tupelo's competitive advantage remained intact.

Another aspect of Tupelo that its boosters didn't emphasize was its pattern of race relations. Day-to-day, the races rubbed along together, but they did it within the usual southern framework of black disenfranchisement, segregation of public facilities and much of private life, petty harassment, and occasionally brutal intimidation. Grisham recounts, for example, the routine humiliations black Tupeloans ex-

Tupelo had often referred to itself as "the city beautiful." This designation didn't apply to the mill housing of South Tupelo or to East Tupelo, on the "wrong side of the tracks" (where Vernon built the house where Elvis was born), or to black neighborhoods like Shake Rag, next door to where the Presleys moved after East Tupelo. But the town had taken great pride in its broad streets and lofty trees. Courtesy of Tupelo Museum.

perienced at the hands of the police. Many responded by joining the Great Migration that took millions of southern blacks from the rural and small-town South to southern cities and beyond, to the cities of the Northeast and Midwest.

Congressman Rankin may have been a great champion of TVA, but he was better known throughout the nation as a race-baiting southern demagogue. His political career began after World War I when he founded a racist newspaper called *New Era*. Grisham summarizes what that paper was all about: "The favorite themes were the defense of lynchings, pleas for the repudiation of the Fifteenth Amendment and alterations of the Fourteenth Amendment of the Constitution, and general assaults on 'do-good troublemakers.'" Rankin used this platform to get elected to Congress in 1920. A black leader commented later, "Thank God Mr. Rankin got himself sent to Washington or I suppose all of us colored people would have had to leave Tupelo." When Elvis was ten years old his congressman was still running against "interests outside the state who literally hate the white people of the South and want to destroy everything for which we stand."[18]

But it tells us something about Tupelo that Rankin was finally unseated in 1952, when his rhetoric came to be seen as an impediment to industrialization. Although being black in Tupelo was no picnic, the town's boosterism spared it the worst excesses of Jim Crow's death throes. Grisham tells a revealing story. He spoke to a segregationist who had sworn to kill anyone advocating desegregation, and asked him about the editor of the *Tupelo Daily Journal*, who had been a moderate, even liberal, voice in race relations. The man replied, "I just knew that George McLean [the editor] was a God-damned Communist, but he was the man who was bringing jobs into the area and if anything happened to him we would have all been sunk." All in all, it seems Tupelo was something of a vest-pocket, Mississippi version of Atlanta, "the city too busy to hate."

So much for the town's economic and political institutions, and they are certainly much of what made Tupelo Tupelo. But there were other institutions that were equally important in shaping the life of the town. Although the WPA guide didn't mention it, Tupelo, like almost every other southern town, was a city of churches—dozens of them in the town and the nearby countryside, ranging from the big Baptist and Methodist establishments downtown to the more modest churches and tabernacles serving the white mill workers and common folk of East and South Tupelo and the black residents of Tupelo's three Negro sections. Two Tupelo churches figure prominently in Elvis's story.

One, of course, is the Assembly of God in East Tupelo, the church the Presleys attended. It was built by the Reverend Gains Mansell, Gladys's uncle, and after World War II Vernon himself became a deacon. The denomination was a new one—founded in Hot Springs, Arkansas, in 1914, it was a mere twenty years old when Elvis was born—but it was one of the fastest-growing of the great family of Pentecostal and Holiness groups that trace their origins to what some have called the "Third Great Awakening" at the turn of the century. Some of those groups are black, some are white, a few are strikingly both, but all believe in such gifts of the Holy Spirit as speaking in tongues; most practice faith healing, foot washing, and other activities found in scripture; nearly all have traditions of lively and powerful gospel music; and none gets much respect from uptown Christians, much less from secular humanists.[19]

The other Tupelo church that figures in our story is the Sanctified Church, which met in a permanent tent in the black neighborhood of

Shake Rag. After the Presley's moved from East Tupelo into town they lived on the edge of Shake Rag, and much speculation has centered on how much exposure the young Elvis had to the black gospel music being performed down the street from his house. After he moved to Memphis, of course, we don't have to speculate.

So this was the town in which Elvis was born and in which he spent his first thirteen years. During the 1930s and 1940s Tupelo's population was growing, slowly, and the rural population of Lee County was declining, as country folk like Vernon and Gladys moved to town to escape the precarious life of tenant farming for the steady, if underpaid, discipline of the factory. Tornadoes, strikes, presidential visits, and bank robberies were the exception, not the rule. For all that it would have liked to bustle, it was basically a quiet, country sort of place, like scores if not hundreds of others, a county seat existing in symbiosis with its surrounding countryside. But it would be a mistake to think of Tupelo as an isolated backwater—a backwater it may have been, but hardly isolated. Remember those sixteen passenger trains a day. And almost exactly 100 miles to the northeast was the big city of Memphis. It *was* a big city, with a population of over 300,000—a railroad center, home to cotton brokers, a major mule market, and the annual Cotton Carnival—and it served a substantial hinterland. The Peabody Hotel was the haunt of white cotton buyers, planters, and debutantes, and Beale Street provided shopping and nightlife not just for Negro Memphis—40 percent of the city's population—but for black folk from miles around. Memphis didn't play the same role for northeast Mississippi that it did for the Delta, but it was always there, just over the horizon. Elvis's great-uncle, the mayor of East Tupelo, used to take the town's schoolchildren on a bus for excursions to the Memphis Zoo, and it was a great day when the East Tupelo Consolidated School's band was invited to play for the Cotton Carnival.

When Vernon lost his truck-driving job in 1948, it was time to move on, time for another fresh start, and Memphis must have been an appealing choice. From time to time Vernon had joined the army of southern men who worked essentially as what the Germans call *Gastarbeiter*—guest workers—leaving their families to do factory work in one big city or another. During the war he had worked for a while in Memphis, and he knew his way around.

When the Presleys left Tupelo for the big city, once again they were a typical part of a larger picture. Vaughan Grisham reports that 20 percent of Mississippi's population left the state during the 1950s, the culmination of a movement from the rural and small-town South that was one of the great mass migrations of human history. In 1960 10 million Americans born in the South were living outside the region altogether, mostly in northern cities. We hear a lot about the Great Migration of blacks, but two-thirds of that 10 million were white.

On May 17, 1954, the Supreme Court handed down its historic decision in *Brown v. Board of Education*, a day that came to be known in some white southern circles as "Black Monday." It marked the beginning of the end of Jim Crow, of de jure racial segregation in the South. Seven weeks later to the day, on another Monday, July 5, Elvis recorded a country-flavored version of the rhythm-and-blues hit "That's All Right, Mama," an act of *musical* integration that set the stage for rock and roll. And he knew what he was doing. He said, "The colored folks been singing it and playing it just like I'm doin' now, man, for more years than I know. They played it like that in the shanties and in their juke joints, and nobody paid it no mind 'til I goosed it up."[20] That spring of 1954 Elvis, like the South as a whole, took a big step into the unknown, and neither would ever be the same.

I heard a story the other day that reminded me of Elvis. It's about an old boy who was out fishing on one of our power-company lakes in North Carolina when he caught an enormous catfish. He hauled it up on the dock and cut it open, and this genie appeared. "I am the genie of the catfish," it said, "and you can have one wish."

The old boy was startled, but he pulled himself together and looked hard at the genie. "Let me get this straight," he said. "You mean I can have anything I want?"

"That's right," said the genie. "Anything you want."

The fellow looked at his boat, and his dock, and the lake, and scratched his head and said, "I believe I'd like a cold beer."

As I say, that story reminded me of Elvis. Here's a southern boy who had success beyond measure and wealth beyond imagining. He could have had anything he wanted, but, in effect, he looked around, scratched his head, and said, "I believe I'd like a peanut-butter and banana sandwich."

Elvis became a pop-culture icon and—never forget—a phenomenal musical influence. As Bruce Springsteen has said, "It was like he came along and whispered some dream in everybody's ear, and somehow we all dreamed it." Eventually, like all too many other southern musicians, he became the classic hero-victim, doomed by his own excesses. But my point is that he remained to a remarkable extent what he was raised to be in the Tupelo years: a polite and humble gospel-singing southern boy, who loved his mama, greasy food, and hanging out with the boys. As we say in the South, he didn't get above his raising—which is why so many of us who never met him feel as if we've known him all our lives.

Howard Finster. *Howard: 1956 Self-Portrait.* ca. late 1980s. Enamel and marker on wood. Courtesy of Larry Clemons.

6 Elvis Presley as Redneck

WILL CAMPBELL

If we are now to academize Elvis Presley, there is one word and concept that must be dealt with at the outset. That word is "redneck." It must be dealt with because it is an ugly word, an invective used to defame a proud and tragic people, the poor, white, rural, working class of the South; a word used often to berate Elvis Presley and his people because the word is used as a synonym for "bigot." If I had said the word we must consider is "nigger," "chink," "Jap," "kike," "dago," "spick," "chick," or "broad," all of you would have been morally outraged at just hearing those despicable epithets said aloud. At least I hope you would have been. You should have been. But hearing the equally offensive insult "redneck" draws not a flinch in most circles, only a chuckle.

I say the word and concept must be dealt with because that is the notion that is most often used by the detractors of Mr. Presley to classify and dispose of him. Albert Goldman, in what claimed to be the definitive biography of Mr. Presley, said, "Of all the dumb activities in this dumb working-class school about the dumbest was shop: Elvis Presley's major."[1] If a center that exists for the study of southern culture needs any rationale for this symposium, that line of Mr. Goldman's is quite sufficient—dumb, working-class laborer, redneck.[2] That was all Albert Goldman needed to say to document that his subject was not to be taken seriously—not Elvis's music, his intellect, his acting, and certainly not his heritage and culture. Nothing about him was to be seen as of any import.

Why, then, did Mr. Goldman need to write about Mr. Presley at all? I do not hold to the conspiratorial interpretation of history—well, that's not quite true—but I think the answer to that question is that Elvis Presley was a convenient symbol and metaphor to that portion of the larger culture with elitist mentality that holds in utter disgust and even hatred the poor, rural, working class of the South: THE REDNECK.

What is a redneck? I have checked every lexicon available to me and the definition does not vary from the following: "REDNECK: Slang. One of the white, rural, working class of the South. Used disparagingly." That is where Elvis Presley came from. That is where I came from. The word does not mean "bigot," does not mean "racist," though a redneck may be a racist, just as one of the fashionable class can be a racist. But "redneck" and "racist" are used interchangeably by America's most sophisticated newspapers and journals today. I think I know why. The word does not mean "ignorant, fundamentalist dolt; amoral, gun-wielding, pickup-driving bumpkin with squirrel tail flying from the aerial, baby shoes hanging from the rearview mirror, and a bumper sticker saying 'SEE ROCK CITY.'" The word means one of the poor, white, rural, working class of the South. Used disparagingly. Period. In every dictionary. I repeat myself for emphasis.

Elvis Presley was a redneck because he sprang from the poor, white, rural, working class of the South. He, by all accounts I have found, was not a bigot. I am a redneck because I, too, descended from the poor, white, rural, working class of the South, Amite County, Mississippi, in the throes of the Great Depression, and you could not come from a more poor, a more rural, a more working-class, a more southern place than Amite County, Mississippi, in the 1920s. In other words, one could not come from more redneck country. But I am not a bigot. Although I don't like to do it, and never recall doing it before, let me document that I am not a bigot, lest you hear what I am saying as simply the words of a self-conscious, defensive southerner when I speak protectively of rednecks.

I was the only white person at the formation of the Southern Christian Leadership Conference with Dr. King and was a longtime friend and ally of Dr. King.[3] I walked with the nine Negro children to Central High School in Little Rock in 1957 to face Governor Faubus's troops with fixed bayonets and a screaming mob.[4] During the Vietnam War I harbored dodgers and deserters in my home and took a number of them to a safe haven in Canada. I was a death target by an extremist group for a time. I am a card-carrying member of the American Civil Liberties Union. I oppose the death penalty. I am a passionate supporter of affirmative action for women and racial minorities, unless used as a partisan political weapon. And three weeks ago I marched hand-in-hand with and in support of my brilliant and beautiful lesbian daughter. Am I a redneck? You dang tootin', as we rednecks are wont to say. And proud of it. Proud, and yet grieved and often ashamed by some of the behavior my people have been maneuvered into by the forces of history, political machinations, and religious deceptions.

And I am growing weary of being the last, the only minority left that is fair game for ethnic slurs from people, considering themselves good liberals, who would (as Dennis Rogers of the *Raleigh News and Observer* said of those "warm-hearted, touchy-feely hypocrites") "go into ethnic shock if you told a nasty joke about women, Jews, the blind, Mexicans or starving Ethiopians but who wouldn't think twice about guffawing at redneck jokes."

I am growing weary of people like Jeff Foxworthy making millions of dollars with their "You may be a redneck if . . ." books and television shows.[5] If what? You may be a redneck if you eat fried squirrel and moonpies for breakfast, for example. Well, I ate fried squirrel for breakfast of necessity, sir, but moonpies were a delicacy for the more affluent. We didn't have the nickel the moonpie cost in Amite County, Mississippi, in those days. You may be a redneck if you mix Jack Daniels with butterscotch malted milks. Don't knock it if you ain't tried it, Mr. Foxworthy, but those of the poor, rural, working class of the South of my youth had neither a surplus of Jack Daniels nor butterscotch ice cream around the house to mix. You may be a redneck if you hang around the bus station all day and pick your nose. Very funny. But put those putdowns in front of the epithets used to describe and insult African-Americans, women, Jews, people of Polish, Italian, Japanese, or Chinese extraction, or any other ethnic, racial, or gender minority, and see how many of your politically correct friends laugh. But redneck isn't indexed yet. Well, let's index it. There comes a time when a body gets weary. There comes a time.

In a recent article in *Newsweek* magazine one of their finest writers used the epithet for the poor, white, rural, working class of the South in the lead article when he stated, "President Clinton can bark orders like a redneck drill sergeant."[6] I wrote a letter of protest, suggesting that perhaps the epithet "redneck" should be dropped, just as other offensive words have been dropped. To tell you that the letter was never published would be redundant. An inquiry as to why it was not published, however, might be appropriate. Is it because the larger culture, the allegedly urbane, sophisticated culture, needs, and will find or create, someone upon whom to place the blame for our interminable racist society? "*We* are not racist. *They* are the racists. Not government. Not commerce and industry. Not the media. Not the mainline churches. Not the academy. *They*, the rednecks, are the racists."

That is a blatant lie. It is the ancient craft of scapegoating. America is a racist society to the core and we all know it. Ah, we have dressed it up now. We don't need a Bilbo, a "Pitchfork Ben" Tillman to scream "nigger!" from the courthouse steps on election eve to keep poor whites voting right.[7] We have code words. Is it not obvious that the 1994 elections had to do with race? When we heard talk of welfare abuse it meant welfare for black people, though statistics show more whites than blacks on welfare. When we heard, "Get rid of affirmative action," it was from those wanting to hang onto the piers of privilege being mildly threatened by enterprising and struggling minorities. "Teenage pregnancies" meant black teenagers having babies. "Crime in the streets and let's build more prisons" was a euphemism for incarcerating and executing more black people. Was that not obvious? And is it not manifest already that the next presidential campaign will be waged on that same cunning and pernicious ground? Perhaps not as brazen as the Willie Horton syndrome, but the message will be loud and clear.

I think I can make a case that the poor, white, rural, working class, the redneck, is guilty of less true racism than any other group in white American society. Not guilty of less prejudice, perhaps, but less racism. There is a distinction that must be made between racism and prejudice—and between racism and racialism for that matter.[8] I am not saying that all or any one of the poor working class are without prejudice. History would not bear me out. We can be educated, or converted, out of prejudice—sheer, raw, naked bigotry. But racism is a condition; it structures the institutions in which we move and breathe and have our being and that give white males the advantage. That is what racism is. Every one of us afflicted with this incurable skin disease called whiteness is a racist. That does not mean we hate black people or wish them ill. It simply means that our skin color has given us ascendance. That is what "racism" is. Prejudice is something else—something on a more conscious level. The redneck is less racist because he operates from a base of considerably less power. It is not the poor, rural, laboring class that produces the rulers, the governors, the managers of this present age that harbors the racist cycle.

All that is to say, Mr. Presley was a redneck. But Mr. Presley was not a bigot. In reality—fairly and critically examined—he and his era might be seen as a crusade for human rights. Consider Mr. Presley's doleful lament, "On a cold and gray Chicago morn, a little biddy baby boy was born in the ghetto. And his mama cried." Those lyrics, written by Mac Davis, tracing that baby through childhood and into early adulthood where the weeping mama's baby was finally gunned down on the street, spoke volumes about, and effectively condemned, America's inherent racism. It was a song of prophecy. So Mr. Presley might be seen, on close examination, to have been an effective social activist whose very being started a revolution throughout the world. Think about it.[9]

Let's explore something of the history of the poor, white, rural, working class of the South from whose loins Mr. Presley sprang. Who is the redneck? Where did he come from and why is he held in such contempt by the more privileged? Why is he the last remaining minority to be made fun of by clowns with the TV cutesies? We can get a clue from the painter and the poet. This man, the redneck, is the one with the hoe. Although the subject of these artists was the French peasant, they also address our subject:

> *Bowed by the weight of centuries,*
> *He leans upon his hoe and gazes on the ground* (ll. 1–2).[10]

And as he so leaned and so gazed his posture left that cervical area from the temporal bones to the first dorsal vertebra exposed to the searing, shriveling, parching rays of the midday southern sun. And we named him "redneck."

Historically, he too was a slave. It was a more subtle kind of slavery—indentured servanthood. Serve me for five, seven years and I will set you free. But freedom to what and in what context? Freedom to flounder, to drift, to wander westward in a frustrating search of what had been promised but never delivered—a secure life in a land of plenty. Freedom to fight a Civil War in which he had no stake and then indoctrinated into believing that the postbellum oppression and poverty were the fault of black people.

Certainly I am not saying that all redneck history can be traced to indentured servanthood. White scholars have not dwelt on it much, but it's a fact of history. In Virginia, at one point, more than 70 percent of the white population was of indentured stock. While African-Americans created a conscious culture out of their slavery—history, art, literature, music—by contrast the indentured servant, the poor white, ashamed to admit that his progenitors had been brought to these shores as servants, would be more apt to tell his grandchildren that his ancestors landed at Plymouth Rock. Such deception was bound to result in a schizophrenia that may account for more of the hostilities of the redneck than any other historical factor. If he were to deny and conceal his own slavery, then he had to dwell on the slavery of others and, with manipulation by the gentry, deem himself better because of the color of his skin.

Here is his real tragedy. Race has been the trump card used to keep the poor white and the poor black as traditional enemies. It is my belief that the phenomenon, the music, the life of Elvis Presley (with all its foibles, all its warts) sought (perhaps unconsciously, something he simply intuited by being redneck, sensitive, and brilliant) to heal that rift, to bring the two to see that their tragedies were the same—the same pain, the same maltreatment and exploitation, the same enemy that continues to promote the cleft between them for political and economic gain. The most recent documentation of this is the poor white buying into the fraudulent Contract with America, which he, and to a lesser extent she, was deceived into thinking was to his or her advantage, when in fact the intent was to their detriment. Race has essentially dictated the history of America and it is bringing us down. Point to one significant political era when race was not a crucial and even dominating factor.

Can you see now why it is important to consider the world of the redneck if you are serious about understanding the historical, social, and cultural significance of Elvis Presley? This is the framework on which so much of the writing about Mr. Presley has been predicated. Many, not all but many, writers have cast him in the light of the redneck, which he was, but the *ergo*, the conclusion, has been that he need not be taken seriously, that he was not one of the strongest influences in twentieth-century America and is not a fit subject for serious research by the academy.[11]

Only recently, a shy, modest, self-effacing major player in the drama, Gene Smith, has stepped forth to share the things he knows for truth because he was there and lived them. From an industry that has seen only lies and distortions used to line the pockets of greedy writers and "tell-all" bystanders, only now are we beginning to get an accurate look at a man whose fame was also his tragedy. Smith's *Elvis's Man Friday* is an important volume for anyone who wants to understand the kind of human being—not what kind of celebrity, star, big-spending media king but what kind of *human being*—Mr. Presley was, what shaped him to be the thing he was and the complex subject that has brought us together.[12]

Yes, Elvis Presley was a redneck because he sprang from the poor, white, rural, working class of the South. But no matter what Albert Goldman and other writers might say, being of the poor, rural, working class of the South did not make Mr. Presley a bigot.

I believe that the nation stands where it is today—neither integrated nor united but moving more and more in the direction the Kerner Report predicted: two nations, separate and unequal—precisely because the rednecks, the poor, white, rural, working class of the South (and now of the nation) have never been a party to any truce that has been drawn.[13] The poor whites have seen government try to make peace between various warring factions, but they have not been brought to the bargaining table (for example, in the truce between the larger society and organized labor). The carnage in the automobile factories of Detroit and the coal mines of Kentucky ceased when the laborers were strong enough to fight back and affect a truce. But when efforts were made to organize the *rural*, poor, working class, for example, as in the Southern Tenant Farmers' Union in the 1930s and 1940s, organized labor, industry, and government backed away and the redneck was left yet again "... stolid and stunned / A brother to the ox."

But the poet was mistaken when he described the man with the hoe as "... dead to rapture and despair, / A thing that grieves not and that never hopes" (ll. 5–6). He is capable of deep grief and robust hope. There was notable hope in that effort, the Southern Tenant Farmers' Union. Here was real, authentic racial integration for the first time, from the highest leadership to the rank and file, perhaps the most valiant effort of poor-white and poor-black rural folk banding and bonding in American history—in Mississippi, Arkansas, Louisiana, Alabama; the most poor, rural, working-class, the most redneck part of America. It is not surprising that the powers that be feared and stifled that movement. It was too much of "We hold these truths to be self-evident." It was fomenting social, cultural, and political revolution. Rednecks and African-Americans were moving out of serfdom by the alignment. It was black and white together, working, socializing, overcoming; tenant farmers and sharecroppers breaking bread and breaking shackles. It could not be, and it wasn't, but what a story while it was—the Southern Tenant Farmers' Union—a revolt that failed. If you would understand the social and historical significance of the life and times of Elvis Presley, I urge you to take a look at the bold but short-lived Southern Tenant Farmers' Union.[14]

The so-called redneck saw a truce being drawn between African-Americans and middle- and upper-class whites as a result of the civil rights movement of the 1960s. But the redneck, the poor, white, rural, working class of the South and now of the nation, was never a party to that truce. They soon said the War on Poverty was not for them. They spoke the truth. It wasn't. It was to affect a truce to which they were not a party. And consequently it was an uneasy truce and did not last.

What finally shall we say of our redneck brothers and sisters? I hope you do not hear me simply as romanticizing my redneck people. I am quite aware of our sins and failures. I know that many poor, rural, working-class southerners joined the Klan, burned churches, lynched, beat little children with trace chains. I know it well. The question, the only question, is where did the poor, rural, working class get the notion that being white meant superiority? To whose advantage was that notion? The answers to those questions are not simple. But one thing is clear. Certainly it was not to the advantage of the poor, white, rural, working class. The only thing to their advantage would have been a federation of the poor of both races. And when that federation was attempted, for example in the Southern Tenant Farmers' Union, it was quickly suppressed.

Today, in the state of Mississippi, people who committed racial crimes thirty years ago are being retried and convicted.[15] The rationale is that we were living in a police state in the sixties and justice in the courts was impossible at the time. I do not argue that we were under a police state. Very well, a police state has someone at the head, someone running it. Why, then, are the governors and senators and congressmen who ranted and raved and preached hatred and defiance from the highest seats of government—why are they not being tried instead of the little people who, after all, were doing precisely what they thought and, yes, knew they were being asked to do? Acts that would be applauded. When will Governor Barnett, for example, be tried for high crimes and misdemeanors and sentenced posthumously for his crimes? Inciting a riot is against the law. Open defiance of a Supreme Court decree is a crime. It was he whose fulminations turned this very campus into a war zone on the night of September 30, 1962, when the first black student appeared. And, yes, there were rednecks here. But at whose bidding? You don't try the foot soldiers for war crimes. You try the rulers. There comes a time.[16]

What I am trying to say is that the so-called redneck is a crucial factor to the social problem of race/poverty in America. And unless they are brought into the dialogue, become a party to the truce instead of being ridiculed, blamed, and scorned, there will be no truce. I am also trying to say that the redneck, even in this postindustrial, technological age, has hung onto a scrap of individualism, and thus offers hope of deliverance from the technological concentration camp we have built. That individualism was well exemplified in the life and music and times of Elvis Presley. President Jimmy Carter put it well at the time of Mr. Presley's death when he said "He was a symbol to the people the world over, of the vitality, rebelliousness and good humor of this country."[17] I am trying further to say that in this vitality, this rebelliousness, this commitment, this dogged determinism, this recalcitrant, complaining, murmuring, seething hostility and seeming helplessness in the face of political and social exploitation, there may yet emerge deliverance from that body of death in the race/poverty that stalks and haunts and infects our land and is getting worse with every national election. If not, then death's shroud will blanket us all.

What form the potential deliverance will take I have no notion. And I know, of course, the greater danger is that it will be no deliverance at all. Instead, the continued exploitation, whether through fun-poking, religious fraud, or political machinations, will result in a fascist theocracy. That, certainly, is the direction in which we are moving. If you doubt that just watch every serious contender for high office during the coming year rush to the TV studios seeking the blessing of the right-wing electronic soul molesters who hurl to hearth and household not the radical and revolutionary message of Jesus regarding the downcast, but rather a milquetoast gospel of "Take up your cross and relax," "Take up your cross and get rich," "Take up your cross and find self-esteem in an edifice made of glass." Great Godamighty! I don't know where this country is headed. But there comes a time to fret. There comes a time.

So I will leave you with the words of the poet, reminding you that when he used the word "dumb" it meant silent, not stupid:

> How will the future reckon with this man?
> How answer his brute question in that hour
> When whirlwinds of rebellion shake all shores?
> How will it be with kingdom and with kings,
> With those who shaped him to the thing he is,
> When this dumb terror shall rise to judge the world? (ll. 43–49)

And judge it, my brothers and sisters, he will. The Age of Elvis, I believe, with all its shaking, its gyrations, its vitality, rebelliousness, dogged determination, songs of murmuring, sometimes seething hostility and recalcitrance, but mounting finally to the screaming, thunderous crescendo in "How Great Thou Art," tried to warn us of the judgment to come. The Lord works in strange, in mysterious ways.

Kinfolk fidelity—Gene makes Elvis laugh while Joe Esposito, Billy Smith, Jimmy Kingsley, and others look on. Courtesy of Larry Brooks Arnett.

7 Elvis's Man Friday

GENE SMITH

I'm Gene Smith, classified as 3-A. I'll explain to you what that 3-A means.[1]

I was drafted around seven weeks before Elvis was. He told me before I left, said, "Gene, I need you with me bad. Why don't you go up there and just act dumb and act like you're about half crazy, you know, because I need you with me." So I went to take my physical. And he was asking me different questions. He'd come to a question and ask me, "Who was the first president?" And I kinda looked at the table and took two or three seconds. I looked up at him. I said, "Hell, I don't know, I wasn't even born then." So he asked me some more questions, asked me, "Whose face was on a twenty-dollar bill?" And I said, "I don't know, I don't hardly ever see a twenty-dollar bill." Then he asked me did I take the newspaper? I told him, "Yes sir." He said, "What sections and parts of it do you read?" I said, "I don't read it." He said, "Well, why do you take it?" I said, "My wife likes to read it. I get it for her."

He asked me a few more questions and I gave him crazy answers. And so he made me an appointment. He said, "I want you to talk to somebody else and I'll see if I can make you an appointment tomorrow." So he did. I guess you'd call him a psychiatrist. He made me an appointment with one of them the next day. I went and met him. He asked me some questions of things and I gave him crazy answers on them, you know. Some of them I didn't really know myself. Then he sent me to one higher than he was. So I pretty well tore his head up too. I got him mixed up about the way I was. Then he studied around there a few minutes and he told whoever was sitting over at the table where they classified you, he said, he just shook his head, said, "Well, hell, classify him 3-A and let him go." So that's the way I got the classification.[2]

I was born in Tupelo, raised up with Elvis. We were the closest two cousins. We played together whenever we got a chance. He lived at first right down the road from me, but they moved to a different place and we didn't get to see each other but every couple of weeks or once a month, you know. I was the closest cousin to him. Me and him always played together, grew up all the way together. I was seven weeks older than he was. I guess he more or less took me as his twin brother that he lost at birth.

His mother told me that she thought that I would be the best thing to be with him and how much she loved me and respected me. She asked me to travel with Elvis. He got up in his sleep a lot. And I was real easy to wake up. You could drop a pin on the floor and I'd jump. But anyway, I traveled with him and he jumped up in his sleep quite a few times, thought somebody was trying to kill him or something.[3]

One time I let him go to see how far he would go. He jumped up swinging. He thought three guys were in the room to kill him. They had knives and he got up swinging and doing a little of that karate kicking stuff. He happened to hit the bedpost with his right foot and just peeled that big toenail off. I could call him right easy. I could say, "Elvis, Elvis," and then he'd come out of it. But if you hollered at him he'd get that much worse. I woke him up and he said, "Well, why didn't you wake me up?" I said, "Well, I wanted to see what you'd do." He had a few choice words.

The reason I wrote my book, *Elvis's Man Friday*, was that I sat around close to eighteen years and I read and saw all this garbage people were putting out about Elvis—and lies. So I figured I'd let the world know the real truth. This is a truthful book. I've run nobody down. I do not lie or steal so this is truth to the best of my knowledge.[4]

We were on *The Ed Sullivan Show* in New York.[5] After the show, you know, Elvis had to get out as quick as he could. They had police officers lined up and down the aisle where he had to go out and jump in a cab. When he left, well, he left running, and a couple of them grabbed him by the arm. I was supposed to get in the cab with him, but when they grabbed him by the arm Chief Pfeiffer got behind us, in between us. I had Elvis's suit on my shoulder. They just more or less shoved him in the cab. I think his head hit the other door on the other side, liked to knocked him out. Then they slammed the door and the cab took off. I hollered, "Wait, man!" There was another cab there. I tried to stop him, but he pulled off, too, real fast. I guess the

Colonel or somebody got in there and left me running out there in the street with his suit.

The fans said, "Look, Elvis's suit!" And, boy, here they come after me. And I was running up the street, I betcha I got up to thirty miles an hour. They got so close I could feel the wind from their hands. And I said, "Well, I can't do this." I was thinking to myself, "I can't let this happen, you know. I know this suit costs a lot of money but . . ." They didn't call my name, they didn't care who had the suit, they just knew it was the suit. I'd run till my legs were getting tired and felt like I was fixin' to fall, so I just said, excuse my language, but I said, "Well, the hell with this suit," and I flung it straight up. I betcha two or three thousand people landed on that suit. Didn't nobody have no big piece of it. Three or four people got hurt in it. I hated that. But I didn't want to get hurt myself.

I had a few choice words when I got to the motel. "Why didn't you hold the cab for me?" Elvis got a big laugh out of it. He said, "What did you do with my suit?" I said, "I throwed it up in the air and let them fans get it." He said, "Man that suit cost me so many thousands of dollars." I said, "Well, I'm here."

Me and the Colonel got along real good because he knew I was with Elvis and he knew Elvis wanted to be with me at all times, so he respected me. Well, we used to pull a few pranks together. Elvis would get some big wheel from the studio, lot of something, and he'd hypnotize me, play like he'd hypnotize me, and I'd lay there and I didn't know nothing, you know. You could ask me a question, I'd give you a crazy answer. One time, he had a guy, he said, "Lay a fifty-dollar bill down in there. I guarantee you he won't pick it up." So he laid a fifty-dollar bill down there, they kept talking, and I was laying over there, supposed to have been out of it. The guy had to get up and use the rest room. And he went and used the rest room and when he come back I wasn't there. Neither was his fifty-dollar bill. Yeah, Elvis had a few jokes because he was always wanting to do something like that.

We had probably six or eight rooms, suites, in the Knickerbocker Hotel in L.A.[6] Elvis and myself, we had one of them pellet guns that shoots caps, you know. It looks like a real pistol. It just blows the powder up and sounds like a real gun. So we got laying around there and didn't have anything to do, got bored, so we just made up a little deal to pull and have a little fun. Elvis goes downstairs and an older man and woman, forty or fifty, got on the elevator and Elvis got on the elevator with them. They were going to the eighth floor and we were on the sixth.

Me and the Colonel got along real good because he knew I was with Elvis and he knew Elvis wanted to be with me at all times, so he respected me. Gene and Elvis on the knee of Colonel Tom Parker Claus. Courtesy of Larry Brooks Arnett.

So I was watching the elevator, the little hand, when it got to six and the doors started to open. I said, "Uh, huh!" I said, "I told ya I'd gitcha!" That man and woman started screaming. I shot him twice, he grabbed himself and fell up against the wall. I shot him a couple more times and he staggered out into the hallway up to the wall and just slid down and made his eyes roll back. That couple was trying to get the door shut and get back downstairs. They went back downstairs and said Elvis had just been shot, that he got shot in the elevator. Police were surrounding, they were coming in the windas and doors and I thought they was coming through the woodwork. Boy, they had that place surrounded in very few minutes. It was so rough the motel asked us to leave. So we went to the Beverly Wilshire. Then we done a little damage down there. We got in a pie fight.

Elvis wasn't prejudiced. He liked all people. He liked you whether you were red, black, green, or whatever color you were. He was brought up in church. He sang in the choir in the church—that's where he learned how to stroke the guitar well enough to make that first record. He wasn't racist. He liked everybody. He had black women in his group. He loved to hear the black guys like the Platters and the Drifters sing. That's the only kind of music we ever listened to, really. The Platters and Ray Charles and the black singers—we'd rather hear the black singers than the white singers we had at the time.

I lived on Mississippi Boulevard in South Memphis. There was a black church three or four blocks away up from me. We used to like to go up there on Sunday mornings and Sunday night, Wednesday night, you know. They sang in their churches and we'd go up there and the preacher would tell us we could sit upstairs if we wanted to or sit anywhere we wanted to. We usually sat upstairs. We liked to hear them sing and you know the way they move around and all.[7]

We would kind of make motions with the hand or with the ear or say something backwards, you know, in a way. If we saw a good-lookin' girl, if she was built good, looked good, we'd kind of sing, you know, sing something backwards and Elvis would know what I meant and I'd know what he meant. It's kind of hard to explain something like that.

Priscilla was in the car with us one day. I was talking to Elvis about, you know, how pretty I thought she was and she was built good and all that. And I was kind of mumbling and saying some little verse backwards. Pulling my ear and running my hand down my face meant she was real pretty, you know.[8] I'd say something about a Coca-Cola bottle or something the way she was built, you know. Just different stuff like that. But Elvis knew what I was talking about and Priscilla didn't. I think Priscilla's got something in her book on that order about me and Elvis mumbling something that she couldn't understand, but she was sure that we did.[9]

I left Elvis in about '63 and I just went down there when he come home to Graceland and all, you know. He'd call me and invite us down. I didn't see too much of a change myself. Well, I saw a change too, but I'd rather not get into that right now.

Joni Mabe. *Afro-Sheen Elvis.* 1982. Glitter collage and sequins on walnut plaque. 8" x 15". Courtesy of the artist.

8 A Revolutionary Sexual Persona

Elvis Presley and the White Acquiescence of Black Rhythms

JON MICHAEL SPENCER

In *Forrest Gump* (the 1995 Oscar-winning movie starring Tom Hanks and Sally Field) there is a scene that shows Mrs. Gump announcing dinner to the guests in her bed-and-breakfast establishment on the outskirts of an Alabama town. One of the house guests is Elvis Presley (although we are not yet certain of his identity), and the young Forrest Gump is in Elvis's room dancing to his music. The two "boys" are interrupted by Mrs. Gump, who first scolds Forrest for pestering the guest and then announces that it is time to eat. Elvis indicates that Forrest is not a bother and thanks the hostess for the dinnertime reminder. As Mrs. Gump leaves the room, Elvis turns back to Forrest and says: "Hey man, show me that crazy little walk you just did there." Sitting on the edge of his bed with guitar in lap, Elvis recommences "Hound Dog," and Forrest (who wears leg braces) moves from the waist down in stiff but syncopated jerks that can best be described as funky. "I started moving around to the music, swinging my hips," says Forrest as he narrates this part of his life-story.

One evening when Forrest and his mother were out walking in town, they saw a surprising sight on the television showcased in the display window of a furniture store. It was that young man, that guitar-playing guest at the Gump bed-and-breakfast establishment, and he was performing that same sassy song—"Hound Dog." Moreover, that young man was doing that "crazy little walk" Forrest had shown him. Forrest looked on silently, taking the scene in unresponsively

First, I want to point out that the syncopated leg and body movements—that "crazy little walk"—that Elvis displayed on television that evening is not attributable to Forrest Gump, but rather to the rhythms that undergird African-American culture and give it its distinctiveness. Collection of Ger Rijff.

due to his rather "slow" intelligence. But he undoubtedly recognized the television star as the guest whose music made him move around and swing his hips. How could he forget? Mrs. Gump, on the other hand, gasped at the young musician's public performance. As she walked away with an expression that suggested an underlying genteel morality and an overwhelming rejection of the new sexual era spawned by the 1950s, she told Forrest that the scene on television was not for young eyes to see.

Using these two scenes from *Forrest Gump* as pretexts, I wish to make two observations. First, I want to point out that the syncopated leg and body movements—that "crazy little walk"—that Elvis displayed on television that evening is not attributable to Forrest Gump, but rather to the rhythms that undergird African-American culture and give it its distinctiveness. Second, Mrs. Gump's gasping at Elvis's performance of "Hound Dog" and her leading Forrest away from the television could not have separated white youths from the black rhythms and the attendant sexualities of the irrepressible black cultural presence in the South (and also in the larger United States). What I intend by this crucial word "sexualities," out of its many possible historical meanings, is: behavioral demonstrations, especially bodily insinuations, associated with libidinal gratification, plus their aesthetic representation or reproduction in art and ritual.

With regard to my first point, when I say that the funky move-ments that Elvis displayed on television are not attributable to For-rest Gump, I mean that those movements are not creditable to the southern white culture in which Forrest Gump was raised or that Forrest Gump represents as a fictional character. Those funky move-ments are traceable to the rhythms that specifically distinguish African-American culture, a culture that Elvis appreciated and to which he acquiesced during his upbringing in Mississippi and Ten-nessee. Of course, this claim is nothing new, for Elvis himself ac-knowledged this acquiescence. "The colored folks been singing it and playing it just like I'm doin' now, man, for more years than I know," he once remarked to a journalist. "They played it like that in the shanties and in their juke joints, and nobody paid it no mind 'til I goosed it up. I got it from them."[1] Additionally, what Elvis told B. B. King on one occasion could have been said just as appropriately to Arthur "Big Boy" Crudup or Big Bill Broonzy or Howlin' Wolf or Josh White or Chuck Berry or Junior Parker or Ray Charles or Nat King Cole or uncountable other black musicians who influenced Elvis: "Thanks, man, for the early lessons you gave me."[2]

So Elvis's debt to black culture is incontestable and generally ac-cepted. But I want to emphasize a particular aspect of this debt by elaborating on a remark made by a Memphis newspaper about six months after Elvis's July 1954 debut recording of Arthur Crudup's "That's All Right, Mama." Beneath a photo of Elvis and his two backup musicians, the caption read: "A white man's voice singing negro rhythms with a rural flavor [has] changed life overnight for Elvis Presley."[3] What I want to underscore in this comment is the view that it was specifically the rhythms of black people that changed life overnight for Elvis. Elvis heard these rhythms on the radio in Tu-pelo, Mississippi, as a youth, when recordings of blues, jazz, and black gospel were taking the country by storm. And as a young teenager he heard the rhythms of the blues, R&B, and black gospel on the radio in Memphis, where his family moved in 1948. In fact, what Elvis loved in the singing of Memphis's white gospel quartets, such as the Sunshine Boys and the Blackwood Brothers, was none other than the rhythms of the black quartets, from whom the guys of these white groups got their "early lessons."[4]

My singling out the rhythms as the distinguishing element in black music (and in Elvis's charismatic performance and success) is based on my premise that African rhythm traditionally has given rise to the characteristic traits in the cultures of peoples originated from Africa.

My singling out the rhythms as the distinguishing element in black music (and in Elvis's charismatic performance and success) is based on my premise that African rhythm traditionally has given rise to the characteristic traits in the cultures of peoples originated from Africa. Courtesy of Jon Michael Spencer.

In this respect, I agree with Leonard Barrett's assessment that "the drumbeats of Africa were the prime method of Africanizing the New World."[5] The drumbeats of Africa, even without the physical presence of the drum itself, endured the slave factories of Africa's west coast and the middle passages of the Atlantic. And those drumbeats were sold right along with the captive black peoples on the auction blocks of the New World. In this strange new land African rhythm languished pitifully at times, particularly in the musically sterile galleries of white Protestant and Catholic churches.[6] But it did so only temporarily, until it could again "steal away" and release itself without reproach among the people who both "possessed" it and knew the secrets of being possessed by it. Thus the Diaspora generally dedrummed the enslaved Africans in America, but it did not derhythmize them. With the drum deferred, African rhythm still generated and appeared in black music, dance, drama, art, and worship.

When I speak of African rhythm (in the singular), I do so as a way of representing the commonalties found in the dynamic world of (at the very least) those African peoples brought in chains to the New World. These commonalties include multimetricity, crossrhythms, and asymmetrical patterning, all expressed percussively, customarily concretized in dance, and involving some form of call and response. This African rhythm was and continues to be found in creolized forms in both the sacred and secular contexts of the New World. The sacred contexts, those intentional places of worship, certainly have been important locations where this rhythmic creolization has occurred through the creations of black artistry and the choreographies of black bodies. The secular contexts, however, have been the most important locations of rhythmic creolization. These secular places, which nurtured the blues and spawned its generations of "juke" offspring, have forever left their imprint on American culture, including that culture's so-called sexual revolution.[7]

The fact that the body itself became the primary instrument through which African rhythm was publicly concretized in choreographies, even amid the genteel morality and bodiless spirituality of New World whites, leads me to my second point. This has to do with Mrs. Gump gasping when she saw Elvis dancing on television to his rendition of "Hound Dog." What disgruntled Mrs. Gump was not Elvis's name-calling, that he was calling some poor soul a cryin' dog—"nothin' but!" Rather, it was that Elvis's performance itself appeared doggish, doggish like that school official who humped Mrs. Gump, a sexual favor for not placing her "slow" child in a "special" school. Elvis's performance not only seemed reminiscent of that school official's humping and yelping, but seemed to bark at the very moralities championed by traditional genteel culture.

From the colonial period through the nineteenth century, that culture had carefully confined sexuality in the home of the conjugal family for exclusively procreative ends, although in the nineteenth century the idea of marital romance had begun to ennoble sexuality. While the early twentieth century saw a shift in values toward consumption, self-gratification, and leisurely pleasure, which included the open commercialization of sexuality in the dance halls and movie houses, the genteel ethic of refined, tender passion between people in love still held sway. Elvis had howled houndishly at this genteel tradition and Mrs. Gump was visibly unsettled. In fact, if we could have heard some elaboration on her sentiments we might have heard words similar to those of a New York journalist who insisted that Elvis's "exhibitions" were "suggestive and vulgar" and "tinged with the kind of animalism that should be confined to dives and bordellos."[8]

What this journalist (in the North) and Mrs. Gump (in the South) both seemed to recognize in Elvis's "exhibitions" were not only public expressions that had long left behind the values of familial, reproductive sexuality, but specifically the public expression of *black* sexualities. That there was an unmistakable blackness to the sexualities

Elvis displayed, and that it is reasonable to view the black rhythms to which Elvis acquiesced as having "carried" these sexualities, can be illustrated in a most obvious way.[9] Namely, it is a well-known fact that, first of all, the words "rock" and "roll" are black colloquialisms that whites used to rename rhythm and blues when they began imitating its rhythms. And, secondly, it is a known fact that these colloquialisms originally referred to sexual intercourse. They meant to do the "shake, rattle, and roll," as Joe McCoy put it in his 1931 blues titled "Shake Mattie."[10]

But not only did the northern journalist and the southern Mrs. Gump probably recognize the blackness of the sexualities "carried" by black rhythms and therefore recognize the alleged depravity of the sexualities; they also seemed to sense that these "illegitimate" sexualities were seductive, which naturally made it all the more necessary that the rhythms "carrying" them be confined to dives and bordellos and not be exhibited on recordings and television. I contend, however, that this attempt to work against nature would have only increased its force, and that Mrs. Gump's leading her son Forrest away from the television exhibiting Elvis's blues-inspired pubis could not have separated white youths (of Forrest's age and older) from delighting in the black rhythms and attendant sexualities of the irrepressible black cultural presence.

That this sexual seduction of whites into blackness was unstoppable was partly due to the fact that, from the 1920s onward, this blackness was coming at them from both possible directions. Starting in the 1910s white entertainers brought the black rhythms and the attendant sexualities across the tracks to the white side of the color line. Starting in the 1920s the performances of black entertainers enticed whites to the black side. By the 1960s, what had burgeoned in the 1920s, in terms of new and acceptable attitudes about sexuality, became the dominant sexual ethic, due in part to the new visibility of sexuality in popular culture that Elvis helped along starting in the 1950s. As the white cultural critic Camille Paglia says, "Elvis Presley, one of the most influential men of the century, broke down racial barriers in the music industry, so that my generation was flooded by the power, passion, and emotional truth of African-American experience."[11]

Although the "first coming" of Elvis was a shock to those genteel whites who wanted to see a subduing of what they perceived to be a raucous sexuality, his coming actually made public a big secret within an unacknowledged crevice of middle-class "civilized morality": the repressed fascination for African rhythm in its myriad black bodily manifestations. Mrs. Gump's turning away from Elvis's television "exhibition" thus represents whites of that day not only resisting the institutions and values of a consumer society that had succumbed to the commercialization of sex, but also their turning away from an acknowledgment of their own proximity to and penetration by black culture. By 1900, middle-class sexuality had moved out of the conjugal bedroom and beyond the procreative framework, but even in the post-1920s the alien and seemingly anarchic sexuality of "underground" black culture was disturbing to the genteel.

Moreover, Mrs. Gump's remark to Forrest that Elvis's exhibition on television was not for young eyes to see represents the prudish miscalculation of whites regarding the proximity of and penetration by black culture. The fact is, as Elvis's blues-generated charisma spread far and wide, thanks in part to the television age, it was principally young white eyes that would be doing the gazing. Furthermore, it was young white bodies that would become aroused by the sexualities riding the back of black rhythms—sexualities that would possess them as though they were its personal devotees.

This theorizing about white proximity to and penetration by black culture is, once again, nothing new. As a result of his first visit to the United States in 1909, almost a half-century before Elvis's first coming, Swiss psychologist C. G. Jung drew some conclusions about this very phenomenon. In an article published in the United States some twenty-four years before Elvis's rise to stardom, Jung explained that he found white Americans to possess "striking peculiarities" when compared to white Europeans. In attempting to account for these peculiarities, he surmised that since the United States was not a completely white nation but was partly "colored," blacks had obviously influenced the mentality, language, movements, and gestures of their white neighbors. The consequence of this living side by side with blacks, Jung concluded, is that underneath their skin whites were "going black." "Below the threshold of consciousness the contagion meets little resistance," the psychologist warned. "Since the Negro lives within your cities and even within your houses, he also lives within your skin, subconsciously."[12]

Upon the release of this article in 1930, one black editorialist remarked that whites might be startled by such discoveries but blacks knew the matter to be an "old story." Specifically regarding Jung's comment that blacks not only lived in America's cities but underneath white skins, the editorialist prophesied: "The Negro has gone deeper into American life than is realized, and he will go deeper still."[13] In later years, seven years before Elvis's death in 1977, Ralph Ellison wrote an article for *Time* magazine in which he stated that black culture was a silent conqueror of whites. It was silent insofar as it was unrecognized or even unacknowledged by whites and was conqueror insofar as this allegedly unimportant culture was a major tributary into the "mainstream." "On this level the melting pot did indeed melt," Ellison wrote, "creating such deceptive metamorphoses and blending of identities, values and life-styles that most American whites are culturally part Negro American without even realizing it."[14]

Despite the racism motivating Jung's warning about these deceptive metamorphoses and blending of identities and values, the psychologist understood something pretty basic, something that our two black writers (the aforementioned editorialist and novelist) understood without the intellectual poison of racism. Namely, in African-American culture something very contagious had infected all who came to intercourse with it: black rhythms (I have been arguing). Jung himself recognized that American music was pervaded by African rhythm and melody, which he said were most insinuating and could obsess listeners for days.[15] The ability of black rhythms to obsess listeners resulted from, in my estimation, a phenomenon that Jung himself championed in his psychotherapy: the reconciliation of the unnatural binary oppositions of body versus soul, flesh versus spirit, and (generally) the profane versus the sacred. What I am saying is that the "insinuation" of black rhythms was none other than the element that activated a reconciliation of the rift between spirit and nature.

It was the blues—the blues itself and the blues as the pith of later secular incarnations—that especially obsessed listeners. To be sure, one does not listen to the blues and lose an appetite for sex or religion. Rather, what the blues suggests, to borrow the language of philosophical theologian Alan Watts, is that, "Without . . . the lustiness of sex, religion is joyless and abstract; without the self-abandonment of religion, sex is a mechanical masturbation."[16] As another theologian, James Cone, put it with regard to black music, the blues all along rejected distinctions between the spirit and nature, which was the acknowledgment of its creators and devotees that there could be no wholeness without sexuality.[17] All forms of black music helped heal the rift of the binary oppositions insofar as they contained black rhythms, but it was the secular genres of the blues continuum that were connected with the necessary context.[18] It was in the secular context that listener-participants (as if in successful psychotherapy) could consciously and confidently own up to this reconciled reality.

In drawing primarily from the blues and secondarily from the myriad musics of its continuum, Elvis brought what Camille Paglia called the "power, passion, and emotional truth" of black rhythms into the world of white youths. The words accompanying these rhythms certainly contributed to the explicit connotation of sexuality, but the words themselves were only representations of the preverbal source of the sexualities. In other words, the expression of black sexualities in language (as well as in "exhibition") has always followed the fact of black rhythms. It has been the rhythms that have generated the ritual-places that are natural environments for the realization of these sexualities, "natural" because the rhythms somehow make such sexualities not only tolerable but comfortable. In fact, such places are so "natural" for the realization of sexualities that an aura of spirituality seems to be cast over them and over sexuality itself.

Whites of Mrs. Gump's era and genteel ethic always sensed the fascination (and repulsion) of the "illicit" sexualities generated by black rhythms, in part because traditional prudishness in the home actually served to heighten the fascination by trying to work against nature. But, to be sure, whites such as Mrs. Gump were not alone fascinated (and repulsed) by the rhythms of black *secular* music. They also felt the allure (and repulsion) of this alleged "illicitness" in black religious music and its generative places. Although many white observers (especially scholars) might have been racist in their interpretation of the sexualities "appearing" in black religious ritual, calling those places godforsaken and pagan, they were not mistaken about their presence.

James Cone's explanation for the presence of black sexualities in black religious music and ritual is that people who do not release their sexualities in dance on Saturday night might find themselves doing so in dance on Sunday morning.[19] Indeed, it is true in a general sense that when sexuality is repressed in its direct appearance it unknowingly rears elsewhere in behavior as well as in such other spheres of life as symbol, so that repression ends up serving roundaboutly in the embellishment of sexuality. Earlier I might have sounded as though this alone was the extent of my own views, for I said that black rhythms have made the realization of sexualities comfortable to the degree that an aura of spirituality seems cast over even the secular occasions those rhythms generate. But I intentionally used the word "seems"—spirituality *seems* cast over secular occasions—for I see this overcastness as merely a matter of perception. My view is that both Saturday-night and Sunday-morning places of black ritual are generated by rhythms that actually reconcile spirituality and sexuality.

Spirituality is not "cast over" Saturday-night places any more than sexuality mistakenly creeps in Sunday-morning places if it is not released the night before. In all black ritual-places generated by black rhythms, spirit and nature are reconciled and returned to their primordial unity. This does not imply that promiscuity is breaking free of the restraint of Puritanism. Rather, it implies the end of people's unnecessary flight from something (nature and sexuality) that is actually inseparable from its seeming opposite (spirit and spirituality).[20]

It is impossible to capture in notation the sexualities conveyed by the rhythms that have activated and accomplished this reconciliation, the rhythms that have long brought the therapeutic black ritual-places into existence. And it is impossible to notate the rhythm-induced sexualities that brought spiritual excitement to the simulation of the black ritual-places that Elvis caused to transpire on white terrain. The best Richard Middleton could do in a scholarly essay was to notate the black rhythms in Elvis's music and then, in nearly a separate act altogether, interpret them. He simply concluded in his interpretation that the syncopations and crossrhythms in Elvis's music had a physical effect: compulsory movement.[21] Middleton thus inadvertently illustrates the impossibility of capturing the compulsion to move, not to mention the even more elusive sexual arousals that accompany that compulsion. Yet I find it quite possible to notate the verbal signifiers of these rhythm-induced sexualities—the words. The words are "signifiers" of the sexualities because they are one and the same with them, one and the same insofar as they are at home in them. Let us look at a few examples from pre–World War II blues, the music that so influenced Elvis from the time he first heard Arthur "Big Boy" Crudup, whose songs he started recording in 1954.

In Blind Clyde Church's "Number Nine Blues" the idea of dance (choreographed rhythm) is intertwined with sex in such a way that doing the "bedspring pop" also conveys the image of a dance step: "Do that dance they call the bedspring pop; you can shut your eyes, begin to reel and rock." Given this juxtaposition of dance and sex, it is difficult to say whether Walter Davis, in "I Can Tell By the Way You Smell," is watching someone dancing or "rocking and rolling" (sexually): "He got the motion and she got the swing; just look at papa out there on that thing." Blueswomen were also concerned about good rhythm and seemed to intertwine its manifestations in dance and sex. In her recording titled "Baby Doll" Bessie Smith says she went to the doctor who said she was perfectly well, which led her to conclude that what she really needed was a loving "baby doll." He

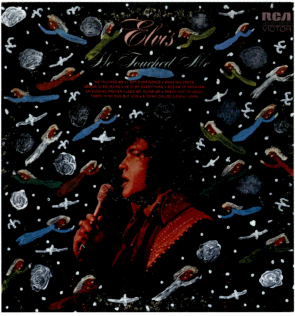

In the crowded marketplace of ideas, Howard Finster appropriates the iconography of famous American presidents, world-renowned celebrities, and global commercial products as the vehicles of his spiritual messages. Howard Finster. *Elvis Album Covers.* 1995–1996. Enamel and marker on cardboard. Courtesy of Larry Clemons.

Alvis was sorta like I am. He was a folk artist. That's what they call him—the man who does his own thing. Howard Finster. *Howard: 1956 Self-Portrait.* ca. late 1980s. Enamel and marker on wood. Courtesy of Larry Clemons.

THE OFFICIAL ELVIS PRAYER RUG

You take this prayer rug into the bathroom and do this ritual for forty days and forty nights to cure arthritis or high blood pressure or if you need money or whatever ails you. Then you send me forty dollars and your prayers will be answered. Joni Mabe. *Elvis Prayer Rug.* 1989. Five-color lithograph with glitter. 28" x 34". Collection of Mr. and Mrs. Richard Boger, Atlanta, Georgia. Courtesy of the artist.

I have a series of prints I call Elvis Mosaics *that I made after I visited the cathedrals of Ravenna in Italy. They're lithographs on handmade paper collaged with acrylic, glitter, and rhinestones. I then sew sequins and lace around the borders and mount them on black velvet.* Joni Mabe. *Hound Dog.* 1989. Lithograph collage. 28" x 34". Collection of CGR and Associates, Atlanta, Georgia. Courtesy of the artist.

The greasy hairstyle for which Elvis became famous was the result of using the hair dressing black men used to straighten their hair. From left, (unidentified man), Nappy Brown, Junior Parker, Elvis Presley, and Bobby Bland. Memphis, ca. 1956. Joni Mabe. *Elvis with Bluesmen.* 1991. Glitter collage. 31" x 32". Courtesy of the artist.

can be ugly and he can be black, she sings, "so long as he can eagle rock and ball the jack."

Although Elvis's songs were not as sexually explicit as the blues that influenced him (directly through itself and indirectly through its incarnations), the blues-based rhythms in his music were not simply inviting of sexual expression. They in fact made whatever sexualities already present in Elvis's words and exhibitions all the more enhanced and suggestive. This is most obvious in his songs with the unmistakable blues beat, blues form, and overall blues persona—"Heartbreak Hotel," "I Want You," "All Shook Up," "Jailhouse Rock," "Hard Headed Woman," and "Hound Dog," to name a few. The textual sexualities in these songs, albeit rather subdued in comparison with the real blues sung by black performers, were also enhanced by such other black rhythmicities as the raspy voice, guttural hums and moans, slippery slides into and out of words, and jazzy glossolalia like "ha-ha-hoo" and "ha-ha-ha oh yeah." Thus, when Elvis sang about needing a woman's love and touch (in his song "Too Much"), about wanting to stick around and get his kicks (in "Jailhouse Rock"), and about kissing a woman in such a way that wild horses could not tear them apart ("Stuck on You"), the sexualities felt like they were being manifested in their God-given context. They felt not godforsaken but good and right, indeed great and righteous, because of the black rhythms and the fact that the resultant ritual contexts were not prudish but permissive for nature.

I have been speaking at times as though the manifestation of black sexualities through black rhythms occurred via the subjective state of the musician doing the expression—that is, as though Elvis poured out through his music the black sexualities he imitated. This is likely a partial explanation for what occurred in the simulated black ritual-places that Elvis brought upon white terrain. Another explanation is that black rhythms themselves imitate (represent or symbolize) black sexualities insofar as they recall the arousing character of particular sexual acts that range from the slippery insinuations of flirtation and foreplay to the funky flow of intercourse and orgasm. Or, to consider yet another theory, it could be that performed black rhythms arouse sexualities in listener-participants and that a black aesthetic is merely selected as a reflection of the aesthetic of the music or performance.

Whether black music is viewed as imitating, arousing, or expressing black sexualities, each of these three means of manifestation is qualified by the way people are brought up to experience music. There has always been a moral strain within white Christian culture that has viewed the musical experience with grudging toleration, in the sense that the slightest suggestiveness of music could immediately transform it into something uncouth. Thus whites were subtly taught to suspect that all music would arouse their nature, except perhaps the most antiseptic of religious chant. And with whites' view that blacks were abundantly or excessively sexual followed the assumption that black music, particularly the rhythms giving it potency and possessability, was also oversexed. Moreover, with the perception of whites that sexuality fell into the binary system of licit and illicit was based the assumption that the rhythms driving black music were forbidden and that surrendering to them would be to embark on a revolution—no less than a sexual revolution. It is evidently in this respect that Camille Paglia calls Elvis "a revolutionary sexual persona,"[22] a man who entered the dreams of whites and "transformed" the way they saw the world.[23]

I want to end with this description of Elvis's significance in the history of sexuality and simply restate my thesis with the added weight of whatever "evidence" I have presented. First, the funky movements—that "crazy little walk" that Elvis exhibited on television—are attributable neither to the white southern culture that Forrest Gump represents as a fictional character nor to white American culture at large. Rather, those movements are traceable to the distinctive rhythms that undergird African-American culture. Secondly, Mrs. Gump's spiritual disgust at Elvis's television performance of "Hound Dog" and her leading Forrest away from that exhibition could not have prevented white youths from delighting in all that blackness and growing up to revolutionize the sexual landscape so as to include blackness forevermore.

PART THREE
ART

Howard Finster. *Elvis Bust* (Paradise Garden). ca. mid-1980s. Enamel on concrete. Photo courtesy of Roger Manley.

9 "It Ain't No Hound Dog, Maybe, But I Believe It's Some Kinda Critter Anyway"

Elvis and Southern Self-Taught Art as Storytelling

ROGER MANLEY

This essay is not so much about Elvis as why I think we need artists like him and artists like Howard Finster. There is something about the stories we hear and the stories we tell ourselves and each other about certain people—the stories that surround certain heroic individuals, not only in our own time, but down through history—that is necessary in order for us to feel like complete human beings. We need to feel that things can happen, that they happen for a reason, and that everything that happens is important. And in order to convey this information in the most deeply satisfying way, we work it into story form.

The southern novelist Reynolds Price once wrote,

> A need to tell and hear stories is essential to the species *Homo sapiens*—second in necessity apparently *after* nourishment and *before* love and shelter. Millions survive without love or home, almost none in silence; the opposite of silence leads quickly to narrative, and the sound of story is the dominant sound of our lives, from the small accounts of our day's events to the vast incommunicable constructs of psychopaths. . . .

We crave nothing less than perfect story; and while we chatter or listen all our lives in a din of craving—to jokes, anecdotes, novels, dreams, films, plays, songs, half the words of our days—we are satisfied only by the one short tale we feel to be true: *History is the will of a just god who knows us.*[1]

The story of Elvis is, I am sure, too familiar by now to launch into at this point for more than a single sentence: It is the old story of a poor boy, born of ordinary parents in humble circumstances, amid suffering, who died young, but who had changed the world before he died. Thousands of people regarded him as a hero—another example of the ideal man. Others have pointed out the parallels to other figures in history and legend—from Jesus or Martin Luther King Jr. to James Dean, Jackson Pollock, Arthur Rimbaud, Abraham Lincoln, or even Clark Kent. Like Kent, the fable was that he lived at home, read the Bible, introduced all his dates to his mother, and didn't drink. He stood for the American way, and when he stepped into his dressing room he emerged a few moments later as a kind of Superman. Or so the story goes.

But there is another kind of hero—what I would call local heroes—people who perhaps aren't so famous and almost never become rich, but who nevertheless may also have a profound effect on everyone whose lives they touch, whether through their personal interactions, their artworks, or through the stories that surround them. They help define us for who we are.

The comparison isn't so far-fetched as it may at first seem. Like Elvis, most of the people I want to discuss were born in humble circumstances of ordinary parents, who endorsed commonly held values. Most of them liked country cooking and fancy cars, feared God, valued honor above self-esteem, probably believed in professional wrestling and almost certainly in the power of evangelism and the likelihood of miracles. Nearly all wanted attention and suffered from the lack of it at one time or another. Like Elvis, they sought to climb out of their situations by discovering a talent and developing it, and they hoped to overcome their self-destructive ways with generosity. For them, as for all of us, sin and salvation were inextricably bound. Most like him, though, they offer the rest of us hope, in our own lives, by showing us that not just they but also we, and everything we do, are vastly important.

This last thing—the hope they offer—is the most critical thing, for that is the essence of anything heroic. The gods put hope in the bottom of Pandora's box for a reason: because they knew that without it, nothing else much mattered—whether bad *or* good. By the same token, it doesn't really matter whether people think of Elvis—or any of the self-taught artists I want to tell you some stories about—as bad or good. He and they both offer hope, just the same. It is this idea of hope that is the essential story that we all have to hear, in order just to stand being alive. And the biggest hope is that someday our lives will change—we'll be redeemed or saved, we'll find the perfect mate, we'll overcome poverty, we'll discover hidden talents, we'll embark upon our true life's work, we won't have to worry about anything anymore. With enough luck, we too may become rich and famous. In its ideal form, we'll never grow up. We'll never even die.

The trouble is, when the changes begin to happen most of the time we don't even realize it until long afterwards. Only a handful among us will ever experience the "Aha!" moment in which we know things are happening—usually it's years later before we realize, counting back, that there were these pivotal points. Seen from the vantage of hindsight, they almost seem preordained. What if Gladys Presley had wandered into Tupelo Hardware and bought Elvis that .22 rifle he wanted, instead of that guitar, for his ninth birthday? What if Vernon Presley had never gotten caught selling the stolen pig that meant they had to move from Tupelo to Memphis? Everything would be different.[2]

In old nursery rhymes, there's a clear description of this process. It's called "For Want of a Nail." You probably heard this when you were a child. I won't try to recite it to you as a rhyme, but the story goes something like this:

> A horseshoe nail works loose and falls out of the hoof of a horse. Because of that, the shoe loosens up and falls off the hoof. Because of that the horse is lamed. The horse was due to carry a rider. The rider was supposed to carry a message. There was a battle going on, and the message was a call for reinforcements. Because the call didn't go through, the reinforcements didn't come. Because the reinforcements didn't come, the battle was lost. And because of that, the war was lost. Because of that the country collapsed and the king lost his head—and all for want of a little nail that got loose.

Heroic artists like Elvis Presley and Howard Finster and others help us hear this story, through the stories of their lives and their creative acts.

I want to tell you one more story about a chain of events like that little nail, since my own life works that way, and I'm sure yours does too. In hindsight, things seem as if they were meant to happen this way. This is the story of one of the reasons why I am standing here in this room today. It began in part because one afternoon in 1969 I had come home from high school in Las Vegas and was slouching in front of the TV. My dad grew up in a gas station outside Prattville, Alabama, and my mother was born on a farm near Hagen, Georgia, and I was born in the South too, but I ended up going to high school in Las Vegas. Anyway, I was watching TV. I wish I could say I was watching an Elvis special, or even Elvis himself—it would be cool to be able to say that, but I can't. I can't even honestly say I ever saw Elvis, even though he was performing regularly less than three miles away my whole senior year. If I'd known then that I was coming to this conference, I'd have made a point of it.

No, I was a classic high school nerd, so I was watching *General Electric College Bowl*, a trivia quiz show for college students. My father came home from work in a bad mood and somehow we got to arguing about where I would go to college. Frankly at the time I couldn't have cared less, but he pressed me on it, so I just pointed at the screen. "I'll go there," I said, to get him off my back, without even knowing quite what it was I was pointing at. A few minutes later, I discovered I was committed to going to a place called Davidson College in North Carolina. I didn't really care. I cared a lot more when I got there, some months later, and all the ramifications of going to a small southern Presbyterian liberal arts college in the middle of nowhere began to really sink in. What's more, I didn't find out it was then an all-male institution until it was way too late to back out. Oh well. All through fall term freshman year I struggled and chafed, dying to get away from the campus. Finally, Christmas break started, and I decided to escape. I didn't have a car, so I hitchhiked. I looked at a map and saw the Outer Banks—a chain of slender, sandy islands off the coast of North Carolina. They looked as good a place as any to go.

When I got there, I began to think I'd made a big mistake. It was pouring rain and there was hardly any traffic. Hours passed—no one seemed to want to pick up a 230-pound wet person with a scruffy beard. Then a pickup truck finally slowed down and I hopped in. I tried to salvage my trip by asking the driver what I could find to do in a place like this. He suggested I might want to take a look at the lighthouse or a walk along the beach to look for shells—there had been some good storms lately and no telling what might have washed up. The lighthouse didn't much appeal. I've never been much on heights and sheer drops. And I didn't feel much like loading my backpack

Annie Hooper led me off on a tour through her house. There were figures everywhere—on top of and under the furniture, in the kitchen, and up the stairs. I had met my first southern self-taught artist. Courtesy of Roger Manley.

down with shells. Then he said, "Well, you could go by and see my grandmother. She does these wood carved things." Christmas was only a few days away and I figured I might buy some bookends or duck-decoy ashtrays or something like that as presents, so I thought about it and decided to do it. He dropped me off at a laundromat where I dried my clothes, and then I followed his directions to her house. When I knocked, the door was opened by a tiny white-haired lady who ushered me inside as if she'd been expecting me. And I think it is fair to say now that when I crossed the threshold into her house, my life changed profoundly.

As my eyes adjusted to the light I began to discern the forms of thousands of faces looking back at me. The floor was so crowded with the figures of angels and sheep and ancient Hebrews that there was scarcely a place to put my feet down. I'd met Annie Hooper (1897–1986). Annie led me off on a tour through her house, pausing every now and then to flip a light switch with a yardstick or to lift and animate a figure, while she spoke in her clipped Outer Banks accent about the Bible, human loss, bravery, redemption, faith, trust, and death. There were figures everywhere—on top of and under the furniture, in the kitchen, and up the stairs; the sun porch was crammed with the Children of Israel following the Pillars of Fire and smoke; more figures were in the parlor and out in the shed where she'd left only a pathway through the Sermon on the Mount to get to her washing machine. I didn't know what to make of it—I only knew it was the most amazing thing I had ever seen. I had met my first southern self-taught artist.

Years later, I began to hear the term "outsider art," but that term hadn't been invented at the time. All that happened was that when I came back from that trip, I tried to tell people about this experience and people found it very hard to believe—they thought I was making it up. So I had to go back out to the Outer Banks at Easter and photograph it, and then when I came back and started showing those pictures to people, something in them started to react to it. They started to say, "Oh, I know someone like that. I've got an uncle who is making dinosaurs out of car bumpers." Or someone else would say, "Oh, I've got a neighbor like that, someone who is collecting mule dung that looks like presidents of the United States." And so I would go by and visit these people. And over the course of the years I gradually accumulated a lot of pictures of these kinds of people without really knowing what I was doing. Later I found out that I was visiting outsider artists.

Roger Cardinal wrote a book called *Outsider Art* in 1972 that named the field.[3] He called it that because this art was not folk—it wasn't traditional, not passed down from one generation to another. It wasn't fine art because it wasn't learned in an academic setting or with the intention of exhibiting it in a museum. It wasn't commercial because the people really didn't intend to sell it. It just didn't fit into any of the other categories, except perhaps the category of people whose stories tell us something about how to survive. And he called it outsider art.[4]

Gradually, I began to visit more and more of these people. I began to discover a plot—I mean, a sort of story line or pattern to the way many of them had lived their lives. For not only do we each have stories about our encounters with eccentric people, but we share our understanding of their lives with one another. Let me offer a caveat, though, by way of another old children's story—this one is called "The Five Blind Men and the Elephant."

Five blind men were wandering through the jungle, hand in hand, when all of a sudden they heard a trumpeting noise. "What's that?" they wondered. One of them said it sounded like an elephant, although he had never encountered one, and none of them had any idea what that meant. They decided to send one of them out to see what it was like. He wandered ahead with his hand stretched out, felt the animal's trunk, and then stumbled back to the others. "Elephants are just like snakes!" he said. "It doesn't sound like a snake," said another. "I better go and check it out." So he went, and felt the ear and ran back to the others. "Elephants are just like fans," he said. "Snakes? Fans? That doesn't make sense," said another. "Maybe I better go." He felt the elephant's leg and came back and reported that the other two were wrong—it was just like a tree. Another went and felt the side and came back to say that it was like a wall, and the last went and felt the tail and claimed that the elephant was like a rope.

Well, all were right, but all were wrong—maybe it's something we should keep in mind when we are talking about Elvis, when we're thinking about things like subliminal anticolonial messages or life in the South or what any of these artists is really like. When I talk about these people, please bear in mind that I'm only one blind man, who's felt only one part of the elephant, trying to tell you some stories about what I found.

I'm into the pattern or plot of the typical life-story of the outsider artist.[5] Typically, the kind of artist who does this kind of work is someone who had a very physical way of making a living—someone like a logger or a farmer or a factory worker, someone who could look at the end of the day and see at the end of a day's work that they had done a certain tangible job. Insurance actuaries and teachers and lawyers are not likely to become outsider artists because what they do is largely invisible. But the kind of people who tend to become this kind of artist are people who can see what they've done at the end of the day. Then something happens that takes away their ability to see that value—something like an industrial accident that prevents them from going to work or an illness or an early retirement or maybe their spouse dies and they lose their energy and ability to work. And over a period of time they become very depressed. For most people that this kind of thing happens to, the depression evolves into something like alcoholism, homelessness, or just general depression. But once in a while, a tiny percentage of people will overcome this experience by beginning to make things, and those kind of people are the people who become outsider artists.

James Bright Bailey (b. 1908) was an asbestos worker in North Carolina, and he fits this pattern really well. He worked in an asbestos factory that made fire hoses and asbestos insulation. Over a period of years, as you can imagine, he had breathed so much of that asbestos dust that he had to retire. He went home and he began feeling very depressed. He began feeling like his life was over before he was ready for it to be over. And he missed all his friends down there at the factory. He was sitting there feeling depressed one day, and just to pass time he began whittling away on a little piece of wood. And something about doing that satisfied him so much that he decided to make another figure. He began to make little figures of his friends and to set them up because those were the people he knew. He was thinking about them so he began carving them. And gradually, as time went on, his little figures began to take over his house—on top of the TV, in the bathroom, down the hall.

Each one represented a particular person, someone that he knew. And this had an actual effect because not only did it give him a sense of value, a tangible sense of accomplishment, but it also attracted people. His friends would come by to see how he had carved them. So they were constantly dropping by, and they would tell each other about it, and that created a sense of community for him. He had to build furniture to set the little figures on. Then he had to build a wing on his house to enclose the furniture with the figures on it. It just snowballed. One thing led to another.

Clyde Jones (b. 1938) was a pulpwood logger working for a textile mill in North Carolina and one day he made a mistake. He felled a tree the wrong direction and it landed on top of him. He broke his leg

James Bright Bailey began feeling like his life was over in a sense before he was ready for it to be over. And he missed all his friends down there at the factory. He began to make little figures of his friends and to set them up because those were the people he knew. Courtesy of Roger Manley.

in about five places; he cut off one of his fingers—it was just a bad day in general. And he stayed at home feeling very depressed about his inability to work any more. During that period of depression, he began to make something. He took a small stump and attached legs to it. It looked like an animal. After

he looked at it, he decided it wasn't a hound dog but it was some kind of critter anyway. That's how he began making things. Something about doing that satisfied him so much that he decided to make an-

During that period of depression, Clyde Jones began to make something. He took a small stump and attached legs to it. It looked like an animal. After he looked at it, he decided it wasn't a hound dog but it was some kind of critter anyway. That's how he began making things. They completely filled his yard and adjacent yards and became something of an attraction. Courtesy of Roger Manley.

other one and another one and pretty soon the little animals began to take over. They completely filled his yard and adjacent yards and became something of an attraction. People would come by to see his yard and to wander through it. Sometimes on a Sunday afternoon there would be bumper-to-bumper traffic. This gave him a sense of value, a sense that he was able to contribute to the community again, that he was valuable once more because he could do something.

Clyde isn't particularly concerned with verisimilitude—that things look like what they are supposed to be. If he gets a pair of plastic poinsettias, he will attach them and make eyes out of it. For him, it's the act of being busy that's important. Often people will bring by things for him to use—industrial carpeting, even old plumbing gear—and he will incorporate that into his work. Just as they had with James Bright Bailey's little figures, people come back later to see what he did with the things they gave him.

Georgia Blizzard (b. 1919) is another example of someone who took suffering and decided to do something with it. Georgia is one of these people who has had every bad possible thing happen to her, so it seems. She got married to a coal miner. One day the mine collapsed and crippled him, so she had to go to work to take care of him. She worked in a textile mill and got brown lung and they had to take out one of her lungs. She raised an orphan who was run over by a train. Her older sister came to live with her and then came down with Alzheimer's. Her own daughter's marriage failed, so she came back home to live with her mother and then became a paranoid schizophrenic. One thing piled on top of another. A lot of people would go out and shoot themselves or take up alcoholism, but what Georgia did was she started to take up clay. She would crawl into a cave on her property and get cave clay and without any tools—with no potter's wheel, no special gear, not even a kiln—she began to shape the clay with her hands. She put it in the middle of a truck tire and set the tire on fire and the burning tire would fire this clay adequately to make these figures that contained all this suffering that she had experienced.

She made a pot that commemorated a run-in that she had with one of her neighbors, who seemed to be friendly at first, but then it turned out that she was just trying to get her land from her. At one time Georgia had a dream that she was sitting on a throne surrounded by people who were begging for her decisions. They wanted her to take charge. This dream became the plaque, *The Unjust Throne*.

Vollis Simpson (b. 1919), another person who took a bad thing and made something great, had an unusual way of making a living. Vollis picked up heavy things for a living in a rural crossroads community in eastern North Carolina. If the Southern Railway locomotive ran off the bridge and wound up in the river, they would call Vollis. He built thirteen cranes and with them could hoist things like locomotives, water towers, and complete brick factories and move them to a new location. A few years ago he was doing one of these jobs when a cable broke, caught him across his chest, and broke several of his ribs and his sternum. As he was laid up in the hospital he realized that he was doing all this work for other people, but that when he died he wouldn't be

A lot of people would go out and shoot themselves or take up alcoholism, but what Georgia Blizzard did was she started to take up clay. She would crawl into a cave on her property and get cave clay and without any tools—with no potter's wheel, no special gear, not even a kiln— she began to shape the clay with her hands. Courtesy of Roger Manley.

leaving anything for anyone to remember him by. He decided he wanted to do something big that would take advantage of his ability to weld things or to lift things. He began building what may be the largest whirligigs in the world. About fifty or sixty feet tall, these immense whirligigs on his farm in eastern North Carolina have thousands of moving parts perfectly balanced to pivot into the wind: people that ride bicycles and play the guitar, people or birds that flap their wings, or angels that fly.

One of the three early-warning signs of outsider artists is strange cars.[6] In a way, Elvis pioneered the car as a public statement of values and beliefs in American culture. Take, for example, Bill Dunn. He had a bad experience. His wife divorced him and she married the lawyer that handled the divorce, and together they apparently worked to bilk him out of all his money. So he painted his septic-tank truck and a hearse—symbolic vehicles for filth and death—with public statements of pain and how he was mistreated. As he drives around, he publicly tells the tale.

Vollis Simpson decided he wanted to do something big that would take advantage of his ability to weld things or to lift things. He began building what may be the largest whirligigs in the world. About fifty or sixty feet tall, these immense whirligigs on his farm in eastern North Carolina have thousands of moving parts perfectly balanced to pivot into the wind: people that ride bicycles and play the guitar, people or birds that flap their wings, or angels that fly. Courtesy of Roger Manley.

Car-customizer Churchill Winston Hill is the creator of the Elvis van. It has buttons that run along the sides that, when pushed, play songs from a built-in jukebox. This involvement with Elvis, which is an example of involvement with heroes in general, runs throughout a lot of this kind of art. Lester Pressley has his own version of the Presley car, complete with a little doll of Elvis Presley surrounded by women receiving praise.

Howard Finster (b. 1916) styles himself as God's Last Red Light. If you were to see his car, a late-model Cadillac like one Elvis used to drive, and were to follow it, you would wind up at Howard's house, Paradise Garden, in Pennville, Georgia. Howard thinks of himself as someone who can try to preserve and celebrate all that is great and good in the world. He does this through his Paradise Garden, where he is trying to collect one of all the inventions of mankind. Howard traffics in heroes, as do many of these artists. Some depict more abstract concepts through versions of eagles or Uncle Sams or angels, or else, as is the case for many African-American artists, portray leaders like Kennedy, Martin Luther King Jr., or Lincoln. In Finster's pantheon, it's Jesus, the Devil, Henry Ford, George Washington, a host

Bill Dunn had a bad experience. His wife divorced him and she married the lawyer that handled the divorce, and together they apparently worked to bilk him out of all his money. So he painted his septic-tank truck and a hearse with public statements of pain and how he was mistreated. As he drives around, he publicly tells his tale.
Courtesy of Roger Manley.

Car-customizer Churchill Winston Hill is the creator of the Elvis van. It has buttons that run along the sides that, when pushed, play songs from a built-in jukebox. Courtesy of Roger Manley.

of friends, and, of course, Elvis himself, though often as a boy. There is something about the notion of potential, rather than Elvis's realized adulthood, that appeals to Finster.

Howard is the ultimate recycler. He is trying to collect one of everything. This is part of his God's Last Red Light or Last Noah approach to things. He wanted to own one of everything and preserve it in Paradise Garden down behind his house. When I say one of everything, I literally mean that. You can hardly name anything that Howard doesn't have or hasn't owned or doesn't own three or four of—even a pair of tonsils floating in a mason jar embedded in the wall of the Garden. There are canceled checks, kidney stones, all kinds of guns, airplane parts, parts of milking machines, parts of cars, typewriters. He has an adding-machine collection, a bomb collection—anything you can imagine Howard has collected it and added it to this Garden. There has been a kind of ebb and flow in and out of it as people have purchased things and taken them away. But at various times it's been an amazing place to see.

In Paradise Garden he also honors all the people who have touched his life, whether alive or dead. There's Henry Ford and especially Elvis. Elvis shows up throughout the Garden and throughout Howard's work. Like his Coke bottles or telephones or trash cans or even his own face, Elvis is a blank slate upon which Howard can project his own ideas and wishes, just as Elvis was for so many other people. Sometimes Howard literally writes these ideas directly on Elvis himself, just like he does on his Coke bottles and other commercial aspects of life, which he takes and reinterprets. He's done this with his own self-portrait.[7]

Elvis has meant a lot to many other outsider artists—like James Harold Jennings (b. 1931), who painted his own version of Elvis. James lives in a school bus about eight miles north of Winston-Salem, North Carolina. Next to it he's built a personal amusement park in which he can feel creative and comfortable. Woodrow Gantt (b. 1911) lives in a house that is actually styled after Elvis's birthplace in Tupelo. He did a carving of Elvis made from a brick.

Henry Louis Holliday (b. 1937) was a welder. He told me, "The only thing I'm afraid of really is lightning." And his house was made of metal mostly. I was looking at it and kind of admiring it one day and he said, "You want to go inside?" I went inside. It had a very unusual decorative scheme. The walls were decorated with chewing gum stuck on in patterns. The ceiling was covered with globs of chewing gum too. This is not the kind of thing you see in *Southern Living* or *Better Homes and Gardens*. The fact is, though, he did it because it satisfied him. He wasn't worried about resale value; he wasn't worried about what the neighbors would think. He just knew that this is something that he wanted to do and he gave in to that whim. Life's too short not to. In a way you can think of this as a poor man's Jungle Room.

Howard Finster styles himself as God's Last Red Light. If you were to see his car, a late-model Cadillac like one Elvis used to drive, and were to follow it, you would wind up at Howard's house, Paradise Garden, in Pennville, Georgia. Courtesy of Roger Manley.

James Harold Jennings, who painted his own version of Elvis, lives in a school bus about eight miles north of Winston-Salem, North Carolina. Courtesy of Roger Manley.

There are the stories we tell about our own encounters with these outsider artists, the blindman type of stories we tell about them, but there are also the stories that they themselves intend for their art to tell. Let me stop trying to describe these elephants and let one of them speak for himself.

Lonnie Holley (b. 1950) lives right under the incoming flight pattern of the Birmingham International Airport, where the planes go directly over his house. He takes the old sand-casting molds from the Birmingham steel mills and carves them into amazing, intricate sculptures made out of what is essentially man-made sandstone. He's done thousands of works that completely fill the entire four-acre property, including inside his house. He lives within his art. Also he takes found objects and makes incredible assemblages. When you see the stuff at his place it looks like nothing so much as just a collection of junk, but actually everything he does is filled with meaning. In fact, it would be possible to examine at great length any individual work of the artists discussed in this essay.

Holley's *Fourth of July Pot* was made just after Independence Day in 1991. At first glance, it appears to be an assemblage with little more than the barest structure to distinguish it from mere chaos—or from modernist sculptures with little more going for them than curious juxtapositions of materials and forms. But it tells a little story, with profound implications. It deals with issues starkly outlined to Holley by the choices and conduct of some members of his neighborhood on the Fourth of July. A mother on welfare chose to spend her government check on a barbecue rather than on her needy children. The family is silhouetted in wire among various mementos of the misguided feast: eating utensils, the pot, a brightly painted pork rib. A videocassette, remote control, gaudy carpet, and tattered clothes re-create their living environment. The steel spring wedged between two halves of tree bark reinforces the splitting effect her negligence is having on her children. "How much one day could take away from our way of living," Holley says, talking about this piece, "if a person don't understand that day." As Lonnie explains:

Henry Holliday's house was made of metal mostly. I was looking at it and kind of admiring it one day and he said, "You want to go inside?" I went inside. It had a very unusual decorative scheme. The walls were decorated with chewing gum stuck on in patterns. The ceiling was covered with globs of chewing gum too. In a way you could think of it as a poor man's Jungle Room. Courtesy of Roger Manley.

A lot of us that can't read or write don't even know what independence mean. They just celebrate because they know that the day is a day to celebrate yearly. We as a people can easily get involved in traditions and ceremonies and join in and become actors in those things. That's good in a way—in a way it's not. We still have to control our habits. *The Fourth of July Pot* shows we're out of control as far as some of those habits is concerned. Sometimes making preparation for a celebration we spend too far and too much.

It's the old way versus the new way: The old way was celebrated after the harvest from the seeds that we planted. Today we're taking from that harvest without all of us being interested in replanting.

The two pieces of wood, the tall bark and short bark, man and woman, show the value of the old, and the cotton they had picked and harvested around the Fourth of July. The bark shows the strength of the outside because we had lost the value of the inside. The cotton is in place of the true tree to show their labor was true at that time.

It's tied up to hold itself in place because of communication. If we had listened as well as watched for the value of the truth of the whole tree, we would have been stronger, and it would have allowed us to fill our pot, not just on the Fourth of July, but every day after that. Our

Lonnie Holley takes found objects and makes incredible assemblages. When you see the stuff at his place it looks like nothing so much as just a collection of junk, but actually everything he does is filled with meaning. Courtesy of Roger Manley.

habits allowed us to take advantage of the pot, and the meat all the way to the bone. The meat gave us very little strength, though, leaving us blue because of high blood pressure and other sickness it could cause.

All the value we put into that day become tied up in many ways from the bed we slept in and it causes a strain and tension of trying to keep enough money for the habits of one day's celebration.

That's how Holley explains that one piece.

The works of so many of these artists—and there are hundreds more—could contribute much more than they do now if we could only learn to hear their stories. Reynolds Price says we need stories, and he is right. We particularly need the kind of stories provided by unknown people like these southern self-taught artists, as well as by those among us who, though equally eccentric, became famous like Elvis did. The lives of any one of these people has the potential for meaning, and that is true whether or not they are liked, disliked, or feared—as some neighbors undoubtedly feared James Harold Jennings—or admired, even worshipped, as Elvis was. The point I am trying to make is about meaning, not entertainment; understandings, not smiles. As frightening as these artists may have been to their neighbors, they learned things—from seeing them and talking about them and occasionally confronting them—that they never would have learned from someone in a house just like their own. The Jungle Room at Graceland is just the same kind of eccentric space that Henry Holliday's chewing-gum room is—a place filled with wonder, where we can feel the real presence of another person's energy and life, one that provides, if you'll forgive the reference to chewing gum, food for thought. We need the hopes and dreams of places and people like these and the stories they enable us to tell about racial injustice, religious doubt, love, loneliness, and personal value.[8]

Driving around on the back roads somewhere between heaven and hell, it's good to be able to think that a young boy playing in his shabby yard could one day be hiding all the hosts of heaven in his barn. If we can think that, perhaps we can glance in the rearview mirror and catch a glimpse of our own selves and tell ourselves the story all of us

Lonnie Holley's Fourth of July Pot *deals with issues starkly outlined to Holley by the choices and conduct of some members of his neighborhood on the Fourth of July.* Lonnie Holley. Fourth of July Pot. 1992. 52-1/2" x 37" x 17". Wood, metal spring, yarn, and found materials. The Arnett Collection. Photo by Nathan Partridge.

most need to hear: that our lives may be waiting to burst forth in creative flower, that we're yet capable of doing something that will make it all—all the worry, all the pain, all the doubt and confusion, even all the boredom—suddenly, somehow, seem worth it.

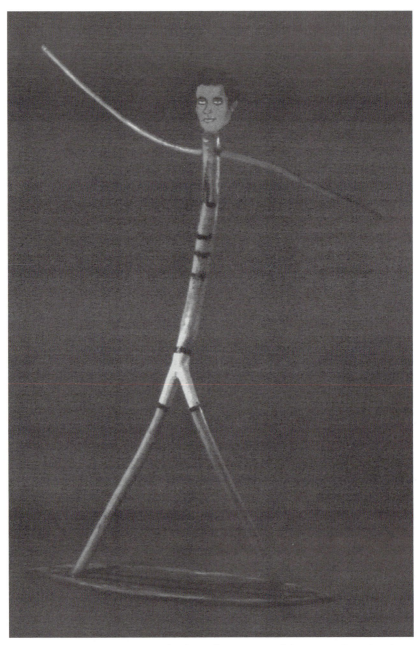

Ivan McClean. *Surfin' Elvis.* Welded metal. Courtesy of the artist. Photo by Jim Ramer.

10 In Search of Elvis

An Exhibition in a Variety of Media

KATHERINE HERNDON

My search for Elvis began three years ago when I moved to Memphis and began my personal immersion in the aura that Elvis left there. I grew up in Hollywood, so the complementary atmosphere of stardom and fandom in Memphis seemed familiar to me. The only difference was, there was just one star—Elvis Presley.

In the fifties, the number of American teenagers grew rapidly as a result of the postwar baby boom. For the first time in American social history, adolescence as a form of identity predominated. The desires of childlike dependence combined with the demands of adult independence produced an ambiguous and often conflicting set of expectations for teenagers. In short, America had reached its adolescence. In a world that was struggling to adjust and adapt to the new postwar conditions, teenagers could find a part of themselves in the heroic Elvis.

Polar opposites harmoniously coexisted in the image of Elvis. Paradoxical aspects of humanity—sensuality and spirituality, tenderness and passion, humility and ambition, masculinity and femininity, the temporal and the intangible, the blurring of distinctions between race and class—could all be found in the heroic Elvis. For American teenagers, Elvis offered a cultural hero that addressed directly what they were feeling.

All of this turmoil came together in a powerful celebration of the vitality of Elvis. The sensuality of his performance style was seen as a threat to the conservative moral atmosphere of the fifties. Parents were shocked by the very aspects of his music that the teenagers embraced. Adults feared that traditional values were being threatened. Even his rapid climb to fame utilized methods that were new and potentially destabilizing to the fifties. Television and clever marketing worked together to produce "Elvis"—his cult of personality—as the first media archetype.

I grew up well aware of the fabulous fame of the icon of Elvis Presley. In one year, 1956, when I was one year old, Elvis became an international celebrity, sold over a million copies of a single recording, earned a million dollars, performed on all the major television shows, and made his first film.

In Memphis, it is easy to see how his adoration spans generations. On my first tour of Graceland in 1984, during the screening of a documentary about his rise to stardom, a very young girl seated behind me whispered to her father, "Daddy, I think Lisa Marie is the luckiest girl in the whole world." The wall outside of the mansion is now a palimpsest of testimonials from the children of those teenagers whose world Elvis endowed with meaning. "I was not born when you died, but my parents made sure I knew who you were and I love you too." "Even though I never saw you sing, I love you, Elvis."[1]

Always a fan of rock 'n' roll, I cannot imagine my life without the associations this music has given me. Incidental riffs of familiar songs bring back memories of times and people now long gone. In Memphis, I began to meet others for whom the music of Elvis had the same effect. I began to feel more and more that our world had been shaped by rock 'n' roll, and that Elvis had been our first real hero. I soon began to get a feeling for the profound impact this one man had on the entire world.

It seemed unbelievable to me that the magnitude of this icon had escaped presentation in Memphis, the *locus sanctus* of Elvis's image. In 1993 I curated at Delta Axis Contemporary Arts Center the first exhibition of contemporary art with Elvis as the subject ever held in Memphis—*Elvis: A Cultural Obsession*. While researching artists to be included in the show, I began to see that this neglect was no simple oversight. Rather, it was evidence that the paradigm of contemporary art was still resistant to the inclusion of elements of popular culture, even though the make-readies of Duchamp had first been presented in Paris in 1914, nearly fifty years before the advent of Elvis onto the world stage. Contemporaneous with the rise of Elvis was Andy Warhol, Roy Lichtenstein, James Rosenquist, and others of the Pop art movement.[2] These artists were using materials, techniques, and images (including that of Elvis Presley) from popular culture to penetrate and enshrine the world of fine art with contemporary cultural values. Despite their enormous creativity and ingenuity, modern art traditions still prevailed.

Contemporary artists struggle with issues of image and communication. Art-making requires the artist to scrutinize and explore our world and produce an observation, depiction, or solution according to the artist's individual view. As members of a subculture, artists often question the validity of traditional institutions. These questions often exert considerable influence on evolving values and cultural trends within the traditional culture. Highly regarded and serious artists are still using Elvis imagery in the years since his death to explore the contradiction between dynamic, creative aspects of humanity and the pressure to conform to tradition. The image of Elvis has become a catalyst in the exploration of fantasy and myth in contemporary America.[3]

People seem hungry to understand why and how Elvis has affected their lives. I found that many of the artists in the exhibition felt some level of personal involvement with the King. Whether or not they had actually met him or seen him perform, Elvis had touched their lives. Questioning, exploring, growing, and changing are all activities within the realm of the artist. Was it any wonder they should look to the Elvis icon for inspiration? In that image can be found the perfect synthesis of unity, tolerance, vitality, and challenge. The subsequent absorption of that symbol into our collective iconography has had an unparalleled impact on American culture. The image that spoke so directly to youthful rebellion also addressed the quest of the artist.

The exhibition of visual art at Delta Axis in conjunction with the University of Mississippi's International Conference on Elvis Presley was intended to be a further exploration of why artists are so drawn to the heroic image of Elvis. We displayed an eclectic mix of work by artists from diverse backgrounds and cultures, of all ages, from within the region and outside it, from academically trained and self-taught backgrounds. Through the works of some twenty-three artists I sought to depict the breadth, pervasiveness, and universality of the meaning of the image of Elvis Presley.

The works of Josef Schutzenhofer from Austria and Petr Lysacek from Ostrava-Zabrac in the Czech Republic present us with two very different European depictions of the image of the man who is the personification of the American Dream—the rags-to-riches story. In the collaborative photographic series *Czech Out Memphis* Lysacek and Memphian David Horan used Elvis's birthplace as a representation of "American" psychologies idealized in Eastern Europe. Schutzenhofer's sardonic etching *Elvis Silenus* portrays Elvis as the potbellied satyr of Greek mythology who had the gift of prophecy and could charm humans and animals with his song. These depictions convey the complex feeling of reverence for an imperfect hero in an imperfect world.

American artists are also exploring the realization of the dream. A welder by trade, Ivan McClean chose Elvis's film career as a reference to their common bond to the work ethic. His *Surfin' Elvis* (see chapter frontispiece) reminds us that although it sometimes appears frivolous, art is produced through hard labor. "I could imagine Elvis," McClean said, "reveling in sweat just like I do when I'm working with metal on hot southern summer days." D. C. Young's photographs *Elvis at the Chenile Shop Hwy. 49* and *Elvis T.V.* and Ceci Smith's simple portrait of Elvis before an American flag, *El Hombre*, suggest the "boy next door" making it big. By contrast, Ke Francis's *Elvis Memorabilia and Gift Shop, Belden, Mississippi*, points up the aggressive marketing to which Elvis was subjected.

Visionary folk artist Howard Finster, whose work can be seen throughout this volume, has produced many paintings that he says the ghost of Elvis has guided him to do. When depicting Elvis as a heroic image, he most often paints the innocent and pure baby Elvis from a well-known early photograph of Elvis at three years old (see Chapter 5).

Though they have very different aesthetics, many of these artists are moved by Elvis's music. In his chain saw sculpture of a Bunyanesque Elvis and hound dog, Tommy Rieben's cedar portrayal of The King literally carves out from a single tree the one among the many. Elvis's guitar has replaced the ax as a mythic emblem of the frontier spirit.

For Elayne Goodman, Elvis is quite simply motif. Goodman's *Elvis Shrine* (see Chapter 15) is just one example of her application of the icon of Elvis to the devotional format accepted in our culture and throughout history. In *Gladys and Child* Ceci Smith uses the "holy family of Elvis" to build on the powerful recognition of the divinity of ordinary life running through American art and literature: "the mechanic's wife with her babe at her nipple interceding for every person born . . . " (Walt Whitman, "Song of Myself," sec. 41).

It is indisputable that Elvis Presley, whatever the style of depiction may be, has radically altered our concept of heroism. Even in death, Elvis remains a close, personal friend to people around the world of every generation and cultural background. He is an American hero, a symbol of freedom and self-expression, the personification of all that rock 'n' roll has given to future generations. These artists are concerned with the qualities that cause people to cling to an image and devotedly praise and cherish it.

Selected Bibliography

Barth, Jack. *Roadside Elvis: The Complete State-by-State Travel Guide for Elvis Presley Fans*. Chicago: Contemporary Books, 1991.

Combs, James. "Celebrations: Rituals of Popular Veneration." *Journal of Popular Culture* (Spring 1989): 71–77.

Dewitt, Howard A. *Elvis—the Sun Years: The Story of Elvis Presley in the Fifties*. Ann Arbor, Mich.: Popular Culture, Ink., 1993.

Hammontree, Patsy Guy. *Elvis Presley: A Bio-Bibliography*. Westport, Conn.: Greenwood Press, 1985.

Hopkins, Jerry. *Elvis*. New York: Simon and Schuster, 1971.

Stanley, David, with Frank Coffey. *The Elvis Encyclopedia: The Complete and Definitive Reference Book on the King of Rock & Roll*. Los Angeles: General Publication Group, 1994.

Whisler, John A. *Elvis Presley Reference Guide and Discography*. Metuchen, N.J.: Scarecrow Press, 1981.

Elvis Silenus. *Josef Schutzenhofer, originally from Austria, received his MFA in painting from the Maryland Institute of Art in 1987. His work is often corrosively satirical, targeting Euro-American culture. He has taught painting in Maryland at Towson State University and Delaplaine Art Center. Recently he returned to Austria to pursue painting full time.* Photo courtesy of Jim Ramer.

Elvis. *Tommy Rieben lives in Oakland, Tennessee, and has created chainsaw sculpture for the past five years. He restores antique automobiles for a living and has done art tournaments and public exhibitions with his chainsaw art. He saw Elvis in a big cedar tree in the woods in Fayette County.* Photo courtesy of Jim Ramer.

Religion, *from* Czech Out Memphis *series. Petr Lysacek, from Ostrava-Zabrac in the Czech Republic, received his education from the Academy of Fine Arts in Prague and has exhibited throughout the Czech Republic and Germany. David Horan has a combined degree in photography and sociology from the University of Memphis. Since 1986, he has been teaching, doing workshops, and working as a freelance photographer. The two artists worked together while Lysacek was in Memphis as a visiting artist at the University of Memphis. They decided to produce a series of eight photographs as a collaborative project using Elvis's birthplace as a representation of the phenomenon of social icons and "American" psychologies idealized in Eastern Europe.* Photo courtesy of Jim Ramer.

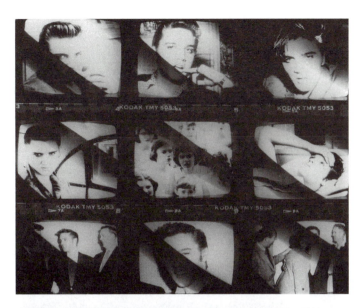

Elvis T.V. *and* Elvis at the Chenile Shop Hwy. 49. *D. C. Young lives in Hattiesburg, Mississippi. She was raised in western Kentucky and studied photography at the University of Kentucky. She has been an artist-in-residence at the École nationale de la photographie in Arles, France, and at the University of Memphis. She has published in books and magazines and exhibited in group and one-person exhibitions throughout France, Mississippi, and Florida. Her photographs are in the collection of the Mississippi Museum of Art and other public collections. She is a cofounder and member of Club Pyramid, an interdisciplinary, intercultural, and interracial artists' collaborative group.* Photos courtesy of Jim Ramer.

El Hombre *and* Gladys and Child. *Ceci Smith, originally from New Orleans, lives in Jackson, Mississippi. She has a degree in Special Education and teaches art at the Mississippi State Hospital. "I was actually in Mexico when Elvis died, so I think I got the Mexican take on it. The reaction there was as if some important part of their image of America had died."* Photos courtesy of Jim Ramer.

Elvis Memorabilia and Gift Shop, Belden, Mississippi. *Ke Francis lives in Tupelo, Mississippi. His art has been included in numerous group and one-person shows across the United States and Eastern and Western Europe. He has received the Rockefeller Foundation Grant, the NEA/Mississippi Arts Commission Individual Artists Grant, and the Polaroid Foundation Grant. In 1987 he won the SAF/NEA Regional Fellowship in Sculpture. His work is in the collections of the Mint Museum, Boston Museum of Fine Arts, Library of Congress, Smithsonian Institution, High Museum, and National Museum of American Art. "I live in the town in which Elvis was born. We had the same schoolteachers. I used the very books he used in the seventh grade. His name was still in them (he wasn't famous yet). Now he's dead and I'm broke and an artist. It would be strange not to have done something with his image."*

• Surfin' Elvis *(see chapter frontispiece). Ivan McClean has lived in Greenwood, Mississippi, since 1991 but is a native Californian. He earned a degree in Farm Management at Cal Poly Tech in San Luis Obispo and worked in the Philippines with the Peace Corps. He and his brother began making "fun things" in their welding shop where they made gates and fences.* Surfin' Elvis *is a departure from his welded metal pieces. He felt a kinship with Elvis while working on the piece. "I could imagine Elvis reveling in sweat just like I do when I'm working with metal on hot southern summer days."*

Joni Mabe. *Elvis Prayer Rug.* 1989. Five-color lithograph with glitter. 28" x 34".
Collection of Mr. and Mrs. Richard Boger, Atlanta, Georgia. Courtesy of the
artist.

|| Everything Elvis

JONI MABE

I didn't become a fan until the day that Elvis died in 1977, and I was totally obsessed with him for a long time.[1] I turned every holiday into an Elvis holiday: Halloween I had an Elvis pumpkin; Christmas I had a Christmas tree with all Elvis ornaments on it. I drove all my friends crazy. I had my Elvis museum in my house until 1983. Then I decided to take it on the road after I graduated from college. The first show on tour I just called *The Elvis Room,* but over the years, as the show grew larger, so did the title. Now I call it *Joni Mabe's Traveling Panoramic Encyclopedia of Everything Elvis.*

I went to the University of Georgia, where I got my Master of Fine Arts, and did my thesis on Elvis, which I don't think had ever been done before in an art program. I almost didn't graduate because my art represented the Elvis Culture, which is a far cry from abstract expressionism, the main thing taught in the UGA art department. I've never won a grant from the National Endowment for the Arts with my Elvis art, but I've won some stuff with my sculpture from my Oddities Museum and for my artists' books. Recognition of artwork with Elvis as the subject matter has come a long way since I started makin' Elvis art over eighteen years ago.

When I discovered Elvis on the day he died, I was washin' my Scout and listenin' to a tribute program on the radio. I didn't know all his early music. When I was first aware of music, mainly during the seventies, Elvis was sorta like what Wayne Newton is today. Back then I was listenin' to Lynyrd Skynyrd, Bad Company, the Allman Brothers—mostly southern boogie and stuff like that. So I really discovered Elvis on the day that everybody lost him, which is sorta ironic.

The first time I went to Graceland I couldn't afford all the souvenirs so I just went home and started makin' my own Elvis objects. I made stuff and then started tradin' with people for objects and memorabilia that they had. So I don't have a lot of my early work. But I'm constantly makin' new works to replace ones I've sold or traded.

I install the museum, floor to ceiling, sorta set up like an Italian cathedral or King Tut's tomb. It becomes a whole Elvis environment or whole Elvis world and I play Elvis music on a continuous loop. It usually takes me two weeks to install the museum—that's fourteen days and probably about 140 hours of hard work, with a lot of nail holes in the walls after I leave. I have in the show Elvis whiskey decanters, Elvis collectors' plates, Elvis costumes, Elvis lamps, Elvis clocks and watches, an Elvis bedspread, Elvis pillows, Elvis T-shirts, Elvis mugs, Elvis caps, an Elvis 1964 jukebox with fifty Elvis 45 records, Elvis bedroom slippers, Elvis towels, Elvis knives, Elvis cologne, Elvis shoestrings, Elvis sweat, Elvis albums, tabloids with stories of "Elvis on Mars," "Nixon Grooming Elvis for President," "Elvis Sightings," "Elvis Is Alive," "Elvis Is Dead at 58," "Elvis Tribe in Africa," "Smelvis—Cow Paddy in Shape of Elvis's Face," "Elvis in Coffin," "Elvis Hiding in Swiss Alps with Kennedy and Hitler"—all things and anything related to Elvis.

Every place I install is totally different because I use whatever is available—showcases and pedestals and so forth. I just have to adapt to the space. I think my museum is one of the most unique collections because it's not just someone buying and showing the memorabilia and souvenirs. A lot of it's handmade, one-of-a-kind objects as well as other people's artwork. A lot of people donate things to me, so every time I have a show somewhere their work gets seen too. My collection is so large now, probably about 30,000 Elvis objects, that I can't travel with it everywhere. I have to leave part of it at home, especially books, records, and magazines. There's no sense in takin' all that. It's easier and more impressive to present objects on the walls than in showcases. Like that sayin'—"Sculpture is something you back into while lookin' at a painting"—my sculpture is usually partially connected to the wall. Some of my shows have been set up like a stage backdrop or Madame Tussaud's Wax Museum (another one of my idols), with my costumes on mannequins in the Elvis bedroom.

I have dirt from Graceland and a lot of Elvis's hair. I got a huge photograph of the rejected stamp from the post office in New York, which I think is more valuable than the accepted stamp. I made an Elvis suitcase that I used to carry all my clothes in. It's got all the bubble-gum cards from 1978 on the inside. I hang my *Angel Elvis,* with love handles, over the bed. I like to use red and gold when I install be-

Some of my shows have been set up like a stage backdrop or Madame Tussaud's Wax Museum (another one of my idols), with my costumes on mannequins in the Elvis bedroom. Joni Mabe's *Traveling Panoramic Encyclopedia of Everything Elvis.* 1991. Interior environment. Tate Center, Athens, Georgia. Courtesy of the artist.

cause those are the first colors that Elvis used at Graceland. He had red velvet curtains with white fringe-ball trim, a long white sofa in the living room, and a solid-gold piano.

I have on display the toenail that I found in the shag carpet in the Jungle Room at Graceland in 1983. This was the first time that I had gone through the house and I wanted to touch where Elvis had touched. I was touchin' the walls. I was in the Jungle Room and the rest of the tour went on outside. I just bent down and wanted to touch where he had walked and not where everybody else had walked. I just felt something in one of the fibers of the green shag carpet and picked it out and it was this toenail clipping. I call it the *Maybe Elvis Toenail* because I'm not a hundred percent sure that it's his.

I also have a wart that I got from a doctor in Memphis who removed it from Elvis in 1957 or 1958, I believe. I keep it in a test tube. It's a huge wart that grew on Elvis's right wrist. If you study the photographs from this period you'll see how Elvis tried to cover it up in various ways, often with a leather wrist band. He was real self-conscious of it because it was so large. I guess that's why the doctor had to cut it out instead of burnin' it off.

I also have a wart that I got from a doctor in Memphis who removed it from Elvis in 1957 or 1958, I believe. I keep it in a test tube. It's a huge wart that grew on Elvis's right wrist. He was real self-conscious of it because it was so large. I guess that's why the doctor had to cut it out instead of burnin' it off. Joni Mabe with Elvis wart. Courtesy of the artist.

You know, I get weird calls all the time, and I thought this Elvis wart was a joke 'cause I've had people callin' me sayin' that their father-in-law was a dentist and they have Elvis's fillin's, do I want 'em? Or they were a nurse at the Memphis Baptist Hospital and have a vial of his blood. I get bizarre calls all the time. But this wart is just too weird not to be true. I don't know why he saved it or anything. But I bought it. To me, it's sorta like P. T. Barnum: This wart is like my Jumbo and the toenail is like the Fiji Mermaid. They are my most prized possessions.[2]

I have my own button maker. My Elvis-button jacket with 270 Elvis buttons was one of the first outfits I made with it. Since then I've made an Elvis-button dress with 800 buttons, an Elvis-button coat with 1,400 buttons, and an Elvis-button hat. I'm workin' on some boots now. I've also made a gold lamé jacket, two *Elvis Fan Dresses*, and a Las Vegas–style polyester jumpsuit.

I have a series of prints I call *Elvis Mosaics* that I made after I visited the cathedrals of Ravenna in Italy. They're lithographs on handmade paper collaged with acrylic, glitter, and rhinestones. I then sew sequins and lace around the borders and mount them on black velvet.

Sometimes I never know what's gonna happen because I usually make mistakes and that's how I make decisions. The reason I got into glitter was I was in school takin' printmaking and doin' lithographs and I couldn't ever get the ink dark enough. And so to the areas that I wanted darker I started addin' glitter to get the right color and then the glitter looked better than the ink, so I started usin' glitter over the entire print. I didn't know anyone else usin' glitter on lithographs, so I figured I had discovered some new technique. Now I'm usin' the computer and the color laser printer to enlarge things and I'm not even doin' the traditional printmaking anymore. But I'm still usin' glitter.

I did my *Elvis Prayer Rug*, a five-color lithograph, in 1988 with an edition of seventy-five. You take this prayer rug into the bathroom and do this ritual for forty days and forty nights to cure arthritis or high blood pressure or if you need money or whatever ails you. Then you send me forty dollars and your prayers will be answered.[3]

I have a series of prints I call Elvis Mosaics *that I made after I visited the cathedrals of Ravenna in Italy. They're lithographs on handmade paper collaged with acrylic, glitter, and rhinestones. I then sew sequins and lace around the borders and mount them on black velvet.* Joni Mabe. *Hound Dog.* 1989. Lithograph collage. 28" x 34". Colletion of CGR and Associates, Atlanta, Georgia. Courtesy of the artist.

I make walnut wood plaques of Elvis. One is called *Afro-Sheen Elvis* (see Chapter 8 frontispiece) because of the shiny black glitter used for his hair. My father makes walnut grandfather clocks so there's always scraps of walnut lyin' around. For every inch thick he ages them a year, so the walnut boards are stacked up everywhere around his shop.

My *Elvis Presley Scrapbook,* which was included in the group show *Elvis + Marilyn: 2 x Immortal*, is one of the early pieces I did in 1983. I would take Elvis's image and other images from fifties magazines and put him in different situations. It's got twenty pop-ups; it's forty pages, with hand-set type on hand-dyed Rives BFK paper, with sequins and lace on each page. It has different stories and quotes from Dave Marsh, Greil Marcus, Clive James, and other writers.

I make other books as well. I've been rejected from so many grants that the rejection letters started stackin' up. So I decided to make a book out of 'em. It's called *The Collection of Rejections*. It contains rejection letters from the Guggenheim, NEA, even *America's Funniest Home Videos*. I've already completed Volume 1 and am now workin' on Volume 2.[4]

I made an Elvis jewelry box and Elvis kitchen matches. You can almost put Elvis on anything and it'd work. A clock I found in the trash can I made into an Elvis clock. I've started now puttin' him with food labels. He looks good with the Jolly Green Giant and Aunt Jemima.

I painted a plaster bust that I bought right after I got my Master of Fine Arts. This older woman came to see me and she just couldn't figure it out. I had gotten this master's degree and she thought I was supposed to be painting like Van Gogh and here I was painting this tacky Elvis bust. It never fails. The first thing I'm asked once anyone finds out I'm an artist is, "Oh, what kind of paintings do you do?" Sometimes I just say "surreal" so I don't have to explain what I do.[5]

I don't know, I just feel really close to Elvis. At first I was totally obsessed, but I have to sorta pace myself now 'cause I'm in it for life. So it's sort of a long-term marriage.

I make my own autograph books. I read one time that Elvis's autograph sold for $1,200, written on a napkin, which will probably rot. So I decided to start collectin' autographs. At home in my house in Athens, Georgia, I have a huge collection of people's autographs. A lot of people have died since I got their autographs, people like Joseph Cotton, Roy Acuff, Robert Mapplethorpe, Raymond Burr, Telly Savalas (who wrote "Who Loves You, Baby"), Conway Twitty,

Lawrence Welk, Mickey Mantle, Johnny Mize (who is my cousin), and Ginger Rogers (who is also my cousin). Johnny Mize is in the Baseball Hall of Fame. I don't have an Elvis autograph. I wish I did.

When I was in Los Angeles this woman just called me up at the gallery and said Elvis's hairdresser, Larry Geller, kept his hair and did I want to buy some of his hair. And I said yes. These people contact me. It's not like I'm searchin' for it. So I couldn't refuse.

The museum sorta has a life of its own. It books itself and I just follow it around and do all the work. It travels in twenty-one Volkswagen-size wooden crates, painted red just like the circus and on wheels. When the museum went to London in 1993, United Airlines hauled and sponsored it. But I had never made an inventory of all the items, and going through customs I was supposed to have a list of every individual object in each crate. And I started to panic. Then the customs guy opened the lid on one crate and said, "Oh, it's Elvis, let it go through."

But coming back I had to have an inventory list. It's forty-six pages long and took me four days to complete. I guess they wanted to keep my museum in London since Elvis never got to tour there.

When I first started makin' Elvis art the only thing in the art world I knew about was Elvis on black velvet and Andy Warhol's prints of Elvis. Since then Elvis art has come a long way, now with the Elvis stamp and Clinton being elected president, him being such a fan. Elvis art is just now being taken seriously, I believe.

Yes, I do see a relationship between P. T. Barnum and Colonel Parker. But I identify more with P. T. Barnum—he's one of my idols.

I don't want to be Elvis, but I really did fall in love with him. There's something so mysterious about him that I can't figure out, which keeps me interested because he's such a contradiction of himself all the time. And he was the first pop icon, I think, to really *unconsciously* combine sex and religion in his music, just like Madonna did twenty-five years later but very consciously.

I think my sense of humor and Elvis's sense of humor are a lot alike. Just as he would get on stage and mock himself, he would probably think what I'm doing is hilarious. And I think he would be honored that someone has created this huge tribute to him in the art world—where there was none before—and taken it to a highbrow level.

Paul MacLeod explains his "Welcome to My World Elvis Lamp." Courtesy of Ole Miss Public Relations.

12 Why I'm the World's Number One Elvis Fan

PAUL MACLEOD

That the greatest entertainer and humanitarian ever born and the world's finest is just now being recognized, I think is long overdue.[1] I think the whole world is gonna find out what they lost on that August day in 1977. I've dedicated my whole life to Elvis. And I couldn't be more prouder of another thing—that I named my son Elvis Aaron Presley MacLeod right here. He was born twenty-two years ago with one "a" and they didn't put the other "a" to his name till Vernon Presley put it on his son's grave.[2]

Like I said, our whole house, which we call Graceland Too, is dedicated to Elvis from floor to ceiling—every room.[3] And if I brought everything down here today I think it'd take three semitrucks to get it here. And I wanted to bring a lot more display, but it turned out to be that I wasn't aware of the size van they was gonna pick us up in. So we were only able to bring these few pieces, but I hope you enjoy what we're tryin' to do here.

One of the rarest things that I brought with me—I got all this on labels and everything—is the printed program from the night that Elvis won the Humes High School talent contest for singin' "Cold, Cold Icy Fingers," April 9, 1953. It's in pretty good shape. There's only a few of 'em that I know of in the world 'cause most kids they destroyed the things that they were given in aisles back then. What makes this pamphlet so unusual is that they got the name "Presley" misspelled—he wasn't famous by nobody.[4] This is one of our prize possessions. I gave up everything I owned in the world to keep doin' the collection that I've got, preserve it for history, for future archives and everything else.

And you ask me what I gave up? I was lucky enough to give up my time to go ahead and devote myself to Elvis. And I gave up another house that I owned that was paid for, a ranch-style home. I had $120,000 in customized furniture in it. I had $30,000 in furniture that we're livin' in now from Graceland Too. I had a Harley-Davidson motorcycle, a boat, a camper, a swimming pool all paid for, $30,000 worth of diamond rings and watches I got rid of, a gold Cadillac, a Cadillac limousine with VIPs and wraparound bars and the whole works. To top that off, my wife was with me for twenty-two years, seven days a week, twenty-four hours a day, and she finally told me to make a decision—either her or the Elvis collection. And I told her 'bye, and that's the last time I seen her.[5]

Here's even a poem—my memory's not as good as my son's—that was kinda dedicated to us and everything.[6] And I kinda memorized it, and I'll try to recite it the best I can. It's called

GRACELAND TOO: THE WORLD'S NUMBER ONE ULTIMATE FAN—UNSELFISH LOVE

It was meant to be from God above
That Paul would be taken with Elvis's love.
For him to follow so patiently
In all he's collected
Shows he had to be favorably selected.
The boxes upon boxes and files upon files
Information on Elvis Aaron that would stretch out miles.
To labor and toil, even though so tired,
You're the World's Number One Elvis Fan
And you're greatly admired.
So we will follow that dream that's fast coming true
For Elvis's spirit is guiding you.
And as tourists walk through so all amazed
They can say to each other that your son's namesake
"Elvis Aaron Presley made our day."

A kinda Clint Eastwood thing. Yeah.

Let me show you some signs of Elvis I've put together from comments of visitors who've come from all over the world to our home at Graceland Too:

ELVIS IS KNOWN AS THE MAN
WHO CHANGED THE TWENTIETH CENTURY

THE KING
OF
ROCK 'N' ROLL

NO BRAG, JUST FACT

THE MOST BELOVED ENTERTAINER
OF ALL TIME

THE SUN NEVER SETS ON A LEGEND

THE ULTIMATE
ENTERTAINER

THE KING OF
ENTERTAINMENT

IT COULD ONLY HAPPEN
IN AMERICA

THE GREATEST OF ALL TIME

THE ULTIMATE HUMANITARIAN

THE MOST CHARISMATIC
ENTERTAINER OF ALL TIME

THE MOST RECORDED VOICE IN HISTORY

THE MEMPHIS FLASH

THE BOY FROM MISSISSIPPPI

THE THREE MOST RECOGNIZABLE NAMES IN THE
HISTORY OF THE WORLD ARE JESUS CHRIST,
ELVIS PRESLEY, AND COCA COLA.

And here's a sign that they got for me and my son here that everybody's been talkin' about kinda worldwide:

THE UNIVERSE'S
GALAXY'S
PLANET'S
WORLD'S
ULTIMATE
NUMBER ONE
ELVIS FANS
PAUL AND ELVIS
AARON PRESLEY
MACLEOD
AT GRACELAND TOO
1853
T. C. B. ©

A lot of folks have called my work a MAGNIFICENT OBSESSION and I think I'll agree with 'em. You wouldn't believe the comments they have made:

TRUE DEDICATION

ENDEAVOR TO PERSEVERE

SOME MEN DREAM OF THEIR VISIONS,
OTHERS REALIZE THEIR
DREAMS AND LIVE THEM EVERYDAY,
I NEED NOT TELL YOU,
PAUL AND ELVIS AARON PRESLEY,
WHICH ONES YOU ARE

I have a gold lamé suit like the one they have on display at Graceland that cost Elvis $10,000, made in Hollywood by Nudie's. I'm gonna be buried in this suit over a tombstone that reads:

HERE LIES
THE
WORLD'S
NUMBER
ONE
ELVIS
FAN
R.I.P.

World's Number One Elvis Fan

Paul MacLeod

Graceland Too
200 East Gholson
Holly Springs, Mississippi

I have a gold lamé suit like the one they have on display at Graceland that cost Elvis $10,000, made in Hollywood by Nudie's. I'm gonna be buried in this suit over a tombstone that reads: "Here Lies the World's Number One Elvis Fan R.I.P."

But the trick is not to die. Maybe I can do what Houdini couldn't do—come back on Halloween night.[7]

When Elvis died, believe it or not, I come up with the idea of a lamp for him after I attended his funeral and everything.[8] I'm gonna put in a switch to a motor that will make the globe of the world go around because in Elvis's fans' eyes, it's become ELVIS'S WORLD now. He did a song on the 1973 Hawaiian special, with a billion and a half people tuned in, called "Welcome to My World." So I'm gonna drill holes around this globe and put a miniature music box inside of it that would play "Welcome to My World," "Can't Help Falling in Love," and "I Did It My Way" 'cause this man did it his way.[9]

I covered the state of Mississippi here where he was born with a heart-shaped "I Love Elvis" pin. He was born in Mississippi, but he died in Tennessee.

I got the red teardrops in it because eighteen years ago this world cried when this man died.

I got the "Number One" on it representin' Elvis fans worldwide—of all, being number one in that man's eyes.

I got the red light bulb in it because it represents how the media around the world caught fire when they learned of Elvis's passin'.

I done the lampshade in five coats of black because it represents the blackest day in Elvis fans' history.

I got the "8/16/77" representin' for the day he died.

I got the crown on top because his recordings are up to a billion and a half and he was THE KING OF ROCK 'N' ROLL, THE KING OF ENTERTAINMENT.

And I done a cross with me and my son's pictures on them and everything. A lot of people been askin' why we done that. What it is, he was THE KING OF ROCK 'N' ROLL, THE KING OF ENTERTAINMENT, but I betcha two dollars he's with THE KING OF KINGS and you won't find another Elvis fan that will disagree with me on that. Yeah.

I'd like to draw your attention to what Elvis did for both blacks as well as for whites. Elvis used to call a black woman by the name of Phyllis Hyman—she just died recently. He used to call her up in the middle of the night and have her sing "He's Got the Whole World in His Hands" all night long to him.

And that's true about him and Muhammad Ali being best of friends. Matter of fact, Elvis used to stay at his training camp a lot, believe it or not. Elvis even had a purple robe made for Muhammad Ali with "PEOPLE'S CHAMPION" on it.[10]

I was there at the funeral, when James Brown came in the back gate when Elvis died. They were really, really good friends. I've got all that.[11]

Matter of fact, I was kinda with Jackie Wilson when he had the stroke and everything. He invited me to his show when he found out what big fans me and my son Elvis were. When Elvis finally got the chance to meet Jackie Wilson, because Elvis copied his record "Don't Be Cruel" and earned five gold records for it, Jackie couldn't believe that Elvis had snuck into his show to see him singin' it and that Elvis kinda even liked Jackie's version better than his own. He come up to Jackie Wilson and he told him, "Don't you think it's about time that Elvis gets the chance to meet the Black Elvis?"[12]

Matter of fact, Elvis turned around in Memphis, eyed an old black lady, and bought her ten different Cadillac cars and a house. In front of the Cadillac dealership in Memphis he went up to some black ladies waitin' in line for the bus and bought 'em brand-new Cadillacs.

And so I don't think there was any kind of hard feelin's toward Elvis by the black people. I think he loved them as much as he did all. And some of my black friends are workin' for Graceland right now—and Elvis still has them out, believe it or not, workin' for his estate, and they are some of the nicest folks you'd ever want to meet.

The first time I ever saw Elvis in concert and on TV was on the Dorsey brothers' show. He made six appearances, and that's what kinda got me goin' on account of Jackie Gleason produced that show and it was called *Stage Show* and he kinda made the statement that Elvis was a "flash in the pan and wouldn't last six months." And I says, "Oh, my God, anybody who looks like that, comb their hair like that, dance like that, and sing like that—something different from Frank Sinatra, Bing Crosby, and Rudy Valley." I started collectin' everything from that day and I haven't stopped and I won't stop.

I collect anything, I don't care what it is—be it a thumbtack with his picture and name on it, it makes no difference to me. The first record that I ever bought was "That's All Right, Mama," and the earliest thing that we got in the collection is that thing from 1953 when he won the talent show at Humes High.

I ain't makin' any money as it is for this. We have to pay out so many utility bills to keep the place goin'. We were chargin' $3 for an hour-and-a-half tour and now we had to raise it up $2 on account of all the utility bills, phone bills, Internet, and everything else. But I'm more happier and makin' me happy for the rest of my life doin' what I do, and I wouldn't change my life for nothin' in the world. And matter of fact—I'm standin' here right now in front of you—if you think I'm lyin' to you about this statement I'm afraid I'm not. There's a couple of people here in this room knows I'm not lyin' to ya. Elvis was loved by millions of fans worldwide, believe it or not, and I think the world's startin' to know that. And anyway, I was lucky enough to be loved by a few. But anyway, Elvis was loved by millions and if I could give up my life right now for that man to be alive here in front of you right now, he'd be here 'cause I'd be dead and gone. That's right, that's a true story.[13]

A friend of mine is named Becky Martin, from down in Tupelo. She went to school with Elvis, matter of fact. And she was there when the first contest took place in 1945 when Elvis, then in the fifth grade, sang "Old Shep" at the annual Mississippi-Alabama Fair and Dairy Show. Matter of fact, they just took the old lady out who lives across the street from me. She's almost a hundred years old, and she changed Elvis's diapers. And strange enough, the guy that went to school with Elvis in Tu-

Graceland Too

1853

Graceland Too is an antebellum mansion built in 1853 in Holly Springs, Mississippi (which is located halfway between Elvis' birthplace in Tupelo and his home Graceland in Memphis).

My house, Graceland Too, was built in 1853. It's 145 years old. We're gonna have it blocked, the roof changed, we're gonna have new columns put on it, a porch, a little wall put out in the front. Everybody's been complimentin' us. As the work gets done it will be an identical twin to Graceland.

pelo he just bought the house. I'm tellin' ya, the whole neighborhood where I live in Holly Springs, Mississippi, is connected with Elvis. It's very strange. Even my mother was born on his birthday of January 8.[14]

And somebody throwed out a little puppy that wasn't even bigger than the hands of any of these women in the audience, an infant puppy that hadn't been weaned by its mother. We turned it around and we fed it, we got a flea collar for it, gave it a bath, feedin' it three cans of dog food a day. She now sleeps on my son's back every night. And you know what we named it? We named that puppy after his daughter Lisa Marie Presley. Matter of fact, there's seventy dogs out in California named after Elvis, believe it or not—all kinds of animals and everything, yeah.

I'll even try to explain this star to ya. It might sound a little nutty to ya, but maybe it won't in a second. Here ya go. What it is, is Elvis has been dead for eighteen years now. And as all astronomers know, they heard of Haley's comet and heard of James Dean, he's been dead for over thirty years, Marilyn Monroe, and her estate's still generatin' money, and Graceland's got about three hundred million a year comin' in now. But here's a star right here that ain't never gonna burn out. This is the Elvis comet and this is the star that ain't never gonna burn out as long as we're alive or we'll all be gone, but this man will live forever. Yeah.

What do I think of Lisa Marie's marriage to Michael Jackson? I believe if Elvis was alive, I would think he would have went to his daughter and asked her, "The only thing I gotta say to ya, 'Are ya in love?' If it is, it makes no difference because you're the only one that's gotta live your life and everything like that." And I don't think it was for the money because like I said Lisa's got about three hundred million a year comin' in and Michael Jackson, as far as I know, he ain't hurtin' for money.

Matter of fact, we had a picture that dropped on the freeway, I guess, that went down at the bottom of this portrait from Elvis in '56. He's layin' in the bed, it's like he's really not gone in the hearts and minds of his fans like me—he's just takin' a rest, well deserved.

My house, Graceland Too, was built in 1853. It's 145 years old. We're gonna have it blocked, the roof changed, we're gonna have new columns put on it, a porch, a little wall put out in the front. Everybody's been complimentin' us. As the work gets done it will be an identical twin to Graceland.

I started this when I was thirteen years old and I've been doin' it for forty years. We had about 21,000 visitors come through Graceland Too in the last four years since we opened. In fact today, August 10, 1995, is our anniversary. We opened up today four years ago.

I was talkin' to one lady and I told her, "Honey, you lied when you said you loved me. And I had no cause to doubt. But I rather go on hearin' your lies than to go on livin' without you."[15] I hope you're enjoyin' what we're tryin' to do here.

The MacLeods of Graceland Too. Courtesy of Paul and Elvis MacLeod.

13 Generation E

ELVIS MACLEOD

I'd like to introduce my talk with the way Elvis liked to introduce one of his songs. The song was called "Walk a Mile in My Shoes." The introduction and the song itself were obscure until a couple of years ago, but now it's part of the mainstream Elvisology as we speak of it here today. He would say, "You never stood in that man's shoes or seen the world through his eyes, stood and watched with helpless hands while the heart inside you dies. So help your brother along the way, no matter where he starts. For the same God that made you made him too, these men with broken hearts." Today I would like to sing my song as Elvis sang, to give my speech in my own voice and in my own shoes.[1]

I'm here as an Elvis fan who is part of a younger generation of fans as abundant today as when Elvis first hit it big in 1956. There are millions of Elvis fans around the world, and they can be classified from the die-hard, which my father and I represent, to the casual listener.[2] Whether you like one of his songs, a movie, a concert, a charitable act, or some other aspect of Elvis's life and career, or if you're not a fan period, in my opinion you have to acknowledge a couple of facts about this man: First, Elvis was a man, I stress, and not a god, as some of the tabloid journalists have made him out to be; second, his fans are not his worshipers and his bodyguards, a.k.a. the Memphis Mafia, are not his disciples. This is wrong! It just goes to show how the media choose to address something that they know nothing about. This being the case, they decide to form their own analogies about it.

Of course, Elvis is the perfect subject to use to illustrate how tabloid journalism has manipulated this person's image, career, and life. This is their own stereotype that makes most people see the image of an out-of-shape, unhealthy figure that most people think of when you mention the name Elvis Presley. It's become the standard that when a person such as Elvis dies, instead of the press remembering a great man for what he was and still is, they focus more on his mistakes in life and magnify them to outrageous proportions. The main reason behind this is because it sells papers. Nobody wants to hear about the accomplishments; only the dark side of everything is illustrated in the news today.

This conference has shed a lot of light on things about Elvis, and, like Elvis himself, it has broken down stereotypical barriers that have been placed in front of his tarnished image. Elvis broke through many barriers not only in the music world but in everything from race relations to popular culture. The embodiment of these achievements is the people that Elvis called "the fans who placed me in a mansion on a hilltop"—Graceland, of course. I'd like to share with you my personal memories and views of how I became an Elvis fan in a way that you may think is babbling; but to others what I have to say will illustrate how I feel about Elvis, the global icon who represents many things to many people.

The press calls the age-group from eighteen to thirty Generation X, pretty much unknown. For me, it should be Generation E—future Elvis fans.[3] These fans are what will make the endless legacy of Elvis grow for a new generation of people, regardless of race, creed, or background. When I hear a song or watch a performance by Elvis, I ask myself how could someone not admire at least one of the many outstanding qualities of this man. This is left up to the observer to decide, and maybe there are a number of things that will interest not only fans but scholars curious enough to investigate his enduring presence.

Fan clubs are springing up everywhere around the world chartered by groups from Generation E eager to discover that they are not alone. The origin of this following is a younger generation of people, the misnamed Generation X, not the teenage bobby-soxers who were first turned on to Elvis back in the fifties. I find it interesting that these young people today have turned to Elvis Presley on their own. He means many things to many different people. For example, he has inspired fledgling musicians to become great entertainers. His image has been placed on posters, shot glasses, lamps, ashtrays, and recently a U.S. Postal Service stamp. Even a nationally respected figure such as the current president of the United States, Bill Clinton, has been influenced by Elvis throughout his life and political career.[4] The mainstream public, tuned in to trends and fads, finds it chic to be part of this new era of Elvis fandom that picks up where the others left off.

My story, though influenced like anyone else's by my age and by our all-pervasive media culture, nonetheless is really more about how

Elvis became a personal part of my life in a way hard for some to understand, but definitive for others. My father, Paul, became an Elvis fan at the early age of thirteen, at the time of Elvis's explosion onto the national scene in 1956. We return again and again to the Dorsey brothers' TV program called *Stage Show*, as if it were the scene of a crime. It was produced by Jackie Gleason, who was quoted as saying that Elvis would be "nothing but a flash in the pan." Well, you know what history has taught us about that. This and other electrifying performances by Elvis would soon be famous for Elvis's "stage antics"— "sexually vulgar movements" that many people criticized Elvis for.[5] My father was just one of millions in the television audience who were turned-on and converted by Elvis on Saturday night in fifties America. But for Generation E today, Elvis might be discovered through books, movies, CD box sets, or Elvis impersonation. Finally, most people of Generation E have become an Elvis fan by picking it up on their own and not having it passed down by a parental figure, as too many, even some here at this conference, still incorrectly assume about me.

Believe it or not, I am rarely asked the question, "How did you become an Elvis fan?" That's kind of hard to understand since I've basically lived, breathed, and slept Elvis Presley for most of my life. Why doesn't someone ask me this? In my opinion, they already have the answer. They assume that I picked up my devotion to Elvis from my dad. Of course, he was a major influence but not the only one. I consider myself someone with a solid memory, especially when it comes to certain details in my life, which I'd like to tell you about now.

When I celebrated my fourth birthday one of my presents was an Elvis album. *Moody Blue* was to become Elvis's last recorded LP; pressed on translucent vinyl, it was RCA's two-billionth Elvis disk. Along with the album I got concert tickets to see Elvis live. The concert was to be given on August 28, 1977, at the Mid-South Coliseum in Memphis. Before this, I had already seen Elvis in four concerts, all of them vocally powerful and visually stunning. Please keep in mind that all the information and memorabilia that you see today displayed at Graceland Too was at this time in storage.[6] I did not grow up in an atmosphere of "Elvis, Elvis everywhere." In fact, I became an Elvis fan by hearing his songs played on the radio and at home.

Most people who never ask me how I became an Elvis fan most likely assume that it was forced upon me by my father. This is not the case. Even at the age of four I knew that I liked the music but wasn't aware of who was singing it. About the only thing I knew was that this man knew a lot of people. You see, when I went to those concerts and saw all those people I thought they were all "friends" of Elvis and that he had invited them there to hear him sing.[7] Matter of fact, that's what I thought about my dad and me. The tickets were invitations, the coliseum was Elvis's home, and we were Elvis's invited guests. So as a child I wasn't aware of who Elvis Presley was and didn't have the slightest bit of knowledge of what he meant to a lot of people.

After moving from Detroit to Holly Springs, Mississippi, where our family is originally from, my father was able to get closer to the man he had devoted his life to. As if by fate, Holly Springs is ideally located halfway between the two Elvis meccas, Memphis and Tupelo. My father would drive the sixty miles up to Memphis, leaving Holly Springs at about eleven and arriving at Graceland at midnight. He would be back at home in Holly Springs around six the next morning. He would take me along, and over the years we became friends with many of the bodyguards and gatekeepers, among them Elvis's Uncle Vester.

We tried to make the trip as often as possible, usually every night. On these trips I became an Elvis fan not by being subjected to the drive or spending time at his home but by asking questions about who Elvis was and what does he do. Already at the age of four I was asking the question that many scholars and critics are asking today— "Why Elvis?" Being inquisitive, then, was probably the single most important factor that influenced my becoming an Elvis fan. I soon realized that when Elvis gave a concert he was in fact performing for his friends—friends he called fans.

So my father and I were going regularly to Graceland, and at one point, in 1976, we were privileged to be at the right place at the right time. We were making the rounds with one of the security guards when the guard stopped by the windows of Elvis's den, where an RCA recording truck was parked. Elvis was inside in the Jungle Room recording material for his second-to-last album, *From Elvis Presley Boulevard, Memphis, Tennessee*. The song was "Hurt," a very powerful piece. Elvis had admired the song for years and had just now decided to record it.[8] To say the least, it was a bone-chilling experience to be so close, to hear the emotion that he put into it, to later buy the record, hear the song, and think "you were there." (This was one of the eight closest occasions my father came to actually meeting Elvis out of 120 concerts he personally attended between 1956 and 1976.)

During this time and up to the present, I consider my childhood and upbringing to be normal. Before I began my career as an Elvis

Presley archivist, I was familiar with just the basic Elvis and was satisfied with that. Like any other child, I had my heroes and imitated them. At my fourth birthday party, for example, I did my best to impersonate Elvis doing the song "Way Down," which I had heard on the radio and wanted played repeatedly. This is one of the reasons why I received the *Moody Blue* album as a birthday present.

Time passed and along came an event that changed a lot of people. The night of August 15–16, 1977, has been engraved on my mind and the minds of many others. It was a day that I had looked forward to as being one of the happiest days of my life, but it became one of the saddest. I don't know what time it was when we got to Graceland. The only thing I remember is that it was dark. We were talking to fans from around the world, many of whom we became friends with through our common bond with Elvis Presley. Around two-thirty in the morning we were among the many people standing near the gates of Graceland when we heard a roaring noise and looked up the driveway to see Elvis, dressed in a leather motorcycle outfit, coming down the drive on one of his Harley-Davidsons, his girlfriend Ginger Alden on the back. The gates opened up and Elvis went flying past, going about a quarter of a mile before turning around and heading back up the drive to Graceland.[9] From there, from what we know, he went to his private court and played racquetball with his cousin Billy Smith and Billy's wife. After this, he sat down at the piano there at the courts and played his last songs, appropriately titled "Blue Eyes Crying in the Rain" and "Unchained Melody."

Later that day, at 2:35 p.m. on August 16, Elvis was pronounced dead at Baptist Memorial Hospital. My father and I were at home. We immediately headed back to Memphis, joined by thousands of other people from around the world who had heard the tragic news. I have never experienced such silence in my life. On several occasions prior to this, Elvis had been taken to the hospital and rumors of his death had circulated throughout the media, when in fact it was nothing of the kind. To avoid embarrassment, the media this time checked out and substantiated the story. WMC TV-5, a Memphis NBC affiliate, was one of the first on the scene with the information. A fire had previously broken out in the WMC studio, and for weeks they had been basically operating out of a trailer facility. They devoted continuous coverage to this tragic event for six straight hours. The media had caught fire, like that red bulb in the lamp my dad made to commemorate the occasion, and one of the flames that touched a lot of people reached out and touched my dad.

When I found out that Elvis was dead, the only emotion I could convey was anger. The reason behind this is because I wanted to see him live in concert at the Mid-South Coliseum and sing the song "Way Down." We arrived at Baptist Memorial Hospital and found out that the death report was official, that Elvis had apparently died of heart failure. A picture of my father and I was taken at the entrance to the hospital. It is an eerie photo. As the hot August sun shone through the picture-glass window, the image of the name "Baptist Memorial Hospital" was emblazoned on our chests. Of all things, I was wearing a Captain Marvel Jr.–insignia T-shirt with the lightning bolt on the chest. Captain Marvel Jr. was a comic-book character that Elvis sought refuge in while growing up in poverty in East Tupelo, Mississippi.[10]

When we turned on Elvis Presley Boulevard it was like entering a sea of every emotion that could be felt. As we stepped out of the car, the first thing I remember was the sensation of being knocked down by the sheer heat. There's no telling how much the actual temperature was in this pandemonium of people sobbing and grieving for the friend that had passed away. We were among the thousands that were there. Everywhere you looked paramedics were attending to fans overcome by emotion and heat exhaustion. To this day, it is still hard to describe what went on there.

After being surrounded by these masses and engulfed in their emotions, I finally started to realize what had happened. What a great man, a great talent, a great figure had been lost to a world to which he had sacrificed himself, a world to which he had given everything of himself! And the world was showing its emotions in return.[11] But it did not truly hit me until I was alone and let this event sink in. I took off my Captain Marvel Jr. T-shirt, replaced it with an "Elvis in Concert" T-shirt, and found myself standing in stacks of newspapers my dad had bought featuring the many articles of Elvis's death. Each paper announced the hour's headlines—"The King Is Dead," "Death Captures Crown of Rock and Roll—Elvis Dies Apparently After Heart Attack"—just more salt rubbed into my wounds. Dad saw me looking at the papers and told me to turn around. I wasn't paying that much attention when he took a picture that hangs today in our collection at Graceland Too—my eyes red and filled with tears after hearing I could not go to the Mid-South Coliseum on August 28 to see Elvis live. As he explained this, I stared off into the distance and my blurry eyes met with a new poster of Elvis to be acquired. The poster depicted Elvis in his Indian-feather jumpsuit on stage and smiling to what I thought at that moment in time was *me*. What irony for Elvis to pose for me in this fashion! I began to understand that he was dead but would always live in the hearts and minds of his fans.

We went back to Graceland and stayed for a couple of days with fans who shared our emotions. While there, we were among the many to witness a tragic event in front of Graceland. A drunk driver plowed into the crowd and killed two girls. Three were hit, but one survived.

Needless to say, this had been a very emotionally packed couple of days for my father and me, only to be followed by the paramount of it all—the funeral at Forest Hill Cemetery. My father and I were joined by thousands of mourners lining Elvis Presley Boulevard. As the hearse carrying Elvis's body traveled by police escort to Forest Hill, a strange thing happened when it pulled out of the gates of Graceland. A great oak tree, probably there for about two hundred years and still a healthy specimen, lost one of its long heavy branches, which fell as the hearse left the driveway—a strange occurrence that strikes me as an analogy of how a piece of us, the fans, was lost when Elvis passed for the last time through the gates of our hearts.[12]

Elvis was laid to rest in the Presley mausoleum, with his mother beside him. Later, for security reasons, they were both moved to the Meditation Garden at Graceland. No matter how many times I go to Graceland, whether to take a tour or to visit the tranquil environment of the Garden, all the emotions I had when he died are suddenly relived as I pass the graves and think how a great man was lost. I believe that his music will be significantly rediscovered by a new generation and it will bring them happiness. For me, it has filled a void in my heart and has given me something to enjoy each day.

Elvis Aaron Presley was a complex figure. By studying his life we try to find out why his presence is just as strong now as it was when he was alive. It is important to understand how he affected the lives of so many people in so many ways. He had an eternal gift—his voice—that keeps on giving.[13] This was more than anyone could ask for, and when he died a piece of me died with him, though it has been replaced by the joy and happiness he brings whenever I listen to his songs or see his picture. In this way I show my love for someone who deserves a lot more credit than people acknowledge—something that our critics, I guess, just do not understand. Critics cannot understand this because they are not viewing the images, thoughts, and emotions through our eyes.

Not many people can say what really brings them happiness and peace of mind. My father and I have dedicated our lives to preserving the legacy of Elvis Presley. This is our way of paying tribute to a man who has given so much to us; it is a way that we, the younger members of Generation E, can acknowledge and remember him. In four years we have had about 21,000 people come through our home, Graceland Too, to visit our tribute to this man.[14] At the end of the tour, after the visitors have heard us talk and tell our stories, we ask them to write down their comments. This one right here was made by a lovely lady in our audience, Miss Mary Hancock Hinds, and I read her words:

> Paul, you and your son, Elvis, have done a truly wonderful thing, not only for Elvis fans but for the world. You are a model for the world for what can happen when individuals dedicate their heart to preserving history so that generations to come may know of someone like Elvis Presley and his love. America and the world are far richer for your efforts. We salute your passion, your commitment, and your spirit. You personify what makes America great.

To the critics of my father and myself: We may not be what you think you see. Even as I answer your question, your question may never be answered.

14 In Search of the Young Elvis

Confessions of a Dutch Archivist

GER RIJFF

Before explaining how Elvis Presley became an important part of my life, let me give you a brief history of life in The Netherlands after World War II.[1] From 1940 to 1945 our country, and many other countries in western Europe, had been occupied by the German army. In May 1945 the war ended; the Germans were kicked out of The Netherlands by both the Canadian and American armed forces. Besides giving back political freedom to the Dutch, they also gave us the first taste of a special form of cultural freedom—American popular music. From 1940 to 1945, no American or English recording artist had been allowed on Dutch radio. For five long years the Dutch people were subjected strictly to German propaganda music and film. And believe me, few things are worse than that. So after the end of the war, the Dutch were introduced to Glenn Miller, Frank Sinatra, and wild jitterbug dancing.

But The Netherlands had to start from scratch rebuilding everything that had been destroyed by the German army. The liberators moved out after a year or so, and it would take some ten years for the Dutch to rebuild everything and get everyday life back on track. Our parents worked hard day and night to give us what they had been missing out on. A proper education came first, but so did the freedom to go and see movies at our local cinema—American movies, of course. I was about seven years old when I got my first taste of Amer-

Jailhouse Rock. 1957. Collection of Ger Rijff.

icana, sitting in the movie theater watching the likes of Roy Rogers, Captain Marvel, and Superman.[2]

It was about this time that my older brother, who was then fourteen, bought his first record. It was "Jailhouse Rock" by somebody called Elvis Presley. From that moment on I no longer daydreamed of becoming a cowboy like Roy Rogers. No, I wanted to be like that American singer who looked so different from everything I had seen before.[3] That hairstyle, the clothes, and his looks. My god, his looks! Every Saturday our parents would give my brother and I some pocket money, and we would rush out to a little bookshop that sold glossy photocards of the stars of the day. We would stand there for ages trying to make a choice of which Elvis photos to buy. Was it going to be the one of him singing to a dog or the one with his legs and arms spread out against a background of prison bars? We had absolutely no idea where these photos were taken or what they meant, but it was his looks that fascinated us beyond words. We had not seen any of his movies yet.

During most of the fifties, Dutch radio banned rock 'n' roll music from the airwaves, and apparently Dutch television also refused to carry any of Elvis's performances—at least we never saw any of them. When radio finally gave in by giving the younger listeners a full thirty minutes of rock 'n' roll a week—yes, thirty minutes a week—it was on a program called *Teenager Time*. Since there was only one radio station covering the entire Netherlands, that's all we got. But no matter how little rock 'n' roll Dutch radio was willing to broadcast, Elvis's popularity among teenagers grew immensely during the second half of the 1950s.

In 1961 my brother graduated from high school and was rewarded by our parents with a copy of Elvis's first postarmy movie soundtrack album, *G.I. Blues*. We had been aware that Elvis was stationed as a G.I. in Germany until early 1960.[4] And although by car it would have only taken six hours to get to Germany, back then the thought of trying to meet up with him never crossed our minds. Both our parents were working-class, with a small income. Most people in our neighborhood came from the same background as our parents, and only a handful could afford a car and a two-week holiday. Traveling outside of The Netherlands was out of the question for most of us in those days.

During the early sixties Elvis's popularity reached its peak in Europe. All of his 45 releases such as "It's Now or Never," "Surrender," "Are You Lonesome Tonight," and "Good Luck Charm" easily made the No. 1 spot on the record charts. By 1964, nearly twenty years

That hairstyle, the clothes, and his looks. My god, his looks! Collection of Ger Rijff.

after World War II had ended, the Brits invaded the music charts with the same immediate impact as Elvis in the late fifties. For a while, my brother and I flirted with the Rolling Stones and some of the more R&B-type of groups such as Them ("Gloria") and the Animals ("House of the Rising Sun"). But no matter how weak some of Elvis's sixties music output was, we knew things would improve one day.

Our loyalty was finally rewarded when The King, dressed in a black leather suit, sneered into the TV cameras and moaned "Are you lookin' for trouble? You came to the right place!" It was 1968, and after years of Hollywood sugar-sweet songs Elvis was back in a one-hour NBC TV special, rocking his way through classic rock 'n' roll and R&B songs. All was forgiven. The King was back on top. A year later Elvis would return to live performing, starting in Las Vegas and touring hundreds of cities in the years that followed. Somehow Elvis never toured outside of the United States. The truth behind this matter isn't clear. Some blame his manager, Colonel Tom Parker; others blame Elvis himself. Whatever the reason, Elvis couldn't make it to see us, so we had to travel to see him.

Let's now take a leap to 1975. That was the year my girlfriend and I finally got the money together for our first trip to the United States to see Elvis perform live in Las Vegas. We joined up with a group of 250 fans from Europe and England on a two-week trip organized by the official English Elvis fan club. First we went to Memphis and New Orleans, and then we flew off to Vegas, arriving the night of August 21. The excitement of finally going to see my hero was too much. I didn't sleep at all that night. I got up very early the next morning, sat down at the swimming pool, and fantasized about the upcoming evening performance at the Las Vegas Hilton.[5] After a quick breakfast, we got into a cab that drove us to the Hilton, where we had to confirm our reservations for the concert. When we got there, Hilton employees were pulling down the "Elvis Now" banners from the walls. "Elvis canceled his shows," said a hotel employee. "He's gone back to Memphis." All around us there were fans in the hotel lobby crying. It was like a funeral. Just horrible. After all these years of hoping one day to see my hero, the "liberator" of my country, I was stunned to hear Elvis had left the building. God, we felt lost standing there. It was unreal.

On the way back to the hotel our cabdriver innocently commented, "Why don't you go see Wayne Newton, he's just as good if not better than Elvis Presley." Luckily for the cabdriver my arms were limp; otherwise I surely would have strangled him. But somehow we managed to pull through and tried to make the best of the remaining part of our stay in Las Vegas.

One of the good things that happened during our stay in Vegas (as you know, we Elvis fans believe only good things happen in the end to those who love Elvis) was a new friendship I made with a guy from Denmark who had a similar fascination with the young Elvis. He's still a good friend and he's here in the audience tonight—Poul Madsen. Back at home in 1976, Poul and I corresponded a lot, and during that time plans for my first book on Elvis were born. We both had an impressive collection of early Elvis photographs and paper memorabilia from the fifties. Because at the time no books on Elvis existed that dealt with the early years, I decided to do one myself. From both our photo collections I made a choice of material ranging from 1956 to 1958 and baptized it *Elvis Presley: Echoes of the Past*. It wasn't a very professional job, but I learned a lot from it for future projects.

Oh yeah, shortly after publishing the book I finally got to see Elvis live on stage in Las Vegas. It was during the winter of 1976, and I will never forget the moment he walked on stage and blew me away with his presence! Although the years of him being the Hillbilly Cat were long gone, he was everything I hoped he would be. My dream had finally come true.

Now it's 1982. Six years had passed since my first publication, *Elvis Presley: Echoes of the Past*. I was working as a freelance cartoonist at the time and had learned a lot about design. I wanted to do another book on the early Elvis and do it right this time. By then, my fascination for the young Elvis had grown even bigger, especially for Elvis's days with Sun Records. Although fellow fans in Europe had done research on Elvis's Sun career, nothing outside of a handful of photographs was *visually* available at the time. Looking back, it's kinda strange that nobody in the United States ever thought about going to Memphis and looking up newspaper articles from the crucial years 1954–1955 to see what was said about Elvis back then. So that was gonna be my goal: researching local newspapers from July 1954 to December 1955.[6] Poul Madsen and I talked at length about how we were gonna work this out, and we added the possibility of visiting the Library of Congress in Washington, D.C., hoping it had copies of *Billboard* and *Cashbox* magazines dating back to these years.

After the library in Washington confirmed having what we were after, we took off. We did research in Washington for two days, photocopying every tiny little write-up on Elvis, and we became so excited with what we found that we let out screams of joy every time we found yet another piece of printed memorabilia from so long ago. We felt like explorers. After all, nobody had laid eyes on this material for over twenty-five years!

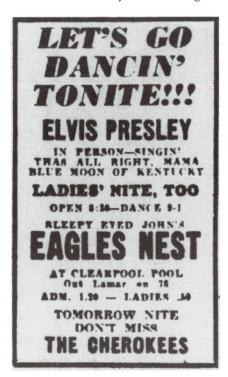

Then we took off again for Memphis, loaded down with what we had discovered. Destination: the Memphis Public Library. For the next five days, from nine in the morning until closing time, I sat in front of a little screen going day by day by day through the Memphis newspapers on microfilm. I nearly had a stroke when on the first day of research I spotted the first ad for Elvis's appearance at the Eagle's Nest only a couple of days after he had cut his first record at Sun. It wasn't discovering the date so much as actually seeing it in print in front of me that was the most thrilling: "Let's Go Dancin' Tonite!!! Elvis Presley in Person—Singin' That's All Right, Mama/Blue Moon of Kentucky . . . Sleepy Eyed

John's Eagles Nest. Adm. 1.00—Ladies .50."[7] It was just a little ad featured among ads for restaurants, movie theaters, and clubs. I was completely blown away. I sat there for what seemed like hours looking at that little newspaper ad in front of me. I was so damn proud of myself. A lot more ads for local Elvis performances followed, including one for his first big-show appearance at the Overton Park Shell on July 30, 1954. His name was misspelled Ellis Presley.

After five days of research in the Memphis library, I had photocopied about everything that had been written about Elvis in the local press. Back home in Holland, I expanded my research by writing to local public libraries all around the South requesting photocopies of concert ads and possible write-ups. That kept me busy for another two years off and on. In 1985, when finally I felt I had enough material, I published my findings in a book entitled *Long Lonely Highway*, a title inspired by Peter Guralnick's book *Lost Highway: Journeys and Arrivals of American Musicians*. Funny thing is, my *Long Lonely Highway* in turn inspired Peter to embark on his monumental two-volume Elvis biography, the first volume of which has just appeared under the title *Last Train to Memphis: The Rise of Elvis Presley*.[8]

Also in 1985 I started my own publishing company, Tutti Frutti Productions, which over the last decade has published about a dozen Elvis book titles. And there's still more to come. The research into Elvis's early years continues. To give you an example, yesterday [August 9, 1995—Ed.], while cruising through some small Mississippi towns, we stopped at a gas station in Randolph to get a drink. When the owner noticed our funny Dutch accents she asked what brought us to Randolph. I was explaining that we were doing some Elvis-related sightseeing in Toccopola, Mississippi, when she began to tell us about having attended an Elvis concert in Randolph back in 1956—a concert fact completely unknown to us Elvis researchers. The lady showed us what southern hospitality is all about when she offered to show us where the concert had taken place. We drove out to the old Randolph High School where Elvis, Scotty, and Bill had been invited to play to the graduating class of 1956 for one early-summer night.

I don't know how to say this in any way other than simply and directly: None of my books has been financially successful. Although two of my titles got huge distribution in the United States, got great reviews, and sold well, I was never happy with my royalties.[9] Yet commercial exploitation is a well-known story in both Elvis's career as well as in the lives of his fans and independent researchers. From the start, however, my goal was not just to make money but to *preserve* photographs and memorabilia of the young Elvis in print through my books. And I've succeeded in that, I think. Recently, I've published photobooks that deal with Elvis on *The Ed Sullivan Show* and on the set of his most famous movie, *Jailhouse Rock.* I've published the memoirs of a lady from Dallas, Kay Wheeler, who tells her story about starting the very first official fan club for Elvis back in 1955. And, most recently, I designed and produced a book entitled *Songs of Innocence* that features over 100 previously unpublished photographs of Elvis at work in New York cutting the multimillion-selling record "Hound Dog"/"Don't Be Cruel."[10]

My books are mainly sold through fan clubs worldwide, and with their tens of thousands of members one might expect a fair sales figure. Not so. If I reach 2,000 buyers, that's tops. Due to low sales figures, production costs are sky-high. If I just break even on my new title, *Songs of Innocence,* you won't hear me complain; though one might wonder why good-quality products like mine are not finding a bigger audience while poorly written and printed Elvis books often sell in the tens of thousands. I guess it must have to do with the price tag on my books or their slightly more "scholarly" subject matter. Or is it just the taste of the general Elvis fan?

For the last thirty-five years Elvis has been a very important part of my life. His music has always been there—in good times and in bad times. I can't picture my life without it. I hope that through my work I have paid back a bit of the debt I feel I owe him. Outside of my parents, Elvis Presley was the person who shaped my life the most. I thank him for that.

PART FOUR
RELIGION

Vern Evans. *The Four Kings.* Courtesy of the artist.

15 Dead Elvis as Other Jesus

MARK GOTTDIENER

My interest is not in Elvis Presley the person, but in the social phenomenon arising around his life after he died, or what the culture critic Greil Marcus calls the "Dead Elvis."[1] With Dead Elvis, the boundary between an aesthetic sublime and a spiritual sublime or between a popular cultural obsession and a religious obsession has become blurred. I locate the social phenomenon of the Dead Elvis at this fuzzy border in contemporary culture that articulates[2] with the commodification[3] of everything Elvis for personal and monetary profit.

The Dead Elvis Phenomenon

In the 1960s a comedian, Vaughn Meader, made his reputation by doing a terrific imitation of Jack Kennedy, and a week or so after Kennedy was assassinated someone whom I don't recall went on TV and said, "Well, I guess Vaughn Meader is screwed!" By implication, of course, what was meant by this remark was that the requiem for President Kennedy was also a requiem for the career of his impressionist. Once a person dies comedians making their living by impersonation usually change their act. There is something quite remarkable going on when people convert a dead celebrity into a social phenomenon that refuses to die. And, if that is the case, then there is something truly unique about Elvis Presley and the life that he has led after his death. Dead Elvis is a phenomenon that has no precedent in human history with the possible exception of the social reaction to major religious leaders such as Jesus, Mohammed, or the Buddha.

In contrast to Elvis, the founders of the major religions, who live on after they have died, remain known principally by what they said. They are deified through printed discourse. Their words are enshrined in text. Jesus is experienced through what the disciples have written about him. Each speech, every word in the New Testament, is poured over by millions of people who are religious Christians. Most American Christians are, perhaps, unaware that there are people in other areas of the world and in some cultures that once flourished even in the United States who came to Jesus not through the text or discourse but through bodily actions and, more specifically, the re-creation or impersonation of Jesus's own experience, especially at the time of his death.[4] The Penitenties, a sect in Latin America, would on the occasion of Easter re-create the crucifixion and in other ways mutilate their bodies in the manner of Christ's wounds. Penitenti cults were quite active in New Mexico, for example, until ritual crucifixion was outlawed by the government. In several cities in Italy, Easter is celebrated by a ritual march to Calvary where participants break the skin to emulate Christ's wounds, using cut glass that allows them to bleed profusely. Some, like several cultures in Latin America, celebrate by crawling on their hands and knees to a ritual crucifixion site.

People in textually oriented Christian cultures might consider these practices grotesque, and for the more squeamish it is possible to participate in a similar activity by traveling to Jerusalem on Good Friday and marching the stations of the cross on the Via Delarosa. The latter activity, despite its ritual re-creation of Jesus's bodily actions, is embraced as normative, while ritual crucifixion is not.

I mention these examples because they define a latent antitextuality in Judeo-Christian-Islamic culture. The grotesque practices, in particular, contrast strongly with the very literate institutionalization of most religions and their worship of a dead, charismatic figure through a sacred text. I am referring here to a different kind of religious impulse in the deification of a particular personage and life that is considered "holy." This impulse is a desire to experience the bodily actions of a god or prophet, the moments of his life—the most critical moments of a sacred life and, in the case of Jesus, the most painful moments of that life by worship through the experience of pain. The latter kind of activity is highly frowned upon, even discouraged by law, in the organized religions of the United States and is undeveloped except in the rituals of minor cults I mentioned.[5]

In contrast to the example of organized religion, people celebrate the communion of Elvis through his material manifestations, not through a sacred text. They seek to feel what Elvis felt, to look like him, to possess the abundance of material objects sacrilized by his aura through commodification, and to be him through impersonation.[6]

Elvis, while he was alive, and the Dead Elvis share something in common: They are both examples of commodification of the body as a desirable sign. When Elvis was alive his career was attended by an immense outpouring of merchandising that exploited his fame. The remarkable aspect of Elvis is that, despite his death, merchandising has never ceased. While Elvis was alive he became a corporate commodity and many people's livelihoods depended on him. Dead Elvis also supports a large number of people all over the world that continue to produce and sell Elvis-related merchandise. Even the current Elvis Presley conference, for example, feeds off the body of Dead Elvis.[7]

In this sense, Elvis is something that Jesus is not. The commodification of Jesus, the reduction of Jesus to an object that inspires merchandising, is quite limited because of the sacrilegious aspects of that commodification or materialization. At one time people produced small statues of Jesus for the dashboards of cars. There still is the familiar portrait of Jesus the "hippie" WASP that is found in people's homes. And, of course, many people sell the most popular commodity—Jesus on the Cross—for hanging in homes or around people's necks. However, this type of material objectification is limited by the bounds of blasphemy. A Day-Glo button with photo and autograph of Jesus would probably not be well received.[8] Yet there is a vast commercialization of songs referencing Jesus and Christianity that is accepted by many people as a form of prayer but that is also mass-marketed for profit.

Dead Elvis, on the contrary, is our *other* Jesus. We unabashedly and actively celebrate his commodification in a million material manifestations. I consider Dead Elvis, then, as the Other Jesus. This claim is not the same as saying that Elvis *is* Jesus or led a life analogous to Jesus. Many people have made the latter observation. When confronted with the Dead Elvis phenomenon, Greil Marcus said:

> The identification of Elvis with Jesus has been a secret theme of the Elvis story at least since 1956. Since Elvis' death it has been no secret at all. In 1982, in Memphis, Sam Phillips told a crowd of fans and followers that the two most important events in American history were the birth of Jesus and the birth of Elvis Presley. The audience didn't know how to respond. Was this blasphemy or the truth?[9]

In opposition to these remarks, I don't think the phenomenon of Dead Elvis can be understood by thinking of Elvis identified as Jesus. Let us dispense with the analogy but keep the contrast between the two and their social roles. Dead Elvis is our culture's *other* Jesus.[10]

Elvis Impersonation

The commodification and objectification of Jesus in material commodities and objects is quite limited and can easily cross the commonly accepted notions of blasphemy, as I mentioned. In contrast, people have been free, since Elvis first became popular, to commodify him and objectify him in any way they wished. From Elvis's earliest days, the market in Elvis mementos has commodified our cultural obsession with his face and body. The sanctified Elvis provides people with freedom and liberation to express themselves through the medium of Elvis objects. The aura of Elvis invests all kinds of objects with a sacred glow—ashtrays, drinking glasses, clocks, liquor decanters, buttons. Just ask Mr. MacLeod, the creator of "Graceland Too," a house infested with Presley artifacts located in Holly Springs, Mississippi.

So Elvis, as the other Jesus, as Dead Elvis, is also a medium of personal self-expression and liberation through material culture in a way that identification with Jesus is not. This aspect, I believe, is the powerful force behind the Dead Elvis phenomenon. Attaching oneself to the Dead Elvis is an act of liberation from the constraints of most religions because it enables you to celebrate popular culture,[11] secular ideas, commodity fetishism,[12] eroticism, black-white integration, and, most specifically, Southern Culture.

The aura of Elvis invests all kinds of objects with a sacred glow—ashtrays, drinking glasses, clocks, liquor decanters, buttons. Just ask Mr. MacLeod, the creator of "Graceland Too," a house infested with Presley artifacts located in Holly Springs, Mississippi. Elayne Goodman. *Elvis Shrine.* Mixed media sculpture. Photo by Jim Ramer.

These impersonations also articulate with every conceivable state of being—there is "the young Elvis," "the midget Elvis," "the apprentice Elvis," "the black Elvis," "the Mexican Elvis." Representations of his materiality, the body of Elvis, possess multiple manifestations much like the Hindu gods or Santeria saints and take on numerous forms. Courtesy of Ole Miss Public Relations.

However, as a sacred sign vehicle, the Dead Elvis can turn almost anything into an object of desire—the city of Las Vegas, for example. The consummate illustration of this characteristic is the popularity of Elvis imitators. The phenomenon of an immense number of active impersonators for a dead individual, as is the case with Elvis imitators, is simply unparalleled in the history of the human race. In our culture Elvis seems to be everywhere, not just in the form of material objects or mementos, but in the form of people taking on the persona of Elvis, of people dressing as Elvis, of textual references to Elvis, and of audiences or groups of people being presented with a display of Elvis imitation. At any given time, at any place in the world, it seems, someone somewhere is doing Elvis. These impersonations also articulate with every conceivable state of being—there is "the young Elvis," "the midget Elvis," "the apprentice Elvis," "the black Elvis," "the Mexican Elvis." Representations of his materiality, the body of Elvis, possess multiple manifestations much like the Hindu gods or Santeria saints and take on numerous forms.[13]

Marcus hints that many people in our society have difficulty expressing themselves and in turning themselves into something that they admire. However, those same people find it very easy and comforting to transform themselves into Elvis or to participate in the worship of Dead Elvis. The transformation of the body by the sign system of Elvis, which is the root of the Elvis imitation, is a vehicle for freedom and self-expression. The Elvis Presley imitator, or the activity of impersonating Elvis, is a ritual form of empowerment. "As a fake," writes Marcus, "the Elvis imitator can do anything: walk onstage drunk, fall over, talk dirty, fondle women in the audience, throw up."[14] Everyone knows the impersonator isn't really Elvis, but his presence somehow lets people relax and push the constraints of normalcy. They loosen up and behave in all sorts of ways through the medium of Elvis that they never would as themselves.

I am intrigued by the popularity of Elvis impersonation, by the fact that an act of imitating Elvis is a major staple of entertainment in places like Las Vegas, private parties, cruise ships, celebrations of fifties rock and roll, and so on. In examining this phenomenon there are some things that immediately come to mind. For instance, when he was alive, if Elvis was an individual that people felt ambivalent toward, if not downright hostile, he certainly would not be revered in death. There are few Richard Nixon impressionists that are still working, for example, although Anthony Hopkins made a good try in 1995. The fact that Elvis is so popular dead, and so widely imitated after death, suggests to me that the presence of Elvis is very comforting to people, and, in fact, that deep down many people love him in the true sense of the word. People have to love Elvis to want to see or be his imitation so frequently. Consequently, above all else, the Dead Elvis phenomenon is about obsessive love for Elvis as the Other Jesus.

The presence of Elvis, the donning of material artifacts that belong to the sign system of Elvis, that signify Elvis, empowers the imitator, liberates the imitator, enables the imitator to violate social norms without sanction. This representation also empowers the audience, gives great comfort to the audience, and allows the people in the presence of an Elvis imitator to feel love for someone else. Elvis is deeply loved, and the popularity of Elvis imitators proves it. When Elvis was alive there were no doubt many fans who loved him—mainly women, but also men. This love was not directed at the actual person of Elvis, but at the commodification of his body by Hollywood and the record industry.[15] However, there were also many people who were drawn to the mass-marketed Elvis, while he was alive, that still could not feel or certainly express their love. Now, the popularity of Elvis imitators consists not so much in the expression of love as in the *invocation* of love, the emotion, the feeling of the emotion of love in the presence of Elvis or the Elvis imitator. When Elvis was alive there were many people, especially men, who could not allow themselves to feel love for him, since the intimacy that that feeling of love would have suggested was a dangerous one because it involved a living person. With the real Elvis dead and converted to a sacred sign system, and in the presence of the Elvis imitator or the boy of Elvis as a simulation, all the emotional "red flags" regarding the feeling of intimacy for another, especially for one of the same sex in the case of men, are removed.[16] We are presented with a fake, but this simulation, this representation, can be taken in our own minds for the real thing, the real thing that is a fake, the real thing that is also dead and resurrected as a comforting and entertaining sign. And in that context, many more people than when Elvis was alive are able to lose their inhibitions and at least at some level feel love for another.

The Elvis imitator brings comfort and familiarity and eases the minds of the people in the audience about participating in the ordinary, mundane forms of popular entertainment. The Elvis imitator invokes the celebration of the commodified body of Elvis. The Elvis imitator brings joy.

Elvis as a Sign System

Andy Kaufman was a brilliant comedian who died in the 1980s. During the previous decade he perfected one of the earliest and certainly the most original imitations of Elvis Presley. The Andy Kaufman imitation of Elvis was done in the 1970s before Elvis died, that is, before the period of the later Las Vegas years that is the referent for almost all Elvis impersonations today. Kaufman's Elvis is a combination of the young Elvis of the 1950s—the rockabilly Elvis, the censored Elvis—and the early Las Vegas Elvis, the thoroughly commodified Elvis.

The Kaufman imitation was part of a comedy routine. It was originally meant as a prop for a single joke that was developed in the typical Kaufman style over an extended period of time (he had a very dry sense of humor). The joke consists of a contrast between another character invoked first in the act by Kaufman, called "the foreign guy," that was his major stage persona, and the thorough, complete, and riveting transformation he performed by becoming Elvis. Kaufman's foreign-guy character was best known through regular appearance on the TV sitcom *Taxi*. In that series his name was Latke Gravis. Latke was a very quiet, unassuming individual who spoke English with a thick but unrecognizable accent. Kaufman juxtaposes, for hilarious comic effect, the shy, retiring Latke character, who then transforms himself into a perfect Presley imitator—outgoing, entertaining, and, most important, sexy.

This vignette illustrates what I had in mind when I described the Elvis imitation as possessing the ability to empower and liberate. By empowerment I am referring not only to the effect on the performer, but also to the effect on the audience in the presence of an Elvis imitation. Kaufman uses Elvis imitation to thoroughly transform the Latke character into a dynamic individual, but he also performs one of the very best Presley imitations and, by so doing, carries the audience as well into that special realm of joy brought about by the presence of Presley.[17] At the time, I don't even know if Kaufman realized what the spiritual and emotional effect of a Presley impersonation would have on an audience. Since then, the millions of imitators are perhaps aware that something in the behavior shift of the audience must be going on to enable them to consistently earn money by such means.

We readily accept the Elvis imitator as comforting because we love the simulation of Elvis. We desire the presence of the body of Elvis so much that we easily accept the imitator. Impersonators are everywhere in our society and many of them are quite bad, but they are all welcomed as a form of entertainment. I am intrigued by a variety of things involved in the Dead Elvis phenomenon, and I have hinted at many so far. But I am especially interested in analyzing the ability of people to assume so easily the Elvis persona, given that his image remains so powerful and uplifting. I believe a way of understanding the importance of the Elvis imitation and the hunger for his commodified body is by considering Presley as a system of signs.

By a system of signs I mean a series of objects that operate as vehicles for meanings that are unified by interpretive codes. A code is an overarching universe of meaning that enables people to interpret individual signs in particular ways. We cannot, in fact, communicate with each other without some understanding of the code we are using.[18] If I talk to you, for example, about the behavior of a "bachelor," you will understand that I am discussing "male seal" only if we have both acknowledged that our conversation is about marine biology. The code of marine biology orders the system of its signs so that two or more people can communicate about that subject.[19]

The sign system of Dead Elvis is structured by a number of intersecting codes. The vast commodified domain of material objects that signify Elvis functions principally through images that iconically represent his body. However, these representations belong to different periods in his life. Each of these phases is structured by separate codes that endow material objects referencing Elvis with meaning. For example, the dominant code used by impersonators is the Elvis of the Las Vegas years. That is, the Elvis that is impersonated bears the closest resemblance to the Elvis of the Las Vegas performances, although some impersonators will use the 1968 TV special or the Hollywood Elvis as a referent. Quite possibly, every Elvis incarnation has the capacity to bring comfort and joy to an audience, but it is the Las Vegas Elvis, the Elvis of the later and last years, that is the most popular impersonation. Ironically, several years ago the U.S. Postal Service ran a contest to choose an Elvis Presley commemorative stamp. Two choices were given—a Las Vegas Elvis and a youthful, rockabilly Elvis. Overwhelmingly, it was the latter that was chosen first. So, while the former is the most popular impersonator incarnation, people still idolize the *image* of the young Elvis.[20]

Impersonating Elvis, then, involves the use of a number of objects and vocalizations drawn from the Elvis sign system that are structured by a particular code belonging to a phase in his life. This constructed representation invokes the mythological image of Elvis worshipped by the audience. Perhaps the most important of these is the hair or wig (since most imitators do not have the thick black hair of The King). This headpiece configuration, including the muttonchop sideburns, is instantly recognizable. It is probably the single most powerful sign in the Dead Elvis invocation. In contrast, for example, I do not think a wannabe Elvis impersonator would be as successful with a wig (without sideburns) representing the hair of the young 1950s Elvis. The Dead Elvis wig of the Las Vegas years is so familiar as a sign of Elvis that I would guess most Americans could recognize it floating alone on a river, lying on the road, flying through the air, or, in other words, disembodied in any one of many ways. We would instantly say, "Oh, there goes an Elvis wig over the falls," or "There's an Elvis-wig roadkill," or "Look out, some aliens are flying an Elvis wig," and so on.

A second critical object belonging to the Las Vegas Elvis sign system is the metallic, overly stated sunglasses. Let's just admit it and say tacky plastic glasses. Put on the Elvis wig and those glasses and you couldn't walk two seconds on any street in America without someone recognizing you as an Elvis wannabe. What was the purpose of those glasses, I wonder? It's not relevant here, but perhaps they were some extra bit of insurance for the older Elvis in looking cool during the later part of his life. For whatever reason they were worn, we know now that Elvis made it real easy for the legion of Dead Elvis imitators that would come after him by choosing those tacky shades.

Another important material object belonging to the Dead Elvis sign system is the sequined Las Vegas jumpsuit and jacket. This too is instantly recognizable because it refers directly to the underlying code—the later Elvis of the Las Vegas lounge acts. Kaufman's imitation used a quasi-Vegas outfit, but that was in the 1970s before the canonized Elvis imitation of the later Vegas years took hold. The ritual wearing of a sequined costume by Elvis impersonators provides a great deal of work for outfit suppliers in the entertainment industry, another blessing bestowed by Elvis on his following.

To the basic objects of wig, glasses, and costume, impersonators often add a silk scarf/towel and occasionally, like Kaufman, a guitar. Then they employ vocalizations that also belong to the same sign system invoking the Dead Elvis, such as the signature phrase "thankyaverymuch," and gestures from his Las Vegas act. Lastly, the ritual of a successful Elvis impersonation usually involves a passable singing imitation of Presley's major hits. The presence of Elvis is already invoked in the impersonation ritual through the use of the appropriate objects of dress. Vocalization adds to the effect of simulation. So, by the time in the act that the well-known music is played and the gesturing is triggered, the impersonation achieves a redundancy that is mythological in its proportions in the Barthesian sense, with signs layered on signs.[21]

In sum, the impersonation of Elvis relies on a sign system, such as the one consisting of the Las Vegas code, relevant material objects, gestures, vocalization, and music. The impersonation layers redundant signs and becomes a *mythical* invocation of the Presley presence. The audience responds not just because it is entertained or amused but because it is liberated and empowered by this ritual. They commune with The King, the Other Jesus, who sanctions fun and common secular pleasures.[22]

Flip-flopping this picture for a moment, the Presley impersonator is also empowered by this very sign system and the ritual of imitation. Much like the Spanish matador, the clergy, the surgeon, or the police, for example, any individual can be transformed by objects of clothing that signify a powerful role in society. The Presley sign system is no exception. Imitators of the Las Vegas Elvis have their own suit of lights. By donning wig, glasses, jacket, and guitar, the sacred Presley objects, if you will, any man, child, or woman can become Elvis and command the power of the Presley presence. Vocalizations and singing, if done in a passable Presley manner, further empower the imitator through redundancy. They build layers onto the impersonation. Within the appropriate setting, then, and by invoking the ritual of Presley imitation, anyone, regardless of who he or she is in everyday life, can, as Marcus observes, act drunk, stupid, wise, fall over, throw up, and so on, within an acceptable or normative context. But these same people can also feel comfort, be entertained, and experience joy, love, peace, and communion. These feelings return to the impersonator just as they emanate throughout the room, making the invocation of the body of Elvis a powerful social ritual.

Dead Elvis as a Commodity

Because the bare essentials of the Elvis sign system are so successful in the ritual of impersonation, all the many other objects that refer to Presley possess some of that ritualistic, mythical power. Elvis is not only the most imitated human that ever lived; he is also one of the most commodified, although in the latter case the manic merchandising by the Disney Corporation of all its products swamps the Presley universe by comparison. Objects invoking Presley have been around since the 1950s when his career first went nationwide. He and his partners founded "Elvis Presley Enterprises" and, beginning with the 1950s, copyrighted all manufactured images and souvenir merchandise. Elvis artifacts have been merchandised with this same corporate logic for the last forty years.

Consequently, an immense quantity of objects now exists. Each one is part of a larger Elvis sign system that is organized by a much more general code than the more particular sign system of Elvis imitators just discussed. Instead of invoking the familiar or comforting Elvis, the old Elvis of the later Las Vegas years, these objects are meaningful in a variety of ways that draw on a less specific and more expansive code. The larger Elvis sign system invokes the experience of an entire generation—youth, middle age, family, children, divorce, death, joy and bereavement, friends, war, the armed services, aging, pain, pleasure, rock and roll, Las Vegas, and on and on. Taken together, all the objects of Elvis merchandising are referents to a generation's memories.[23] Each object individually invokes a time and place for us. They mean different things to different people. We relate to them in different ways when we see them used or worn by others. Our feelings and experiences are united simply by the familiarity of Elvis himself and their centrality in the life of a generation. We remember time and place when exposed to these objects because some aspect of Elvis is connected to what we were experiencing during that time and at that place. For each one of us, that memory is different.

As the ritual of Presley imitation becomes more uplifting and powerful in people's lives, the objectified Dead Elvis—the million objects of his commodification—will become increasingly more sacred. These objects and the new ones made each year, such as the posters for the Elvis Presley conference, revitalize the revering of Elvis and also play a part in the liberatory celebration of his life.

16 Sermon on Alvis

HOWARD FINSTER

Good afternoon.[1] I'm really enjoyin' my trip to Mississippi. On the way out here I drawed six Cadillacs in the backseat. Every time I come to a little town, I'd holler to my granddaughter, I'd say, "What's the name of this town?" And she'd tell me, and I'd put on the back of my Cadillac what town I was goin' through while I was a-drawin' on it. And I come to another town, do the same thing. And I had about six there started from subjects and town to town. And when they said, "We're now crossin' into the Mississippi line, we're right now crossin' over into Mississippi," I put on the back of that'n—"We're now crossin' over into Mississippi. This is Howard Finster's first Mississippi Cadillac."[2]

I got 'em all kinda hulled out and they're sort of a special thing for this special trip.[3] I have lots of requests for paintings and so much more paintings that I couldn't never, save my life, do if I was in perfect health at this time. I just done a piece for Tennessee's two hundredth annual[4] and done a bird habitation picture to help build houses for the unfortunate people. And I made an album cover along that line for the Jimmy Carter administration. All of them things. And finally got to where I was just workin' to help folks and about ready to starve out myself. I got back into doin' a few pieces and sellin' 'em, you know.[5]

I was asked to take a little block out of my life of one of my subjects. I've always dwelled on different subjects in my life and what things are here for and all. I found myself in this world writin' a lot of stories at the same time and them goin' down on the history and all, like that song I sung, "I'm just a little tack in the shangle of your roof." Things like that.

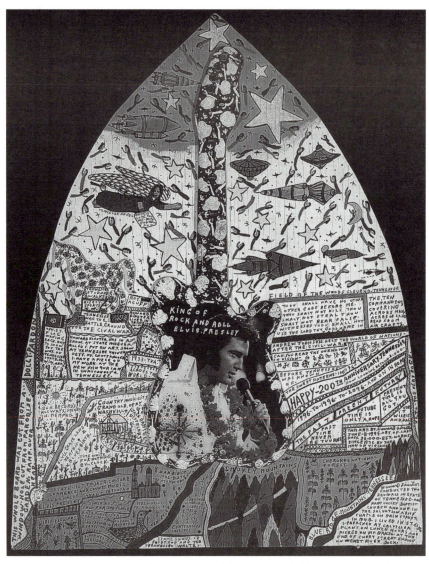

Howard Finster. *Happy 200th Anniversary Tennessee.* 1995. Enamel and marker on wood with mounted electric guitar. Courtesy of Larry Clemons and Tennessee State Museum.

And it come down to the point that my chapter on Alvis[6] Presley is due. And I was asked to speak on Alvis, what I knew about Alvis and all of that. So that's what I would like to try to do in the few moments I've got is to speak on Alvis Presley in my life as a minister.

I was just had got big enough to feed the stock and start workin' a little in the fields when Alvis was born.[7] My father just missed the Civil War and was there with me on the farm. Then come up World War II and went through with all of that. And all that time, through all that, there was Alvis. Alvis was here. Alvis was over there. And Alvis was over here. And I realized this in my ministry and time, when I was pastorin' churches most of the time when Alvis was singin' across the world. And I hardly missed anything about Alvis. I got just about everything on radio that you could get on radio. Then TV come on. I got everything on TV about it that you could get. And part of my life's story is a Alvis Presley story, a little slice of my life and my time. And not only Alvis but Edison, Einstein, the Wright brothers, and all of them. God sent 'em here for a purpose. They filled in a block.[8]

When Edison come, I was tryin' to get by with oil lamps. Our house was sorta dark anyhow, not very many houses painted inside at that time. And Edison come along and we soon had lights, you know. And then we was gettin' behind with war equipments and things, you know, and the Wright brothers come along and sorta put us in the air. I've seen all of that. Sixty-five years of it from the time it started. And I seen Ezekial come to pass, which he spoke of the horseless chariot— Henry Ford and his horseless chariot. And I worked on that. It had a part of my life story. He put the world on wheels and picked up the coal industries and sold the oil all over the world and put the rubber tree people to work. He just done a great job. And me and my father bought one of his old T-model trucks that had solid tires on 'em. And they finally got to where they put holes in there, make 'em a little more flexible. That Henry Ford story goes on, you know.[9]

One day there's a fella come there, I didn't sell'm my art. I thought art—had been taught—that art was kind of a holy thing. You didn't sell art. You just kept it, you know. Wrong to sell it. But God showed me a different story. I had a vision. I ain't got time to tell you that vision, but you may read it some day, that God showed me when to become an artist just like he showed Alvis when to make his best strikin' songs. And that's what I begin to do is to work on these. And time went on and there I had so many stories in my life that it was hard to divide 'em out. And I couldn't tell 'em all at one time so I

Henry Ford put the world on wheels and picked up the coal industries and sold the oil all over the world and put the rubber tree people to work. He just done a great job. That Henry Ford story goes on, you know. Howard Finster. *T Modle Ford.* ca. 1989. Enamel and marker on wood. Collection of Peter Paul.

wrote two or three small books, one poem book. And I begin to do things like that and my art kept growin'. And people was askin' me, "Why do you do George Washington? Why do you do Einstein? Why do you do this and that and the other? Why do you do Abraham Lincoln?"

Well, Abraham Lincoln is about the only Bible motto we've got left in history—"In God We Trust." Abraham Lincoln is preachin' from the penny. And they gonna soon take that off of it. And then all of these things begin to happen, inventions, and also Alvis Presley burstin' out into the world, into the news.[10] And it was all a great thing to study all of that, especially for a uneducated young feller like me who didn't understand a lotta things. And I begin to trust in God and God called me into the ministry work to preach. And the first church I pastored I stayed there four years.

And Alvis at that time was a young feller about fifteen, sixteen years old. He was havin' a time gettin' established and gettin' his parts out of life and his royalties and everything. And he had a man's job and he was a kid. His father and mother wudn't able to help'm much along that line. He loved his family. He's been in my life ever since he's been in the world just about it. And I just went right along by the side of him from his Cadillac all the way down. That's been one thing in my whole lifetime that I heard about and looked at and listened to was Alvis Presley. And he finally was just part of me, part of my ministry.

And the Church of God people really got the Holy Ghost. They was really, truly borned-again Christians. And they come to the place where they wanted to use stringed instruments. And they sung it with a different time to it. Howard Finster. *Elvis Album Covers.* 1995–1996. Enamel and marker on cardboard. Courtesy of Larry Clemons.

And I got to studyin' about it, you know. Millions of people love that man. I love him. Why do I love him? Same reason why they love him. There's somethin' about him. And it come to me that millions of people and everybody in the world loved Alvis just as God loved him too. There's no way around that. You tell me God don't love somebody that the whole world loves and you tryin' to get me tangled up. And I thought too about God's love fer him and how many places he got to that he couldn't work things out and God worked 'em out fer him just like he worked things fer me in my ministry work.

And they finally called me a folk artist. I built my first turnin' lathe out of two T-model generators and a starter and a cornplaner wheel. And I made my first turnin' lathe and started turnin' out art—little bottles and lamps and all kinds of things. And I run it by foot treadle, foot power. And I went on and other parts of my story come and then the Church of God they broke out in the world. They played stringed instruments in their services. And the people at that time in the old-fashioned Baptists from way back, they thought it was quite difficult to see string music in church, you know. And they didn't understand it.[11]

And the Church of God people really got the Holy Ghost. They was really, truly borned-again Christians. And they come to the place where they wanted to use stringed instruments. And they sung it with a different time to it. And I've used their time several times like "get on the farin' line."[12] And their music sounded full of life to me. And they was called Holy Rollers. And I remember from the time they was born. But they had somethin' besides just that. And what they was a-doin' at that time wudn't very popular. But tonight this Baptist man here didn't criticize them about their stringed music. He comes up here with a stringed instrument and plays for Howard Finster and all you people. Of one thing, one time that the other churches condemned, and now then they're doin' it too.

And that's the way sorta in on my part of Alvis's life is Alvis come along as The King of Rock 'n' Roll. And he had timed his singin', pure and alive, sort of like the Church of God had. And come to find out, I think Alvis was pretty well raised up in that kinda faith. And I'll always love the Church of God. I have their story from the beginning. And when they set their mind to do somethin', they're gonna do it. And I pastored several churches and I'd wanna do things and the people was contrary about it. One place I was at we had enough timber on our property, church property, to frame a new church. The old church was about gone. And I jumped on to 'em about it and, ahhh, they didn't want to cut the trees. They'd been there so long, you know. But I finally got that thing over—one of the deacons was a sawmiller—and we done that, we cut them trees and framed that church and built that church. You just had to stay in there with it.

And there was another church and it was just ole dark-lookin' moldy wood. And one of the old fellers there in that church—I wanted to paint it inside so we could see how to read our Bible at the stand, you know. There was no volume of light in there. It was just pitiful. And this feller he didn't want to paint that church 'cause he said they wudn't no knots in that lumber and he hated to paint that church. And I think to myself, "My God, man, if there was a knot in there you couldn't see it. You couldn't tell if it was all knots, whether it was all wooden knots."

And I got to the place pastorin' churches that I just figure out things that I needed and everything and set in on 'em about it until I got it done. And Alvis was like that. When he set in on a thing he'd do it hisself. He didn't have to go to New York and get somebody to write his poetry. He didn't have to go somewhere and pay several thousand dollars and get somebody to help him write a song. He was sorta like I am. He was a folk artist. That's what they call him—the man who does his own thing.[13] And I done my own thing from a kid—made my printin' tools, made everything, all of my stuff. And they call me a folk artist. I got to teachin' and I only finished the sixth grade. Man, I never got no education. I'm still a unfinished student. I never even finished high school. And I felt like God sent me here for somethin', but I didn't know what it was. I couldn't figure out nothin' for myself because I felt down sorta, uneducated, only one man of his kind. No chance for me. I couldn't get inside of a school-house door. I'll never even be invited to go and look over a university and see what they look like.[14]

I had a dark life out there lookin' at it and it was all true. And then they's one thing that I learned. In our school the teacher always every morning read a verse in the Bible to us. We all stood to our feet and quoted the Lord's Prayer together. And then at last we stood up on them benches and I'se so little I could just barely get my head up over them benches, standin' on the back footrail. And then sang that old song, "When the roll is called up yonder I'll be there." And that ole teacher had a roll call he called.[15]

Our schoolhouse wudn't too big, but they had their revivals in our schoolhouse. My father was a sinner. He was not a Christian. I grew up tryin' to get him to God. And he's part of my life's story like Alvis is and like Edison, George Washington, and Abraham Lincoln.

I was listenin' on Abraham Lincoln the other day. I thought I knew everything about him, but I don't know nothin' much about Abraham Lincoln. Abraham Lincoln had a little son like I had five kids. And he lost that little son. And I seen him go through all that and I never knew it before and I'm seventy-eight years old. And so they wanted to know why I use Alvis, Abraham Lincoln. I said, "Well, the reason I use 'em is the same reason that Jesus Christ used certain things to get his message over." And I'd ask Jesus a question, "Lord, why did you use a mustard seed to describe faith? Why did you, Lord?" Well, everybody in the world knows what a mustard seed was. And no doubt that he used that for everybody to know what he was talkin' about.

And then another great subject come up, the Resurrection. And Jesus was wantin' to explain it. What did he use? He used the wheat, a grain of wheat seed for that great subject of the Resurrection, the changin' of our bodies into immortality. He used that wheat seed. Why did he use a wheat seed? Everybody in the world, from a baby on up, knows what a wheat seed is.

And people ask me about why you do Alvis, why you do Abraham Lincoln? I said, "Everybody in the world knows 'em. And I do 'em because when they see them they know who they are and they come to see what the thing's all about."[16] And they find me there speakin' and they call me a folk artist because I do my own thing. And I've said to myself, and said this very day, that's what Alvis was. He was a folk artist of music. He was a folk artist of what he was called fer to do in this world. God says many are called but a few are chosen.

And Alvis's character, the way I seen it in his young days, from the time he was born, God took a likin' to him. And he had him marked out for somethin' special. And the time come when he fulfilled that commitment and he made other commitments, Alvis did. And when that commitment was fulfilled, he had this strong feelin' and assumption to get out there what he was gonna do and all through life. I've seen the hardships he had a-doin' it. And how he finally got that ole guitar and got out there and got up to where he could make somethin' and then the con artists were standin' all around to grab that. And I know what that means. I've been used to that for the last few years, about things like that.

But he finally did, God finally got him into a good workin' staff that could work with him and could help him maintain the things he deserved. And them men that's a-livin' today that supported him and helped him pull through them hardships are my friends today. Some of 'em been here interviewin' me today, some of the people that was with Alvis and worked with Alvis.

And when I was in California five days in a big show and was guest with stars and with Art Linkletter, all of that, I had Alvis's fans that worked with him in Hollywood. They hunted me up because I'm just a state or two away from where Alvis was born. And they come to me and tellin' me about workin' with Alvis and all, and I finally got the feelin' like that Hollywood was home to me. They was haulin' me around in that Lincoln and I was with the president of the association and everything.

And Alvis was everywhere that I've ever been. Alvis comes up. And when he comes up he comes up a question. When he comes up he comes up with people who want to condemn him. When he comes up he comes up with people who wanna support him. And that's the way Jesus Christ come up. He had some of the worst enemies a'tall, Jesus Christ did. They worked on him until they got him dead. And his death was for all of our spiritual lives.

And I looked that over and studied it. And along about, I say I was gettin' on to the youth of Alvis, he's about sixteen years old. And I first took up a little study about him when he was three years old. And I had a feelin' to do a ten-inch Alvis standin' up where you could put it on your desk as a close personal thing, that you could set it on your desk or in your office. That little one is right here.[17]

I was gonna make a ten-inch of Alvis at three years old and I wanted one a little smaller because some people don't have a big desk and this was for the smaller desk and this was for the business desk. And you'd be surprised at how many of the ten-inch Alvises right now that are in dignities' offices and that's in companies' offices. And that and this one. Right here on the bottom of this leg right here I started puttin' on there a short little verse, says, "Alvis at three was an Angel to me."[18] There's a big newsman come there one day, course I knew Alvis's enemies and I knew his friends. And I had a feelin' what he was a-workin' for and I'd found the faithless and the truth that was in Alvis and the principle and God that was in'm.

And there was a lot about Alvis that I liked, though I was a pastor of a Baptist church and though, and all of that, I still had somethin' about Alvis that they didn't have there and he had that helped me, you know. And I always wanted to see Alvis in person and I never was fortunate enough to do that. And I have a little story about that a little later to tell you about it. After all, I'm here talkin' about Alvis Presley, my Alvis Presley that I knew all my life.

And this newsman come a long ways. He said, "Howard, I've come a long ways," and me and him was walkin' in the Garden, says, "I've only come to ask you one question Howard, that's all. That's all I'm a-askin' you is one question." And I'se a waitin' fer it and had no idea what it was. "I said all right, what is it?" He said, "Why do you put an angel on Alvis Presley? Why do you put an angel on Alvis Presley?" And he got me wound up. I answered him, I said, "The reason I got it there," I said, "when Jesus Christ was here on this same earth he was settin' there and the mothers were bringin' their little three-year-old kids to him just to get him to lay his hands on 'em and bless 'em. That's what they was doin'. They just wanted to get their little baby blessed, they just wanted to see Jesus's hand come down on it and bless it."

And his own disciples, like lots of our church workers and deacons today, they's out there and didn't know much about Jesus Christ and them his disciples. And they begin to talk one to another. "Let's stop these mothers from bringin' them kids in there to Jesus. He's got all he can do. He's a-healin', he's doin' this, let's stop them from bringin' them kids in there and botherin' him, he needs to rest, you know." That's what they been on to me fer today. "You're not restin' enough now. You get in there and rest." And interviewers are waitin' for me to interview and I don't need no rest when I got people wantin' to interview me. I don't need no rest. I don't know of anything I done to rest. Because I enjoy a-givin' my story to the people more than anything else. And so that was the story about him.

And then I thought about Alvis a lot and I thought he, at sixteen years old, fifteen along there, that he was one of the nicest lookin' kids that I nearly ever seen. I decided I wanted to draw him at the age of fourteen to fifteen to sixteen and I'd call it "The Youth of Alvis." And that's what I done. I done "The Youth of Alvis." I put him on checkered shirts. I put him on striped shirts. And all kinds of things like that that I think he might like, things that's plain. And this man right here come to me in my Garden and visited me because I had never seen him and I always wanted to see him and Alvis Presley come to my Garden several years after he was dead and visited me. And I want to bring that in on it.

And so I made that and I liked it. And other people liked it. And they come wantin' to reproduce them. I said, "Mister, you have to see Graceland." I says, "I wouldn't reproduce them for anything." I said,

"You have to see them about that." I said, "I can draw him with my own fingers and my own brain and my own heart, but I cannot reproduce him. You have to call them and find out about that."[19] Same way with the Co-Cola Company. I can't give you permission to reproduce a Co-cola bottle and I've been makin' Co-Cola bottles till ain't no tellin' how many thousands Co-Cola bottles I made and they got all over the world before the Co-Cola Company even found out I was makin' them bottles.[20]

And that Co-Cola bottle went oversea and was in a three-year show oversea in Europe that Co-Cola didn't know nothin' about it. And a lot of people would think, "Well, I'd be afraid to do that, they're liable to sue you, they're liable to sue you." Well, if they sued me they wouldn't a got anything more than what they got.

And so finally the president of the Co-Cola Company 'umbled down and come to see me. He said, "Howard, we're proud that you're usin' our bottles to put your message on 'em."

Ain't no tellin' how many thousands Co-Cola bottles I made and they got all over the world before the Co-Cola Company even found out I was makin' them bottles. Howard Finster. *Mr. Coke.* ca. 1989. Enamel and marker on wood. Collection of Peter Paul.

And I said, "Well, you go back seven years and look at the height you've growed in seven years and that bottle helped put you up there." So then he wanted me to put his picture on that bottle. So I said, "Well, that'll be five hundred dollars instead of three hundred dollars because I get five hundred dollars for drawin' a personal human being." And so he had me put his picture on there and I made that five hundred dollars extree.

And then the assistant president come to see me. He walked around in my Garden, seen what I was a-doin'. And he said, "Howard, I like fer you to put your messages on our bottle." I said, "Well, thank you, sir," I said, "I been doin' that a good while."

And as Alvis grew and become great so did I pastor churches and become more useful to God and begin to work out what God had fer me to do in this world. I come into this world I was willin' to be a door-keeper. I was willin' to be a servant or anything. I felt like a kicked out thing that never had no opportunity and I had to farm to help my mother and father make a livin' while I was goin' to just regular school. And we wudn't hardly able to buy my books. My book only cost sixty-five cents and you bought 'em at the drugstore. And God started doin' a few things for me and I got acquainted with him like that.

My teacher was a Christian and then God started to doin' a few things for me and I got acquainted with God like that and one day I'se studyin' about how I'm gonna get my *First Reader*. I don't have no sixty-five cents. And my father and mother don't have it. And what am I gonna do?

Sometimes so many years after the World War I they was regiments of soldiers passed our house and it was four or five hundred horses and soldiers to each squadron. And they'd go by there all day long and the roads was chopped all to pieces and stable manure was every-where from one side of the road to the other. And them horses had tracks and just cut that road all to pieces a-goin' all day long, one group right after another. And when I was a kid I sat and watched and seen them things.

One day I run out of the house and was crossin' the road to go down to the barn to feed the animals like, you know, and I seen in a mule's track, the water had gathered in that mule's track. And I seen somethin' unusual in that mule's track. And I picked it up and it was one of those big ole dollar bills, you know, they're almost bigger than a handsel. And they's three corners tore off of that. There wudn't but one sangle corner on that dollar bill. And I took that to the house and showed it to my parents and they washed it off and cleaned it up fer me.

And I went down to our little hometown by the head at the drug-store and I hand that to him to buy a *First Reader* with. And I know I looked pitiful standin' there. And I didn't know whether he'd give me change on that or not. I just didn't know. And he looked at me a time or two 'fore he give me change on that. And he finally looked at me agin and give me change on that and I had enough to buy my reader and forty-some cents left over—from a mule's track with water in it. And that's where God showed it to me and that's what I done with it. That's some of the first faith of me believin' in God Almighty.

And then I was ruptured for two or three years that I'd lifted heavy things and ruptured myself. I wore a trust till it wore the iron knobs off of it. And I was still ruptured. All of that trouble. And I got to talkin' to God about that. "If you can give me a dollar bill out of a mule's track, you can do somethin' about this rupture." And I prayed about it. And one weekend it healed up and was gone. And that's the way I learned about God.

I think if you'll read the Bible long enough you'll find out that's the way Abraham found out about God and Billy Graham and all the other great preachers that found out about him. And I listened to the doctrine preachers. And I read the Bible and I found where it was plain enough for a ten-year-old kid to understand that. It says, "The earth and the works therein shall," which is positive, "be burned up." "Burned up"—that means this earth will completely be consumed. And there'll be no place found for it, even in what fossils is left of it, won't even be there to go in another planet that might be created.

And the two-million-old rocks that they're findin' in this earth today I assume they come from some other planet or some other star and they come into the makin' of this planet and that's the reason they find 'em that old. But that don't mean the earth is that old. If the earth was that old there'd be them kinda rocks at all four corners of it. And they found some of the fragments out of old planets that could be hundreds of millions of years old. And I see their mistake and everything and they just don't understand. But God does understand.

I come to the place where I begin to learn about God. And this is one place right here I learnt somethin' else that God learnt me. I drawed Alvis and called it *The Youth of Alvis by Howard Finster.* And this is my thirty-seven-thousand, a hundred-and-sixty-third piece, right there. And one day after I'd made a few of these and all, I was a-lookin' at the back of it one day and I just turned around and I seen an image of what I thought was an image of Jesus on the back of that. And I couldn't hardly believe it. And I think to myself, "Am I seein' things?" And every one of these I start right here and do that just like you see it on the back. And I put on there, "The front face line makes the back face line and you have two faces with one line." Now there that line is right there all the way down. Now turn it over and that's the backside of the line right there all the way down. And that's not somethin' that I figured out. And it's not somethin' that a folk artist done. I had nothin' to do with that. I just seen it. And it meant somethin' to me. It's tryin' to tell me somethin' about Alvis. There he was on one side and that's how close Jesus was with him on the other side.[21] And that Jesus loves all people.

And this painting right 'chere. I had an overhead Garden, the first beginnin' of my Garden some beautiful pictures, more beautiful than what they get now. And I had this one made of Alvis at three years old. And I had it hangin' under the trellis, the rose trellis, and anytime I was a-workin' I could nearly see it all over the Garden. And it was always a-movin' a little. The wind kept it alive. This is one Alvis that was always a-movin' every time you seen it. It doesn't take but a very little air to move him. And when you looked and seen him hangin' there he was movin'. And that's right close, where I had this a-hangin', that's where Alvis later come into the Garden to me and visited me in person. And that's where this hung.[22]

I come to the place where I begin to learn about God. And this is one place right here I learnt somethin' else that God learnt me. I drawed Alvis and called it The Youth of Alvis by Howard Finster. *And this is my thirty-seven-thousand, a hundred-and-sixty-third piece, right there. And one day after I'd made a few of these and all, I was a lookin' at the back of it one day and I just turned around and I seen an image of what I thought was an image of Jesus on the back of that. And I couldn't hardly believe it. And I think to myself, "Am I seein' things?"* Courtesy of Ole Miss Public Relations.

And this particular one, I don't make too many of them, but people that have large galleries and people takin' pictures a long way off that makes this one here down about the size of this one over here. That there is for people who take pictures because you know that's one of the mediums that really carried Alvis out was photographs and pictures, pictures taken by his fans.

And this feller here that come askin' that question, while ago when I broke down, "Why, why did you put Alvis on there as an angel?" The thought come to me, you know, "Why? Are you a-buckin' up agin him?" I thought to myself, "Don't you like it 'cause I done that?" And I found people that looked like they'd just give anything to bring up somethin' agin Alvis and turn him into a regular old sinner or somethin'. And that's jealousy. And jealousy is cruel. And there's an early history of that. And believe me people was jealous. And when they get that a-way they'd do anything to pull a guy down to their level or to where they could pass him even. I've learned all my life that jealousy is a cruel thing and that's one thing that I have fought when I was a kid and had brothers and sisters. I've fought it since I was married. I've fought it since I raised my family. And that's jealousy. If I can keep jealousy out of my heart and really get shut of it, I'm gonna be a better man. And God's gonna like me more. And Alvis done a lot of things that made me like him. And if he can make me like him, God likes him.

And now then finishin' this story. I've told this man that's over this to give me some kinda signal when I had broke the limits or got over time and he's supposed to stop me 'cause that's one thing I don't know anything about—if I'm in Washington, if I'm in the Library of Congress, if I'm in the Smithsonian, and I've been in all those places. And that's one thing I wanted to tell you. God has give me some miracles in my own life like he give Alvis Presley miracles. When Alvis Presley woke up one mornin' and heard the "Hound Dog" was a top-seller in the world, that was wonderful. That was good news for a feller that's waitin' for good news. And that hound dog is one of the 'umblest things I nearly ever seen. I do bird dogs. And bird dogs are the 'umblest dogs I ever seen.

When they made up that song about the hound dog that led me over into the Bible where Jesus was settin' there one day and there was a poor old woman come along and she went in and told him, "Jesus, my daughter is about to die and I want you to come and save her." And Jesus was a Jew and the Gentiles and the Jews had no dealin's with one another at that time. And Jesus spoke to her and

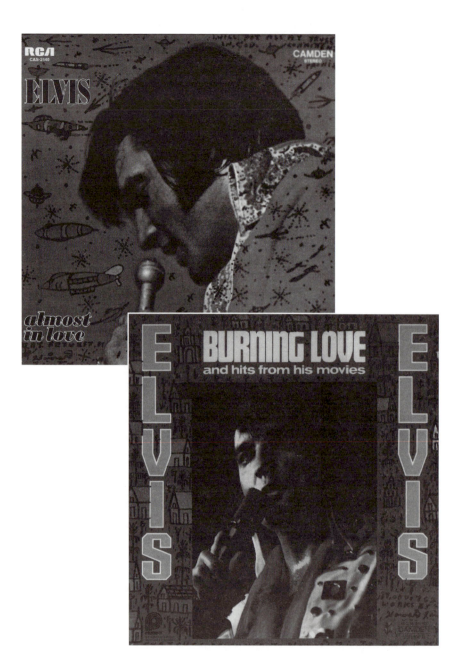

God has give me some miracles in my own life like he give Alvis Presley miracles. When Alvis Presley woke up one mornin' and heard the "Hound Dog" was a top-seller in the world, that was wonderful. That was good news for a feller that's waitin' for good news. And that hound dog is one of the 'umblest things I nearly ever seën. Howard Finster. *Elvis Album Covers.* 1995-1996. Enamel and marker on cardboard. Courtesy of Larry Clemons.

said to her, "Is it meet to give the children the bread? Was it meet to do that?" And this woman said to him, "Jesus, they did give the dogs the crumbs." She was sayin' to him, "I know I'm not worthy. I may be the dog, but they give the dogs the crumbs." She was tellin' him, "Can't you give me, Lord, the crumbs from your table? Even though you can't give me the real food, can you just give me the crumbs?" She was in the principle of the dog and that's what Jesus used. "Shall I give the children's food to the dogs?" And she told him that she, you know, maybe'll get the crumbs.

And that touched Jesus Christ, touched him, and he said, "For this sayin', go thy way. Thy daughter is made whole." She just said somethin' that touched Jesus. "Lord, though you can't give me the real kid's food you can give me some crumbs, can't you?" And that's when he said, "For this sayin' I heal your daughter. You go home, she's healed." And that's where that comes in. And that's the way that is.

And I believe that Alvis done several things in his lifetime that pleased Jesus Christ. And though my daddy was not a Christian, and though I worked with him six years to try to get him saved and he was my first convert, yet though he done some things somewhere that probably Jesus liked. And I been tryin' to do a few things that Jesus would like. And so that song is a type of 'umbleness, and I've owned bulldogs, and right at this particular time I have a poodle dog.

Don't never get a poodle dog and keep him in your home. My wife thinks more of that poodle dog, I believe right now, than she does me. And I worry about that poodle dog. If somethin' was to happen to him, that'd just be like one of her children dead. And I'm about the same way with the poodle dog. I just don't show it like she does. But he is a wonderful little angel and when he gets into your heart and life and comes around at your bed and looks up at you a few times, you've got somethin' that's gonna be hard to give up. And that's the way that Alvis and his charm of majesty, of fellowship, of human being, and all of that charmed people like that. Nobody wanted to give him up. And I've wondered how my wife will ever do without that little dog. That learnt me somethin' and learnt her somethin'.[23]

I was down in a flower bed that the road comes to this a-way from the east and whirled around in the front of the barn like that.[24] And I was right in front of the barn here, and this picture was hangin' on another road that went due west up here about fifteen foot from where I was stooped over. And I was stooped over here a-workin' in this flower bed here on this side, right here like this. There is a flower bed here, a horseshoe flower bed. I was a-workin' on the flowers right

Howards visions OF ELVIS.

1. WAS. DOWN IN A FLOWER BED, THAT THE, ROAD. COME TO THIS AWAY. FROM. THE EAST. AND WHIRLED AROUND IN FRONT. OF THE BARN, LIKE THAT, I WAS RIGHT IN FRONT OF THE BARN. HERE. AND THIS. PICTURE. AND THIS PICTURE. WAS HANGING ON ANOTHER ROAD, THAT WENT DUE WEST UP HERE. AND HERE ABOUT. 15 FOOT. FROM WHERE I WAS STOOPED OVER. HEAE WAS, WORKING IN FLOWER BED. HORSE SHOE FLOWER BED. RIGHT HERE. I DIDNT TURN AROUND. I HAD A FEELING SOMEBODY IS BEHIND MEO AND WHEN AND WHEN I. DIDNT TURN AROUND. EXCEPT. I TURNED AROUND LIKE THIS AND I LOOKED UP. AND SEEN HIS FACE AND SEEN DOWN THE WHOLD FRONT OF HIS BODY. HE HAD A LIGHT BLUE SHIRT. AND OPEN COLLER. AND DARK BLUE PAIR OF PANTS. I TURNED BACK AND. I. THINK TO MY SELF, THIS CANT BE, IT WAS ALL MOST LIKE I WAS ABOUT TO HAVE. A. HEART ATTRCT OR. A STROKE. I COULDENT BELIEVE IT.

"Howard's Visions of Elvis," from the manuscript of a sermon preached by the Reverend Howard Finster at the Ole Miss Elvis Conference, August 8, 1995.

BECAUSE I HAD ALLWAS WANTED
TO. SEE HIM. AND THERE HE. WAS
JUST AS PLAIN AS IT COULD. BE
AND WHEN I SEEN THAT I TURNED.
BACK. HERE. AND STARTED. WORKING
AS THOUGH I DIDNT SEE NOTHING OR
HADNT. HEARD NOTHING. AND WHILE
I HAD MY BACK TO HIM. I SAID TO
HIM. THE ONLY THING ~~TO SAY~~. I COULD
THINK TO SAY. AND THE ONLY.
THING I. KNEW I REALLY WANTED.
~~TO~~ I SAID ELVIS. CAN. YOU STAY
A WHILE WITH ME. AND HE TALKED
BACK. AND SAID. HOWARD IM ON
A TIGHT. SCHEDULE.

here. I didn't turn around. I had a feelin' somebody's behind me. And when I did I didn't get up. I didn't turn around except I just turned around like this and I looked up and seen his face and seen down the whole front of his body. He had a light-blue shirt and open collar and dark-blue pair of pants. I turned back and I think to myself, "This can't be." It was almost like I was about to have a heart attack or a stroke. I couldn't believe it. Because I had always wanted to see him and there he was, just as plain as it could be. And when I seen that, I turned back here and started workin' as though I didn't see nothin' or hadn't heard nothin'. And while I had my back turned to him I said to'm the only thing I could think to say and the only thing I knew I really wanted. I said, "Alvis, can you stay a while with me?" Like that with my back turned. And he talked back with those two words and said, "Howard, I'm on a tight schedule."

Now, when I come up from there that was embedded in my brain cells like the first vision I ever had—my sister come to me when I was three years old.[25] I remember that vision and that was embedded in my brain cell 'cause it's never been moved a jot or a tittle. That vision is just exactly like it was the first time I seen her. And that's the way it is when I seen Alvis. It went down on my brain cell and it's just exactly today like it was three or four years ago when I had that vision. And I've been tryin' to figure out a way to tell what year that was, that there may be a connection there on that.

And so that's my story of Alvis. I believe that God sent him here for a purpose just like he sent Edison for a purpose. And along about that time, you know, we'd been stripped of population. We lost several million people in the Civil War and that isn't put back in class very fast. And we just had a World War I that took millions of our people out and our population was comin' to a place to where that we needed more people in our population and that Alvis Presley was a stimulant to the sex of the young people. He stimulated the sex of young people.[26] And you know what sex is? It's a very important thing. It's so important that if they was no such thing as sex, in a hundred thirty years there wouldn't be a livin' thing on this earth.

Now another thing, another thing is sex has a rule.[27] I preach sex not as a plaything or a joke. I preach sex as one of God's superglories that he made for human beings. And without that we couldn't regenerate the world and that's used from his creation to reproduce this world.

I'm not in the White House and thank God I ain't. And the ones that's in there I don't believe they know what they're really doin'. I don't. I had a vision twenty years ago that Russia and the United States was gonna come together. Because I'd been preachin' that on my heart and tellin' 'em, "If y'all come together as one big global power, y'all be able to police the world and arrest any country that has the atomic bomb." And I put on that big thirteen-foot bottle,[28] "The only way to get shut of the atomic bomb is for Russia and United States to come together, develop into one power, police the world, and arrest all of the countries that had the atomic bomb." It's the only thing that'll stop it. And that's what they been tryin' to do, that's what they're tryin' to do now, and they're havin' a hard time.

What I done is I give you a little bit of Alvis that's in my life, and I don't know what your story is about him but I'll almost guarantee that Alvis is in your life too.

After I done this peculiar picture of Alvis there, I got a note from a feller and it said, "Howard," says, "I was in Alvis's room." Now Alvis had lots of friends and there's lots of people knows him and lots of people that he had friends, just like me or you, that he could call 'em over anytime he wanted. And one of them friends was there. And Alvis was settin' at the table and he was writin' little notes. And he wrote one and just rolled it up with his fangers and he throwed it in a waste can. And this feller messed around there till Alvis went into another room and he went 'n' grabbled out that little roll that Alvis throwed in there and opened it up and read it. And he sent what that said to me. He knew that I had a story of Alvis and he sent that to me what Alvis said on that note.

And on that note Alvis said, "Oh God, I have prayed." He says, "I have got no answer." He says, "Oh God, I will put all of my trust in you." Right there was a commitment. Alvis Presley made a commitment. God didn't hear that prayer he prayed right then. And he wudn't satisfied about it. And, "Lord, I'll put all of my trust in you." That's what the boy said, that's what Alvis said, "I'll put all of my trust in you." And somewhere down the line I believe Alvis kept that commitment. I believe one time somewhere along there he said, "God, everything I've got I'm rakin' it back out between me and you. I've come now to offer it all."

And that's when God saves and that's the onliest one he saves. You say, "How long does it take God to save ya?" Less than a half a minute, just long enough for Jesus to say, "Alvis, I understand, I forgive you." That's how long it takes. And I had a feelin' that that's what happened, that he finally pressed that commitment and done it. And that's the way I feel about it. And I have that governmental rights from my conscience, from my feelin's on that. And I tell anybody if they talk to me, I say, "If you gonna go to hell to see Alvis," I said, "you better change your course," I said, "I don't believe he's there, I believe he's at the other place."

I'm tellin' ya my story of Alvis—me and Alvis and God, that's all. And I wouldn't want to come up here and misconstrue anything about God's work or anything about what God does. Because I'm in his hands and I believe before it was over Alvis was in his hands. And I believe he's here for a purpose and most of the people might never know what that purpose is, but you can work on it and you can find out that he was sent here for a purpose. 'Cause God wouldn't give that much publicity to the population of this world without they wudn't something there that God was gonna use him for.

And I'm sorry that I can't finish my message. And I never have been able to finish it.

PART FIVE
EPILOGUE

Larry J. Coyne. *Incredulity. Memphis Press-Scimitar.* Courtesy of Neal Gregory.

17 When Elvis Died

Enshrining a Legend

NEAL AND JANICE GREGORY

Neal Gregory

Every speaker at this conference has been giving his or her bona fide, so let me give you mine. I was born in Tupelo, Mississippi, about a year and a half after Elvis. I can't really say I knew him, although most people in Tupelo say they did. We were at Milam Junior High School at the same time. He was a grade ahead. I am a graduate of the University of Mississippi, and I remember once as a student at Ole Miss driving over to Tupelo from Oxford with an older coed, who was embarrassed to ask her steady to take her to the Elvis concert at the Tupelo fair. The main thing I remember from that concert were all those screaming girls, including an awful lot of coeds from Ole Miss.[1]

Later, after military service, I went to work for the *Commercial Appeal* in Memphis before moving to Washington, D.C., some thirty years ago. When I worked at the *Commercial Appeal* in the early sixties, we would get those rumors—the rumors that Elvis had died. He had fallen off his horse; he had drowned in a submarine. There was an incredible mystique around the man, even though at that time he was not quite the celebrity we know today. I would pick up the phone at the city desk and somebody would tell me that they were parents of some runaway teenager who was at Graceland and had no money to get home. I remember one time Elvis was at the cemetery kneeling at his mother's grave when some crazed woman on a motorcycle tried to run him down. Most of the time those calls didn't amount to any-

225

thing. If we had a police report or a hospital admitting officer that we could quote, it was worth looking into.

Early in my career I was a police reporter and encountered Elvis in the emergency room at Methodist Hospital in Memphis. A kid had been hit by a truck out on South Bellevue, across from Graceland. It looked like a charity case, and the doctors were making sure the kid was in good enough shape to be transferred to the city's charity hospital, then called John Gaston Hospital. Suddenly in walks Elvis. He was dressed just like a lot of his publicity photos—tight black pants, a shirt unbuttoned almost to the navel; he was wearing a white-billed hat with gold braid as if he were the skipper of a yacht. It turned out that the kid was his cousin and Elvis said that he would be responsible for all the bills. No thought of transferring this patient. The doctors canceled plans for that transfer and started calling in specialists and experts for every possible contingency. The kid was pretty banged up—broken legs, internal injuries, a blow to the head—but I doubt if he needed that much medical attention and consultation. You never saw so much fee-splitting going on in your life.

While we were standing there, I went over and introduced myself, told Elvis I was from Tupelo, and asked him if he remembered Mrs. Camp, a favorite teacher of mine who had talked about having Elvis in her class. Yes, sir, he did. Elvis was very polite. He didn't volunteer anything. He was pleasant enough and seemed to identify with someone who shared his same hometown. But he was kind of nervous. Two things struck me about that incident, my one encounter with Elvis: the shyness of the man along with that generosity he was showing to his cousin. After all, I was just a cub reporter, about a year and a half younger than he was, but he was saying "Yes, sir" and "No, sir," addressing me in the manner that southerners use when they address someone older. He was deferential. I suppose it was because I was with the press and he was uncomfortable—he was always uncomfortable with the media. Yet he wasn't trying to hide. If anything, his clothes were those of someone who was going out of his way to call attention to himself. He certainly wasn't trying to be inconspicuous or travel around incognito.[2]

Because it was Elvis's cousin, that pedestrian injury was worth a couple of paragraphs in the next morning's paper. Even in those days everything that involved Elvis was worth a mention. Later on, I was the Sunday city editor desperately trying to dream up something for the Monday-morning paper. On more than one occasion, I would assign someone to see if Elvis was in town. If he were, we usually could create a story. I recall a photo layout of Elvis and his friends in a touch football game. Or Elvis riding around in a go-cart. There were stories about visitors who came to Graceland or some star-struck kid or some other activity that made for interesting reading on an otherwise slow news day. August 16, 1977, was anything but a slow news day.

To try to make some sense out of the man/myth of Elvis, it is important to go back to the roots of the legend as the conference has done this week—to look at the rural South of the Depression years and trace the unique black and white musical cultures that came together in this part of the country and influenced his formative years; to look at Elvis's incredible career, the recordings, the concerts, and the movies. But it is also important to take the shorter look back to August 16, 1977, when Elvis died. That was the date of a seminal event, and the reaction that followed impressed it on the world. Indeed, some have said that Elvis Presley permanently changed the face of popular culture, and his death had a lot to do with it as well.

How many people remember where they were when they heard that Elvis had died? For another generation it was the death of Franklin Roosevelt, or Pearl Harbor, or V-E Day, or the assassination of John Kennedy, or the murder of Martin Luther King Jr. When something significant happens, people remember where they were, who they were with, and what they were doing when they heard that news. But wasn't Elvis just an entertainer? Why this phenomenal reaction when he died? You can understand the mourning that follows the death of a national leader or even the grief of an entertainer's fans. Did he have that many fans? But for millions of people the world over, the news of Elvis's death brought a feeling that wasn't exactly grief. There was consternation and incredulity. There was a massive sense of loss. Even for those who had not really thought about Elvis for years, there was a great feeling that something had changed. A generation felt middle-aged; a part of their youth was gone. And social critics began trying to figure out what it all means.

The media reaction was incredible. Radio and television reported the news of the singer's death extensively, and the print media followed up for days thereafter. There were photos of startled fans reading the *Memphis Press-Scimitar* with the headline "A Lonely Life Ends on Elvis Presley Boulevard." Elvis's hometown newspaper, the *Tupelo Daily Journal*, ran the headline, "The King Is Dead: Entire Nation Mourns Death of Tupelo's Own Elvis Presley." In Memphis, the *Commercial Appeal* declared, "Death Captures Crown of Rock and Roll—Elvis Dies Apparently After Heart Attack." And, of course, the story received extensive coverage in Nashville. *The Tennessean* reported: "Apparent Heart Attack Cuts Elvis' Career Short at 42."

But further afield, in paper after paper, in city after city around the country, there were massive headlines and photos "above the fold," as we say in the business, reporting Elvis's death: the *Plain Dealer* (Cleveland, Ohio)—"'King of Rock' Presley, 42, dies"; the *News and Courier* (Charleston, S.C.)—"Heart Attack Kills Rock Idol Elvis Presley"; the *Indianapolis Star*—"Elvis Dead At 42; Started Rock Music Era"; *Los Angeles Times*—"Elvis Presley Dies at 42"; *San Antonio Light*—"'The King' Is Dead!"; *Chicago Tribune*—"Young, old mourning Elvis—Crowd waits to pay respects to 'king'"; the *Morning News* (Paterson, N.J.)—"Elvis Presley is dead"; the *Cincinnati Enquirer*—"'King' Presley, 42, Dies of Heart Attack"; *Washington Post*—"All Shook Up On The Day The '50s Died."[3] Some papers ran headlines above the masthead as well. Others printed the headline in red ink, and there wasn't much color in our newspapers twenty years ago.

Of course, the tabloid press had a field day. The *New York Post*, for example, hinted at more than Elvis's death—"Millions Mourn Presley: New book tells of his decline in a drug nightmare." And, too, all the supermarket tabloids, those that exploit the fears of working-class men and women, got in the act. The ultimate was the *National Enquirer*, which ran a photo of Elvis in his casket. This paper sold more than 6 million copies, the greatest sale in the history of the *National Enquirer*.

But that's not the only place where the story was. It was in the *New York Times*, "All the news that's fit to print," the nation's elite arbiter of taste, the paper to which the networks, the newsweeklies, and others look to determine what is important. And there was the story, top left, front page, with a photo, a news story, and a lengthy analysis that continued inside.

If anything, the news coverage was bigger overseas. The British papers covered the story extensively: the *Sun*—"Elvis Dead"; *Evening Standard*—"Presley's Body Lies in State"; *Daily Mirror*—"Elvis Presley Is Dead." The headlines read "Elvis Presley," without any further explanation—everyone knew who he was. And it wasn't just the English-speaking world, but also in every place where music is heard. The Memphis dateline led papers all over the world: in Germany, *Das Bild* (Stuttgart)—"Elvis Presley: Sein Todeskampf"; *Express* (Cologne)—"Elvis Presley tot! Erstickt!"; *Abendzeitung* (Munich)—"Selbstmord-Welle nach dem Tod von Elvis Presley"; in France, *France-Soir* (Paris)—"Elvis Presley est mort pour avoir voulu maigrir." Most French newspapers at the time did not run photographs, but they did in their coverage of Elvis's death.

Elvis had died late in the afternoon—right on deadline for the evening television shows and those editors who had to start making up the morning newspapers. Editors and TV producers scrambled to determine how to play this story about the death of a man that many called The King. Even on the day he died this man, who had stirred controversy throughout his adult life, provoked controversy among the powers that be in the nation's media. You have to remember back. We didn't have the extensive cable news network of today. There was basically just the three television networks, and two of the three decided that this was the most important story of the day—the story from Memphis.[4]

The leading news organization, "the Tiffany network," declined. At CBS News, Roger Mudd was substituting for Walter Cronkite. He argued that this was clearly the top story, but the New York producers said no. Instead, CBS led with the news that former president Gerald Ford had decided to endorse the Panama Canal treaties, and it was not until after the second commercial that they got around to telling that Elvis had died. And, of course, millions of viewers wanting to know about the news from Memphis had already switched channels. Television viewing went up a full 10 percent that Tuesday night over the Tuesday night before, even though audiences traditionally shrink as the calendar moves further into August vacation.[5] In city after city, local media were flooded by callers wanting confirmation and details. Radio stations played Presley's music, and the wire services moved reaction stories from around the world.

David Brinkley, who was then the evening news anchor for NBC television, told us in an interview that he preferred traditional jazz and chamber music.[6] He admitted that he did not care for Elvis's music, but he knew that millions of other people did. More important, said Brinkley, "Elvis Presley *changed* things. He changed the way that then teenaged America *thought* about things . . . about public entertainers and popular music and popular attitudes toward *living* and *behaving* and *dressing* and *talking*." "It didn't even matter a great deal whether you liked Elvis or not," said Brinkley. "He was a part of our lives."[7] Brinkley also thought that a special late-night program was called for, and he stayed around to anchor it. ABC television announced at the end of the hour that it too would have a late-night tribute to Elvis. But not CBS.

It was on Brinkley's late-night show that a minor uproar was produced following from a casual remark from Steve Dunleavy, author of the then recently published *Elvis: What Happened?* Dunleavy let it be known that Elvis Presley came from "white trash." Although such terms as "white trash" and "redneck" were rarely used in the mainstream media, this was the image that a lot of the media still had of Elvis. Dirt-poor, white trash, redneck, working-class—nothing was important about this story.[8] Brinkley told us that for weeks afterward he got angry mail from people who felt wronged by Dunleavy's putdown of Elvis. He said that he would never have used the word himself and that he was shocked when he heard it.[9] But the mail continued to pour in from people complaining that this was not at all true about the Elvis they loved.

The next morning the ratings came in and CBS discovered that it had registered what was probably its lowest ratings of the decade for CBS News. It tried to play catch-up by sending a top producer to Memphis on the *second* day of a breaking news story. It also scheduled a late-night special for the night of the funeral. Recall that CBS was the network that had helped Elvis to stardom through his appearances on *The Ed Sullivan Show,* one of the most famous television events in history. Also in its files was the tape of Elvis's last concert tour, which CBS was preparing to air later that fall. Yet the news department failed to grasp the importance of Elvis. Almost two years later, Burton Benjamin Jr., who was executive producer of CBS News at the time, tried to explain to us the decision by citing the lack of news film and the network's inability to get clearances, but he stuck by his decision. "If on my epitaph it reads, 'This is the man who did not lead with Elvis Presley,' I can live with that."[10]

This sort of debate about news judgment extended to many in the media. Some of the argument was generational, with older editors wondering what all the fuss was about. At major newspapers, editors argued over the proper role of the media in determining standards of taste in art and music.[11] Harry Rosenthal, a top reporter with the Associated Press, was leaving his office in Washington when he saw the news of Elvis's death moving on the wire. He thought to himself that this was going to be quite an event, the funeral of The King of Rock 'n' Roll, and he wanted to go. He called his editors in New York and they said, "No, just let the folks in Memphis handle it; it's a story of regional interest, nothing more." Two hours later at home he got a call to head for the airport. The editors at the Associated Press had decided, after all, to send their top reporter down to Memphis.[12]

He thought to himself that this was going to be quite an event, the funeral of The King of Rock 'n' Roll, and he wanted to go. The gate at Graceland. *The Commercial Appeal.* Courtesy of Neal Gregory.

At the *New York Times*, which prides itself on maintaining a prewritten obituary on every important person in the world, a moment of panic ensued with the discovery that there was no "canned obit" for Elvis. The assignment editor looked around the newsroom and tried to ascertain which one of his highly educated reporters could write this story. Molly Ivins, who got the assignment, thinks she got it because she was from Texas—she talked funny—and for this reason her editor thought she was bound to know something about Elvis. Her chief difficulty in writing the obituary, though, was in following the formal style of the *Times*, which required her to refer to Elvis only as "Mr. Presley."[13]

This uncertainty about Elvis's importance was not limited to the media. We all know about the controversy that raged for years over whether the U.S. Postal Service should issue a stamp for Elvis; there were some who cited the law that anyone so honored had to be demonstrably dead for ten years. Even at the White House, the speech writer who was assigned the task of penning a presidential tribute to the rock star thought this was a terrible idea and beneath the dignity of the office. So he deliberately wrote a bad statement in order to kill the whole idea of a presidential statement, praising Elvis for just being a good soldier and truck driver during his stint in the army.[14]

On his own, however, another speechwriter decided that Jimmy Carter must honor this fellow southerner who had joined the black-white musical roots of their culture. That writer, Hendrik Hertzberg, who is now editor of *New Republic*, penned a second statement. In 1972, Hertzberg had been working at the *New Yorker* when Elvis made his first-ever New York appearance at Madison Square Garden. His piece about the mesmerizing power of this "apparition" called Elvis Presley, which appeared in "Talk of the Town," is now used in journalism textbooks as a model for how to capture the mood of a moment. Based on this experience, Hertzberg knew the entertainer's appeal was not limited to a single generation or region.[15]

The statement that Hertzberg wrote and Carter edited is today regarded as a classic of American self-definition. "Elvis Presley's death deprives our country of a part of itself," read Carter's official statement to the press. "He was unique; irreplaceable. . . . A symbol to people the world over, of the vitality, rebelliousness, and good humor of his country."[16] That is as good an explanation as one can get for the tremendous outpouring that continues to this day for Elvis Presley. Losing a part of oneself hurts. There is feeling there—real, often unexpressed feeling for a man and a symbol.

What's going on now? What's the future going to be? Are we going to be communicating through newspapers and media? Probably not. But we're using the Internet. If you look up Elvis on the Internet, you get lots of homepages, including one at Princeton University called "PElvis." Pelvis—the joke again? But here too Elvis has already anticipated these modern developments. We found this statement on the Net the other day:

> *Computers may out think us one day, but as long as people got feelings we'll be better than they are.*
> —Elvis Presley[17]

We all know how Elvis expressed his rapport with his audience through his music, but sometimes we wonder about the feelings or maybe even about the common sense of others in the entertainment business. For example, Elvis has never been honored by the Country Music Hall of Fame. Yet Elvis, as much as anybody, is responsible for

The statement that Hertzberg wrote and Carter edited is today regarded as a classic of American self-definition. "Elvis Presley's death deprives our country of a part of itself," read Carter's official statement to the press. "He was unique; irreplaceable. . . . A symbol to people the world over, of the vitality, rebelliousness, and good humor of his country." Photo by Wanda Davis Lewis from When Elvis Died. *Courtesy of Neal Gregory.*

the resurgence of that music, reinvigorating it and imparting to most of today's young entertainers their enthusiasm for their music. Would we really have a Garth Brooks as he is today if it were not for Elvis?[18]

Neither has the recording industry ever given Elvis his due, even though this is the man who sold more records than anybody in the history of the business. Only two of their awards went to him, and those were Grammys for his gospel music.[19]

And Hollywood? Elvis frequently showed flashes of an emerging dramatic talent, but his movies basically reflected the view of his manager, Colonel Tom Parker, who once said that scripts were not important; the only thing needed were a few songs and some pretty girls around his boy. Who could argue with the formula? As bad as the movies were, they all made money. But there were some musical gems among the mediocrity.[20]

A dozen years ago we attended a reception on Capitol Hill, where an industry group had come to lobby the Congress on the issue of copyright. There were artists there whose names were unfamiliar but whose works were recognizable—the composers of the most popular songs of the day. Members of Congress heard them play their music, and they noted the familiar tunes. But when one song was played, the room got strangely quiet, the cocktail party conversation stopped, and everyone listened. The song was "Can't Help Falling in Love," and its composer was George Davis Weiss, head of the American Guild of Authors and Composers.

When Elvis was planning a movie, Weiss told us, the word went out that songs were needed. Every composer would send demonstration tapes to the producer in hopes that they could share in the royalties of an Elvis soundtrack recording. For *Blue Hawaii*, Weiss submitted a song for a scene in which Elvis and his girlfriend visit her grandmother and present her with a music box. When the box is opened, the lilting melody begins and Elvis sings: "Wise men say, only fools rush in . . ." That song became the theme that later closed every Presley concert, as his capacity crowd cheered till the announcer's last "Elvis has left the building."

But those in charge of *Blue Hawaii* initially rejected this song. As Weiss tells it, Elvis heard it, overruled the producers, and insisted that the song be included in the movie. When the movie was released, a billboard went up on Hollywood Boulevard promoting the movie and the song that RCA Records had picked to be the next Elvis hit, "Rock-a-Hula Baby." Relegated to the B-side of the record was "Can't Help Falling in Love." That B-side was one of the most popular songs of the year, but it did not even receive a nomination for an Academy Award.[21]

What about the music of Elvis Presley? Throughout his career, many commentators had little to say that was favorable. Mike Royko, the Chicago syndicated columnist, wrote: "I think what Presley's success really proves is that the majority of Americans—while fine, decent people—have lousy taste in music."[22] Royko is not a musician, just a curmudgeonly old man writing a column. But Steve Allen, a man who does have good musical ability and who used Elvis on his television program to counter Ed Sullivan, said: "The fact that someone with so little ability became the most popular singer in history says something significant about our cultural standards."[23] Allen's statement appeared in *U.S. News & World Report* shortly after Elvis died, and more letters to the editors came in complaining about it than anything in the magazine's history.[24]

Then there was Leonard Bernstein, probably the foremost musical genius of our era, who said: "Elvis Presley is the greatest cultural force of the twentieth century." As far as we can ascertain, this statement, which was made to a *Time* magazine senior editor, was reported neither during Elvis's lifetime nor, apparently, during Bernstein's. Rather, it seems to have first appeared in David Halberstam's book *The Fifties*, published in 1993.[25] Many musicians had favorable comments when Elvis died, but few defended his musical talents when he was the object of harsh criticism during most of his career. But more and more we are encountering these "closet Elvis fans" as the reassessment of his career continues.

Janice Gregory

There are many points of view on Elvis. Our standpoint could be described as political in the sense that we pay attention to what moves people and how they either unite behind or divide over various issues and personalities. In a way, we find the continuing controversies about Elvis comforting.[26] If Elvis ever becomes completely acceptable, then we will have lost something important. If thinkers and intellectuals and the privileged ever stop asking "Why? How can this be?" we will have lost something important.

Elvis followed the path of the poor boy made good, the American Dream. But lots of people do that. What Elvis did was something else that we think cannot be overemphasized, at least from a political point of view. He never strayed from home, in every sense of that word. It is one thing to be a self-made enterprise. It is quite another, having done that, to keep dressing in strange clothes, to decorate your house in a way not likely to be approved by *House Beautiful*, to give away Cadillacs instead of endowing a hospital wing like one is supposed to do, to stay in Memphis rather than move to New York like John Lennon did or to Hollywood like countless others did, and to keep your same friends, year after year. We think it is somewhere in that loyalty that Elvis showed to his roots, his family, his friends, and to himself that the secret lies to Elvis's ability to speak for so long to so many people around the world.[27]

For anyone anywhere who has ever struggled or wanted a better life, who has ever felt shunted aside by someone who thought they were of a better class, Elvis is a powerful symbol. He produced better music, filled more auditoriums, and sold more records than the privileged. But he shut no door behind him. Elvis's open door allowed us all to think that he belonged exclusively to each one of us. We can recognize this spirit of belonging in the CBS documentary that was broadcast October 3, 1977, drawn from concert footage filmed just two months before Elvis died. At the end of the show, Elvis's father, Vernon Presley, came on camera and expressed his appreciation for the messages of condolence the family had received. Said Canadian fan Kay Parley: "It was a neighborly touch, a recognition that we have thought of Elvis as one of the family, and Vernon was returning the compliment—treating us as members of the family, or at least as friends."[28] So Elvis becomes ours, but he is, if you will, a family member with a statement. What Elvis seems to be saying around the world is that it is possible to come from nowhere, to make the big time, and still be true to who you are.

Mississippi author Eudora Welty, writing not about Elvis but about place in fiction, gives us some insight into why Elvis's insistence on being Elvis—untamed—was important. In 1957, she wrote:

> Mutual understanding in the world being nearly always, as now, at a low ebb, it is comforting to remember that it is through art that one country can nearly always speak reliably to another, if the other can hear at all. Art, though, is never the voice of a country; it is an even more precious thing, the voice of the individual, doing its best to speak, not comfort of any sort, indeed, but truth.[29]

Unless the artist in question is speaking the truth of what is acceptable and established, this "voice of the individual" Welty describes can be a very upsetting situation for the establishments of the world. One does not have to experience poverty to be an Elvis fan or to appreciate his art. After all, his music is superb and that alone is enough for many people. But there are many other threads to the Elvis phenomenon and to Elvis's attraction that help explain his continued popularity. Elvis's loyalty to his own artistry and roots, his message of strength and hope to all common people, is one of those threads, one that Neal and I hope we do not lose unless we reach that improbable day that prejudice and suppression are no more in society.

So Elvis is upsetting, still, and we say "Good!" But, as we have noted, the establishment consciously and unconsciously tries either to ignore Elvis or to shunt him aside as a strange, fringe phenomenon.[30] For those who have trouble dealing with Elvis, focusing on the most bizarrely dressed fan in an attempt to marginalize and dismiss his following does not work so well anymore. For one thing, it doesn't seem to bother the fans or to slow down the fanfare. For another, in our greatly loosened cultural climate that Elvis himself helped to create, it is becoming harder to tell what constitutes "bizarre dress" anymore.

But the media establishment has recently taken a different tact—to characterize the Elvis phenomenon as a fringe religion. It started with all the hype about Elvis sightings, which began occurring about ten years after Elvis died and which have been parlayed into countless stories and jokes, many of them indeed funny. Elvis sightings became a staple for those stand-up comedians who nightly command a national audience, shaping our attitudes and moods. In his *Kudzu* comic strip, Doug Marlette reported Elvis miracles in the church of the Reverend Will B. Dunn. NFL coach Jerry Glanville announced that a pair of tickets in Elvis's name would be held at the box office for every home game of the Atlanta Falcons. In *The Far Side* Gary Larson depicted Elvis and Salman Rushdie peeking through the venetian blinds of the apartment they share in mutual exile. An "Elvis Tour: 1988" T-shirt appeared, listing all the sightings of the year: in a bedroom window at Graceland; at a Burger King in Kalamazoo, Michigan; on a parachute ride at a carnival in Denton, Texas; and so on. Finally, *USA Today* published a map with reports from forty states where The King had been seen in recent months.

About the same time the sightings began, Graceland started getting calls for Elvis. In his 1987 book, *Elvis After Death*, Raymond A. Moody Jr., a Georgia psychiatrist and author of two best-selling books on near-death experiences, examined the stories of psychologically normal people who had what they believe were psychic experiences involving Elvis. Examples: A young divorcee, terrified at being alone during the birth of her child, is reassured by Elvis in the delivery room; a Georgia police officer, distraught over his runaway son, receives from Elvis in a dream the information necessary to find the boy. Dr. Moody, who holds an M.D. and three philosophy degrees and who apparently took these stories seriously, found in them not a new religion but very familiar tales of mourning: stages of shock, preoccupation with the deceased, and denial. Bereaved spouses, for example, often report seeing their deceased mates and conversing with them. The difference this time was that the object was not a spouse or a charismatic public figure like John Kennedy or Martin Luther King Jr. but a celebrity. Moody offered the proposition that we are so barraged by messages from the media that we use celebrities as a way to order the flow. Elvis as a supercelebrity was particularly well-suited for this, especially since, in Moody's view, people seem able to project onto Elvis any quality they admire. It didn't really matter to Moody whether the experiences were real.[31]

While Moody examined the psychology of Elvisian grief, dozens of scholars have begun to look at the religious facets of the Presley phenomenon. They draw parallels between the treatment of Elvis and the veneration of medieval saints (including pilgrimages to shrines, the collection of relics, marvelous events) or contend that Elvis has achieved a priest-like status because he reconciles conflicting ideals of mainstream America.[32] Then in 1994 a British television documentary, *The King and Me*, raised the question of Elvis worship. But fans interviewed for the program made it clear that they do not consider Elvis to be God, and some noted that Elvis would discourage such speculation. In Portland, Oregon, there really is a twenty-four–hour Church of Elvis—a coin-operated place to pray, be blessed, or get married. But some think this is more parody than church. Recently, we received a telephone call from a reporter at Radio Tokyo who was seeking information about the Elvis church and the Elvis cult—cults being a matter of some legitimate concern in Japan today.

So how much is parody? How much is serious? What is religious and what is less than religious? And what will people do with it? Apparently, Elvis kept himself straight with the Almighty. He did not hold himself up as a religious prophet. The conversations he had with his friend Janelle McComb about the chapel he wanted built in Tupelo are instructive. She reminisced,

> I asked him if he knew who gave him his talent. And he said, "Oh, yes," and pointed up in the sky. And I said, "Well, this brings me to something. If we ever did anything in your memory in Tupelo, what would you like?" And for a moment he stopped and he said, "Why don't you build a chapel so my fans can go and meditate and reflect on their own lives and know that no matter what station they reach in life, if they place their talent in the hands of God he can bless it and they can make a contribution to the world."[33]

And so it is. The chapel is to God and there are no pictures of Elvis in it.[34]

We do not doubt that some persons out there have gotten Elvis confused with God, but that hardly explains the Elvis phenomenon. In my town of Washington, D.C., various inhabitants of the White House, all of whom live under unbearable pressure, have been quoted as saying they walk the halls of that mansion at night and speak to the spirit of Abraham Lincoln or other previous occupants, and we don't turn that into a fringe religion or even think much odd about it. Stepping into the Lincoln Memorial stills the rowdiest school groups, and the memorial is said to have at least one visitor in its templed hall at any time, day or night. When the Kennedy Center opened, the management had to hastily install a souvenir shop (dare I say a relic shop?) because visitors were stripping the place clean, taking door knobs, pieces of the light fixtures, anything that wasn't, and much that was, nailed down. This was the "normal" reaction of people who wanted mementos of the slain president, we were told.

But I suspect there will be little such leeway given to interpretation of Elvis religious and psychological phenomena and art, even though there is much to look at of legitimate psychological, sociological, and cultural significance in the Elvis world. You see, if we make Elvis a fringe religion, then once again we do not have to take him seriously—either culturally or musically.

The *Washington Post*, responding to the British documentary, noted that the true test of when Elvis had reached religious stature will come when a citizen's group tries to ban the playing of "Don't Be Cruel" at a high school graduation.[35] The *Economist*, in January 1995, intoned that Elvis had become more myth and icon than artist.[36] The Russian fans, for their part, are having none of this. By making Elvis into a cult idol, they told a *Post* reporter in 1993, America has degraded his true significance as an incomparable vocal artist and unsurpassed performer.[37] But even the Russians, who take their Elvis seriously, seem to have missed something that we think is important and that a future conference should look at.

Although it was little noticed at the time, Jimmy Carter's statement was one of the few to note the importance of humor in Elvis's appeal. He was "a symbol to the people the world over of the . . . *good humor* of his country" (our italics). Everyone here knows that Elvis and Elvis fans have felt the brunt of derisive humor. But that does not obscure, should not obscure, the powerful way that Elvis used humor and the joy that he has brought to Elvis fans and Elvis wonderers alike. Furthermore, throughout the week of this conference, which has included not only scholarly presentations but musical performances and excursions, our hosts have repeatedly asked us, "Are you having a good time?" Now how many scholarly programs do you know that open with that question?[38] When we hear stories from Elvis's friends and associates, somewhere comes up the statement, "We had a good time," or "Elvis liked to have a good time," or "We were havin' fun."

And Elvis carried this spirit of fun to the stage. As early as *The Ed Sullivan Show* appearances, his teasing, self-mocking sense of humor was evident as he engaged in patter between songs. He introduced "Love Me Tender" as his new "RCA Victor escape—er, release," and led into his final song of the set with "Friends, as a great philosopher once said, 'You ain't nothin' but a . . . '"[39]

The same humor appeared in interviews. Here's Charles Kuralt interviewing Elvis after his discharge from the army:

> KURALT: Elvis, you have some screaming fans out there. Do you still like screaming girls?
> ELVIS (laughing): If it wasn't for them, I'd . . . I'd have to re-up in the army, sir, I tell you.[40]

You can't watch Elvis long without encountering him making some joke or a parody of himself—sneering that sneer and saying, "Wait a minute, my lip's stuck," as he did on the 1968 television special. Or playing sexually with his audience. We see it as reporters ask us, "What would Elvis think of all this serious inquiry?" And the best response I know is the one Bob Greene of the *Chicago Sun-Times* made back in 1977: "Elvis would have laughed, and then sneered that sneer."[41]

It continues, this laughing with Elvis. For a Halloween plot on *Roseanne*, actor John Goodman dresses up like Elvis. Ted Danson's character on *Cheers* seeks Elvis's advice on marriage. The characters of *The Golden Girls* and *Designing Women* discuss trips to Graceland. The star of *Miami Vice* has a pet alligator named Elvis. In an episode of *Murphy Brown,* actress Candice Bergen wonders if the male secretary with the southern accent could really be Elvis. And there are the thousands of impersonators who perform in clubs and arenas across the country and around the world. There is even a team of Flying Elvises. And it goes on and on and on, each year with each new crop of shows and popular entertainment. Sadly, the late Lewis Grizzard of the *Atlanta Journal-Constitution* gave one of his books the title *Elvis Is Dead, and I Don't Feel So Good Myself*. But I must admit, I sure laughed when I first saw it.

"Call it the Elvis Stamp-eed," leads *USA Today* when the Elvis stamp was launched.[42] What fun! The U.S. Post Office, of all people, had fun as it ran the contest for the stamp design. And the public responded by lining up around the block, and then they produced their own imaginative twists on the enterprise, like this friend of my eighty-six-year-old mother-in-law who went to great trouble to ensure that not only would she receive a first-day cover but one with a "Return to Sender" post office stamp on it.

A colleague of mine who runs a group called the Committee on State Taxation in Washington, D.C., was faced with putting on a conference on the incredibly boring topic of state sales taxes on mail-order products. He had his most successful state taxation conference ever. He used an Elvis mail-order catalog as his text. He walked around in an Elvis jumpsuit. And for a mock judicial proceeding at the end, they hired an Elvis impersonator as the expert witness who interspersed his state tax responses with verses from strangely appropriate Elvis songs. They loved it. They laughed. They whooped it up, even screamed on cue. And, of course, they lined up to have their photos taken with the expert witness.

Elvis humor is everywhere. It has become part of our common language. Too often we are embarrassed that our national fun-loving nature, which is carried out most of all in our popular culture, has had a major impact on the world. Why this embarrassment? The humor that Elvis himself first introduced into his public persona made Elvis more accessible; it cemented his relationship with those who came in contact with him personally or over the airwaves. And, as Jimmy Carter noted, this good humor struck a deep chord in the American psyche and the attraction the world feels for the American character. This is what the largest newspaper in Zurich, Switzerland, was getting at in 1977 when it wrote: "Vier Dinge hat Amerika der Welt gegeben [America has given the world four things]: Baseball, Mickey Mouse, Coca-Cola, und Elvis."[43] And British social critic Clive James, writing in the *Observer*, put it this way: "Elvis Presley expressed the rhythm of pure happiness, and there is nothing more pure than pure."

Elvis symbolized the rebellion of common folk against all forms of restraint. He showed us that it was possible not just to be somebody but to do it in a distinctly American way—to be somebody and to have a good time doing it.

Notes

Introduction

1. I have identified some 325 articles, ranging from small-town presses to the nation's most prestigious newspapers and news networks, of an estimated five to six hundred titles published and broadcast on the conference between April 1995 and January 1996. Clearly, for at least one week in August 1995, the Elvis conference was as famous as Elvis himself.

2. A minor civil war of cultural politics was fought in Oxford over competing claims of "Faulkner" and "Elvis" for the representation of southern identity. The situation is strikingly reminiscent of the Ole Miss integration controversy of 1962. In unwitting parody of the governor of Mississippi who physically "stood in the schoolhouse door" to bar admission to the first black student to the university (see Chapter 6), city and university officials attempted to block Elvis's admission to the school by way of a conference according him academic equality with Faulkner. Curtis Wilkie has chronicled this ongoing controversy in a series of articles written for the *Boston Globe*: "Sound and Fury Arising Over Elvis at Ole Miss," July 4, 1995; "Some Want Elvis Invitations Returned to Sender," July 16, 1996; "'Junior' Saves Elvis Conference," July 24, 1996; "University Announces Elvis Has Left the Schedule," August 7, 1996. See also "Ole Miss Kills Elvis," *Oxford Eagle*, July 30, 1996. In southern Negro dialect, "Ole Miss" is the wife of "Ole Massa," the rich white overlord who occupies the "big house," the Greek-columned plantation mansion.

3. This country could go by other names: Muddy Waters, Howlin' Wolf, Jerry Lee, B. B., and so on. But as this book seeks to demonstrate, "Elvis" is the master key that unlocks the worlds of southern and American musical cultures: Elvis Presley opens the door, backwards and forwards, for the discovery and rediscovery of these and many other musicians, artists, and ordinary people, as well as the scholarly issues they raise. For an overview of the territory surveyed by "Elvis Country," see Bill C. Malone, *Southern Music/American Music* (Lexington: University Press of Kentucky, 1979). For the extraordinary contribution of the state of Mississippi to American popular music, see *All Shook Up: Mississippi Roots of American Popular Music* (Jackson: Mississippi Department of Archives and History, 1995).

4. See, for example, Dale Maharidge and Michael Williamson, *And Their Children After Them: The Legacy of* Let Us Now Praise Famous Men, *James Agee, Walker Evans, and the Rise and Fall of Cotton in the South* (New York: Pantheon, 1989).

5. See my essay "Camp Elvis: Totem and Taboo, Hawaiian Style," *Southern Reader* 6 (1991): 1–2, 24–25.

6. The term "popular culture" fails to distinguish between a grassroots culture arising from the people and that top-down, corporate form of culture called popular entertainment imposed by mass media. See Douglas Kellner, *Media Culture: Cultural Studies, Identity, and Politics Between the Modern and the Postmodern* (New York: Routledge, 1995), p. 33 ff.

7. For at least half a century now, social scientists have employed literary theory and notions of the literary text for the analysis of culture. In a richly divergent, interdisciplinary field that includes semiotics, structuralism, hermeneutics, and poststructuralism, this emergent "textualism" has at least one feature in common: the idea that texts are *systems* of the production of meaning, not only through words but also things, images, customs, rituals, gestures, and so forth. "Elvis as text," as the essays in this book demonstrate, solicits a multiplicity of reading styles: historical, sociological, literary, semiotic, aesthetic, personal, and political. Both as a whole and in its parts, *In Search of Elvis* constructs what American anthropologist Clifford Geertz calls a "blurred genre" that cannot be reduced to a single principle, theory, model, or method, nor to a single dominant perspective based on race, class, gender, or any other patriotic allegiance. See Clifford Geertz, *Local Knowledge: Further Essays in Interpretive Anthropology* (New York: Basic Books, 1983), p. 20 ff.

8. In his role as Trickster, as "signifying hound dog," as it were, Elvis has the power to turn the tables on those who insist that he represent nothing but illiterate, lowbrow, trashy southern culture and even cheesier American consumption (see Chapter 4). The "textual Elvis" identifies subversive, countercultural, outsider forces in the fabric of the American experience and marshals them. For a parallel study of African-American Trickster hermeneutics, see Henry Louis Gates, *The Signifying Monkey: A Theory of Afro-American Literary Criticism* (New York: Oxford University Press, 1988).

9. I have in mind here what Chandra Talpade Mohanty calls "public cultures of dissent" within the academy: "[A] public culture of dissent entails creating spaces for epistemological standpoints that are grounded in the *interests* of people and which recognize the *materiality* of conflict, of privilege, and domination. Thus creating such cultures is fundamentally about making the axes of power transparent in the context of academic, disciplinary, and institutional structures as well as in the interpersonal relationships (rather than individual relationships) in the academy. It is about taking the politics of everyday life seriously as teachers, students, administrators, and members of hegemonic academic cultures. Culture itself is thus redefined as incorporating individual and collective memories, dreams, and history that are contested and transformed through the political praxis of day-to-day living." Chandra Talpade Mohanty, "On Race and Voice: Challenges for Liberal Education in the 1990s," in *Between Borders: Pedagogy and the Politics of Cultural Studies*, ed. Henry A. Giroux and Peter McLaren (New York: Routledge, 1994), p. 162.

10. I signify on this genre as Garrison Keillor does in his *A Prairie Home Companion* radio series.

11. See André Breton, *Nadja* (Paris: Gallimard, 1928); *Les Vases communicants* (Paris: Editions des Cahiers libres, 1932); *L'Amour fou* (Paris: Gallimard, 1937); also Anna Balakian, *André Breton: Magus of Surrealism* (New York: Oxford University Press, 1971), especially "Toward a New Structure of Writing: *Nadja, Les Vases communicants, L'Amour fou*," pp. 102–124.

12. Milan Kundera, *The Art of the Novel*, trans. Linda Asher (New York: Harper and Row, 1988 [1986]), "(1) a new art of *radical divestment* (which can encompass the complexity of existence in the modern world without losing architectonic clarity); (2) a new art of *novelistic counterpoint* (which can blend philosophy, narrative, and dream into one music); (3) a new art of the *specifically novelistic essay* (which does not claim to bear an apodictic message but remains hypothetical, playful, or ironic)" (p. 65).

13. For example, *The Birth of the Clinic* (1963), *Discipline and Punish* (1975), and *The History of Sexuality*, 3 vols. (1976–1984). See Christopher Tilley, "Foucault: Towards an Archaeology of Archaeology," in *Reading Material Culture*, ed. Christopher Tilley (Oxford: Blackwell, 1990), pp. 281–347.

14. Ava Collins has assessed the stakes of this pedagogical debate, Right and Left: "The Right wants to 'reclaim the legacy' (Bennett), quite literally reinstituting an educational system based on nineteenth-century models that ignore changed conditions of circulation of information and knowledge in the technologically sophisticated twentieth-century arena, and in effect banish popular cultural forms from the classroom. The Left is struggling to develop analytical models that take into account changed social, cultural, and material conditions." Ava Collins, "Intellectuals, Power, and Quality Television," in *Between Borders*, p. 56.

15. "Just as they questioned the authority of any text, now they are questioning the authority of people to interpret, make sense of that text. The fact that one person has spent years in research, learning methods of analysis, means nothing to them because they think all observers are equal. In all fairness, the professors organizing this jamboree should resign their positions or at least set up a rotational basis where they teach one semester and the Elvis impersonators get the other." Stephen Balch, president of the National Association of Scholars, quoted in "When Scholars Dig Not Only Tassels but Sequins," *New York Times*, August 6, 1995.

16. Mikhail Bakhtin, *Rabelais and His World*, trans. Hélène Iswolsky (Bloomington: Indiana University Press, 1984 [1965]), p. 224. See John Docker, *Postmodernism and Popular Culture: A Cultural History* (Cambridge: Cambridge University Press, 1994), especially chapter 13, "Bakhtin's Carnival," pp. 168–185.

17. David Ray Griffin has described this new pedagogy as a "postmodern spirituality." See "Postmodern Spirituality and Society," in *Spirituality and Society: Postmodern Visions*, ed. David Ray Griffin (Albany: State University of New York Press, 1988), pp. 1–31.

18. What pundits viewed as a dumbing-down of higher education to the level of that "illiterate redneck" Elvis Presley (this is how a British reporter described the situation to me), can, on the contrary, easily be seen as a project too sophisticated, too intellectual, and too subtle for the average academic and journalist to handle. With regard to the necessity of addressing the ground of the university as the concrete site of authentic questioning, I take my cue from Martin Heidegger's Aristotle lectures of 1921–1922: "If philosophical questioning is to take place, here and now, then it can determine itself only in the direction of that factical circumstance of life we have indicated with the term *university*." "Phänomenologische Interpretationen zu Aristoteles," in *Gesamtausgabe*, vol. 61, ed. Walter Bröcker and Käte Bröcker-Oltmanns (Frankfurt am Main: Vittorio Klostermann, 1985), p. 64. My translation.

19. See Russell H. Barrett, *Integration at Ole Miss* (Chicago: Quadrangle Books, 1965); James Silver, *Mississippi: The Closed Society* (New York: Harcourt, Brace, and World, 1966), enl. ed.; David G. Sansing, *Making Haste Slowly: The Troubled History of Higher Education in Mississippi* (Jackson: University Press of Mississippi, 1990), especially chaps. 9–12.

20. See Chapter 16.

21. Bakhtin has given the most erudite and powerful assessment of the crossfertilization of laughter and seriousness in Western literature and culture: "By the end of the Middle Ages a gradual disappearance of the dividing line between humor and great literature can be observed. The lower genres begin to penetrate the higher levels of litera-

ture. Popular laughter appears in epics, and its intrinsic value is increased in mysteries. Various genres, such as moralities, *soties,* farces, are developed. Buffoon societies, such as 'Kingdom of Basoche' and 'Carefree Lads,' are found in the fourteenth and fifteenth centuries. The culture of laughter begins to break through the narrow walls of festivities and to enter into all spheres of ideological life [including the university]. Official seriousness and fear could be abandoned even in everyday life." Bakhtin, *Rabelais and His World,* p. 97.

22. Such "radical contextualism" is a key concept of cultural studies. See Lawrence Grossberg, *We Gotta Get Out of This Place: Popular Conservatism and Postmodern Culture* (New York: Routledge, 1992), ch. 1.

23. As early as 1959 Norman Mailer advanced this thesis with his notion of the "White Negro," which included Presley among other white hipsters of the period. See *Advertisements for Myself* (New York: Putnam, 1959).

24. See Peter Guralnick, *Last Train to Memphis: The Rise of Elvis Presley* (Boston: Little, Brown, 1994), p. 27 ff.

25. The term "attunement" translates Martin Heidegger's *Gestimmtheit,* which combines connotations of "mood" (*Stimmung*), "voice" (*Stimme*), and "definition" (*Bestimmung*) in a phenomenology of human comportment oriented by the "ear" of understanding. See *Being and Time,* trans. John Macquarrie and Edward Robinson (New York: Harper and Row, 1962 [1927]), pp. 172–179.

26. Peter Guralnick told me that the model for his magnificent biography of Elvis, *Last Train to Memphis,* was Taylor Branch's *Parting the Waters: America in the King Years* (New York: Simon and Schuster, 1988).

27. For source materials of this reception history, see Ger Rijff, *Long Lonely Highway* (Amsterdam: Tutti Frutti Productions, 1985).

28. With regard to the pedagogy of this book, the current underfunding of arts education in America, exacerbated by a failure to grasp the concept of "cultural ontology" as explicated here, demonstrates the superficiality of present initiatives to combat social and moral decline in the United States. Elvis names this too. See Carol Becker, "The Education of Young Artists and the Issue of Audience," in *Between Borders,* pp. 101–112.

29. In its relative independence from formal educational institutions, cultural studies has played an important role in advancing concepts of democratic pedagogies outside the university. For example, one of the most influential men in the unofficial civil rights movement in the South, Sam Phillips, single-handedly changed the climate of race relations from his headquarters (Sun Studio) in a converted radiator shop on Union Avenue in Memphis. As Raymond Williams observes (*The Politics of Modernism: Against the New Conformists* [London: Verso, 1989], p. 152), ordinary people (as opposed to formally trained students) read "in a context to which they [bring] their own situation, their own experience." "But I saw—and I don't remember when, but I saw as a child— I thought to myself: suppose that I would have been born black. Suppose that I would have been born a little bit more down the economic ladder. So I think I felt from the beginning the total inequity of man's inhumanity to his brother." Sam Phillips, quoted in Peter Guralnick, *Lost Highway: Journeys and Arrivals of American Musicians* (Boston: Godine), p. 328.

30. Much has been made of JFK as a role model for Bill Clinton's aspirations to the presidency, while his personal fondness for Elvis has been only a source of amusement. Yet a strong argument could be made for the equal, if not greater, influence of Elvis on Clinton's formidable political skills of communication and empathy that helped him win the White House in 1992. For many Elvis fans in the South, Graceland is clearly a southern White House and its famous owner a more presidential figure than the real

one, as that notorious photograph of Nixon and Elvis would suggest. See Sebastian Mallaby, "Bill Presley and Elvis Clinton," *Economist*, August 10, 1996.

31. "Music has been one of the great natural resources of the South and one of its most valuable exports." Malone, *Southern Music/American Music*, p. 1.

32. Linda Ray Pratt, "Elvis, or the Ironies of a Southern Identity" (1979), in *The Elvis Reader: Texts and Sources on the King of Rock 'n' Roll*, ed. Kevin Quain (New York: St. Martin's Press, 1992), pp. 101–102.

33. The controversy over "Elvis at Ole Miss" is a case study of institutional politics of representation. The clash was not only between the classical canon and popular culture, traditional scholarship and cultural studies, as university officials alleged, but rather a power struggle between two competing systems of representation symbolized by "Faulkner" and "Elvis"—in other words, between two constructions of race, class, regional identity, and their respective histories, values, and interests: aristocrat and redneck, Colonel Reb and Hillbilly Cat, the fabled Old South (of gentility, slavery, and plantation romance) and the real New South (of poverty, racism, and industrial blight), and so on.

34. For the notion of a critical pedagogy of representation, see Henry A. Giroux, "Living Dangerously: Identity Politics and the New Cultural Racism," in *Between Borders*, pp. 47–52.

35. For the best collection of contemporary Elvis art, see *Elvis + Marilyn: 2 x Immortal*, ed. Geri DePaoli (New York: Rizzoli, 1994).

36. For the classic discussion of the concept of *bricolage* and the work of the *bricoleur,* see Claude Lévi-Strauss, *The Savage Mind* (Chicago: University of Chicago Press, 1966 [1962]).

37. See my review article, "A Portrait of the Young King as Outsider Artist," *New York Observer*, October 31, 1994; also Michel de Certeau, *The Practice of Everyday Life,* trans. Steven Rendall (Berkeley: University of California, 1984).

38. "The work as work sets up a world. The work holds open the Open of the world." See Martin Heidegger, "The Origin of the Work of Art" (1935–1936), in *Poetry, Language, Thought,* trans. Albert Hofstadter (New York: Harper and Row, 1971), p. 45. For a good gloss on Heideggerian "regions" and their ontological dynamics, see Michael E. Zimmerman, *Heidegger's Confrontation with Modernity: Technology, Politics, Art* (Bloomington: Indiana Univeristy Press, 1990): "Human openness arises within and from a greater, non-human 'opening' or 'region.' This 'region' makes possible a non-anthropocentric clearing in which entities may gather each other into a mutual play that constitutes the 'worldhood' of the world" (p. 237).

39. Paradise Garden is the artist's backyard sculpture park in Pennville, Georgia (see Chapter 10).

40. In this respect, my strategy in this book resembles that of Jean-François Lyotard in his essay "the jews": "I write 'the jews' this way neither out of prudence nor lack of something better. I use lower case to indicate that I am not thinking of a nation. I make it plural to signify that it is neither a figure nor a political (Zionism), religious (Judaism), or philosophical (Jewish philosophy) subject that I put forward under this name. I use quotation marks to avoid confusing these 'jews' with real Jews. . . . 'The jews' are the object of a dismissal with which Jews, in particular, are afflicted in reality." Jean-François Lyotard, *Heidegger and "the jews,"* trans. Andreas Michel and Mark Roberts (Minneapolis: University of Minnesota Press, 1990), p. 3. With my "names of Elvis" I attempt my own rewriting of the name of Elvis by taking it out of the province and propriety of the proper name. It is also worth noting that the historical Elvis was part Jewish (see Chapter 4).

41. See Joanne Glasgow and F. David Kievett, "Teaching Queer: Bringing Lesbian and Gay Studies into the Community College Classroom," in *Creating an Inclusive College Curriculum: A Teaching Sourcebook from the New Jersey Project*, ed. Ellen G. Friedman et al. (New York: Teachers College Press, 1996); Alan Sinfield, *Cultural Politics—Queer Reading* (Philadelphia: University of Pennsylvania Press, 1994); Patricia Ticineto Clough, *Feminist Thought: Desire, Power, and Academic Discourse* (Cambridge: Blackwell, 1994).

42. Pratt, "Elvis, or the Ironies of a Southern Identity," p. 97. Pratt paraphrases C. Vann Woodward's famous thesis first advanced in *The Burden of Southern History* (1960): "Where the rest of America has known innocence, success, affluence, and an abstract and disconnected sense of place, the South has known guilt, poverty, failure, and a concrete sense of roots and place" (p. 96). Elvis had far more burdens imposed on him than just those of fame and wealth at a young age. The unwillingness of southerners to examine these special burdens of southern identity as exemplified in Elvis is not only a sign of the effacement of (white) ethnicity imposed by a certain regime of representational politics; it is also a symptom of deep psychological denial. Moreover, the unwillingness of nonsouthern Americans to acknowledge Elvis's conquest of the American Dream testifies to a deeper need in the American character than democracy: the need to repress its Others. The fact that this repression takes the form of amazingly petty jokes about Elvis's weight, diet, accent, taste, dress, hairstyle, etc., while completely disregarding his unprecedented record of achievement and irrefutable significance in American and world history, says something frightening about the power of prejudice and where that power resides: in the semiotics of the trivial.

43. Consider the following views of local officials and university spokespersons regarding Elvis and the Elvis conference: "It's just not a very academic thing. They're gonna talk about stuff like his drug addiction. It's not the kind of image we want for the university" (Oxford, Mississippi, Mayor John Leslie, quoted in *Seattle Times*, July 20, 1995); "As far as I'm concerned, this will be the last year the university is involved with the conference. The university can spend its time, energy and money on more rewarding efforts" (Ole Miss Provost Gerald Walton, quoted in *Oxford Eagle*, July 30, 1996); "The university may finally wash its hands of this whole undignified business and move on to more worthwhile projects" (Rob Robertson, editor of the Ole Miss student newspaper *Daily Mississippian*, in a front-page editorial, July 31, 1996).

44. No doubt this has much to do with the rise of the New Right in states like Mississippi that now feel politically empowered to reassert the old "states' rights" white hegemony behind a fake progressive rhetoric of decentralization, local control, personal responsibility, welfare reform, and the perennial call to "return to basics." For such "conservative southern progressives," aberrant social forms like those inspired by Elvis (see Roger Manley, Paul and Elvis MacLeod, and Howard Finster in this volume) are a threat to the politics of cultural control. Behind its appeal to the intellectual and moral superiority of "high art" and the "classical canon," one detects an overriding fear of anything with independent energy to indict the status quo. For a contrasting view, see Diana West, "Against Conservative Cool," *Weekly Standard,* August 5, 1996, pp. 20–24.

45. Religious themes began to appear in news coverage of the tenth anniversary of Elvis's death: "A Decade After Elvis: Faithful at the Shrine," *New York Times*, August 13, 1987; "Saint Elvis," *Washington Post*, August 13, 1987; "Words on the Wall Leave Heartfelt Passions to Elvis," *Baltimore Evening Sun*, August 13, 1987; "Candles in the Dark: 2 Sides of Elvis," *New York Times*, August 16, 1987; "King Elvis Still Reigns in Southern Lore," *Los Angeles Times*, August 17, 1987. In the last decade, the subject has been explored in dozens of mainstream articles and books (not to mention the

tabloids): "New Fast-Growing Sect Worships Elvis Presley as a God," *Baltimore Sun*, July 26, 1988; "Elvis Used Miracle Healing Power to Cure Sick Fans," *Baltimore Sun*, December 19, 1989; "Thousands Worship Elvis and He Answers Prayers," *Boston Globe*, January 9, 1990; "Elvis of Nazareth," *Economist*, July 1992; "Among the Believers," *New York Times Magazine*, September 24, 1995. Book-length studies include Ted Harrison, *Elvis People: The Cult of the King* (London: Fount/HarperCollins, 1992); Peter Eicher, *The Elvis Sightings* (New York: Avon, 1993); Stephanie G. Pierce, *Strange Mystery at the 24 Hour Church of Elvis* (Seattle: Where's the Art!!, 1994); John Strausbaugh, *E: Reflections on the Birth of the Elvis Faith* (New York: Blast Books, 1995). For the best scholarly treatment of the theme, see the work of art historian and medievalist Gary Vikan: "Graceland as *Locus Sanctus*," in *Elvis + Marilyn: 2 x Immortal*, pp. 150–166, and his forthcoming study *Saint Elvis*.

46. A life centered around the care and maintenance of the ark, cross, shroud, or shrine is sustained by the same *qualitative* relationship as that, say, of the modern suburbanite to the care and maintenance of his lawn. See Virginia Scott Jenkins, *The Lawn: A History of an American Obsession* (Washington, D.C.: Smithsonian Institution Press, 1994).

47. For the role of "charisma" in social formation, see *Max Weber on Charisma and Institution Building: Selected Papers*, ed. S. N. Eisenstadt (Chicago: University of Chicago Press, 1968), and Edward Shils, *The Constitution of Society* (Chicago: University of Chicago Press, 1982).

48. It's worth noting that Rosenbaum's critical observation, which required objectivity toward *both* Elvis and Christianity, was perhaps made possible only by virtue of his journalistic independence from the university. The ability of the Elvis conference to generate such media interest and in some cases cutting-edge analysis can hardly be underestimated. The crossover and outreach power of the academic Elvis has the potential to disengage both academia and the media from their respective professional dogmas reining in the free pursuit of truth.

49. See Stuart Hall, "The Question of Cultural Identity," in Stuart Hall, David Held, and Tony McGrew, eds., *Modernity and Its Futures* (Cambridge: Polity, 1992), pp. 273–325.

50. Not a second passes in global media without some reference to "Elvis." For example, in this morning's paper the Associated Press reports a warning to Somali Muslims from the chairman of the Islamic Court: "Those who shave like Elvis Presley, Sylvester Stallone and the U.S. Marines will not go unpunished" (September 16, 1996). For theories of identity from the perspective of postmodernism, media culture, and identity politics, see Jean Baudrillard, *In the Shadow of the Silent Majorities* (New York: Semiotext(e), 1983), Arthur Kroker and David Cook, *The Postmodern Scene* (New York: St. Martin's Press, 1986), and Stanley Aronowitz, *The Politics of Identity* (New York: Routledge, 1992).

51. Sigmund Freud, *Jokes and Their Relation to the Unconscious,* trans. James Strachey (New York: Norton, 1963 [1905]).

52. Pratt, "Elvis, or the Ironies of a Southern Identity," p. 102. The *Memphis Press-Scimitar* unwittingly captured this larger significance of Elvis as the embodiment of a region in its headline announcing his death, "A Lonely Life Ends on Elvis Presley Boulevard," August 16, 1977.

53. For a moving account of southern life and change during this period, see Will D. Campbell, *Brother to a Dragonfly* (New York: Continuum, 1992 [1977]). Campbell grew up during the Depression with his brother, Joe, on a farm in rural Amite County, Mississippi. Against a subtle, hermeneutic background of rural southern life, Campbell

recounts the story of his relationship with his brother, who, at the age of 41, died of a heart attack after years of prescription drug abuse.

54. It is probably true that more websites are devoted to Elvis than to any other topic in cyberspace. As Mojo Nixon reminds us, "Elvis is everywhere," a disembodied persona enveloping the globe, a viral force colonizing worlds.

55. Vernon Chadwick, "Papa's Got a Brand New Flag: Confederate Symbolism and the Funky New South," *Southern Reader* 7 (1991): 1–2, 26–27.

56. See Hans Blumenberg, *Work on Myth,* trans. Robert M. Wallace (Cambridge, Mass.: MIT Press, 1985 [1979]).

57. Cynthia Rose, *Living in America: The Soul Saga of James Brown* (London: Serpent's Tail, 1990), pp. 46–47.

58. Rose, *Living in America,* p. 24.

Chapter One

1. Testimonies about Elvis's transforming power abound in American popular culture. One of the most revelatory, most often quoted, and certainly the funniest, accounts is that of the deceased Bob Luman, who recalled his experience as a seventeen-year-old student in Kilgore, Texas: "This cat came out in red pants and a green coat and a pink shirt and socks, and he had this sneer on his face . . . he hit his guitar a lick, and he broke two strings. Hell, I'd been playing ten years, and I hadn't broken a total of two strings. These high school girls were screaming and fainting and running up to the stage, and then he started to move his hips real slow. That's the last time I tried to sing like Webb Pierce or Lefty Frizzell." Quoted in Peter Guralnick, *Last Train to Memphis: The Rise of Elvis Presley* (Boston: Little, Brown, 1994), pp. 182–183.

2. *Billboard,* vol. 55, no. 9 (February 27, 1943): 94.

3. Country music's first great surge of economic growth is discussed in Bill C. Malone, *Country Music, USA* (Austin: University of Texas Press, 1985), ch. 6.

4. George Lipsitz explores the hopes and promises implied by American victory in World War II, and says that "much of the turmoil and tumult of the postwar period can be read as a battle over those promises in virtually every area of life and culture in the United States—from partisan politics to poetry, from church pulpits to popular culture." *Rainbow at Midnight: Labor and Culture in the 1940s* (Urbana: University of Illinois Press, 1994), p. 46.

5. The best general account of the attitudes spawned by abundance is Godfrey Hodgson, *America in Our Time* (Garden City, New York: Doubleday, 1976), particularly pp. 48–98.

6. It should be understood, of course, that that assumption was held most strongly by people who played dominant roles in the relationships described.

7. See Lipsitz, *Rainbow at Midnight,* ch. 2.

8. For a discussion of the origins and evolution of honky-tonk music, see Malone, *Country Music, USA,* ch. 5.

9. Postwar southern evangelical Protestantism has still not found its definitive chronicler, but David Harrell has come close. See his account, for example, of healing revivalism: *All Things Are Possible: The Healing and Charismatic Revivals in Modern America* (Bloomington: Indiana University Press, 1976). Howard Dorgan, *The Airwaves of Zion: Radio and Religion in Appalachia* (Knoxville: University of Tennessee

Press, 1993), provides an instructive account of the radio preachers of Appalachia and reminds us of a phenomenon that was once widespread in the South.

10. Curtis Stewart's "Lord, Build Me a Cabin in Glory," published in 1944, is the classic statement of rustic humility in modern gospel music. It is also an example of a virtually vanished breed of songs and a statement of faith that most modern southern Christians would probably reject.

11. White gospel music, unfortunately, has attracted few historians. Charles K. Wolfe, however, has long been working on a general history. He has provided a general summary of the subject in Charles Reagan Wilson and William Ferris, eds., *Encyclopedia of Southern Culture* (Chapel Hill: University of North Carolina Press, 1989), pp. 1013–1014. Elvis's own relationship to gospel music has drawn much written attention, including the fine accounts written by Cheryl Thurber and Don Cusic in *Rejoice!* (Summer 1988): 5–13.

12. Albert Gannaway produced a widely syndicated series of television shows in the 1950s, featuring Nashville musicians and filmed in staged "rustic" settings. Singers generally sang to pretty young women who dressed in gingham dresses and sat on hay bales. Some of those shows have been made available on videos by the Shanachie label. See, for example, Shanachie 601 (featuring Webb Pierce and Chet Atkins), Shanachie 602 (Marty Robbins and Ernest Tubb), and Shanachie 603 (Ray Price and Jim Reeves).

13. The best general survey of black-white musical interchange is Tony Russell, *Blacks, Whites, and Blues* (New York: Stein and Day, 1970).

14. A fine introduction to country musicians who experimented with black music, although limited to those who recorded for Columbia and its offshoots, is the CD collection *White Country Blues: 1926–1938, a Lighter Shade of Blues* (in the Roots 'n' Blues Series), Columbia/Legacy C2K 47466. A more recent manifestation of the affinities between soul and country music is *Rhythm Country and Blues*, MCAD 10965, a CD collection that features the singing of black and white singers on a number of shared performances.

15. Scholars disagree strongly about the degree to which white country musicians borrowed directly from African-Americans. That is, did early musicians learn from black performers, or did they learn from white interpreters such as the black-face minstrels of the nineteenth century? For varying interpretations, see Robert Toll, *Blacking Up: The Minstrel Show in Nineteenth-Century America* (New York: Oxford University Press, 1974); Robert Winans, "The Folk, the Stage, and the Five-String Banjo in the Nineteenth Century," *Journal of American Folklore* 89 (1976): 407–437; and Cecelia Conway, *African Banjo Echoes in Appalachia: A Study of Folk Traditions* (Knoxville: University of Tennessee Press, 1995).

16. See the references in footnote 14, but also consult Nick Tosches, *Country: The Biggest Music in America* (New York: Stein and Day, 1977), for a fine discussion of Jimmie Davis and other country musicians who have dipped into the "underworld" of American music for material. Other recorded samplings of this music are described in Malone, *Country Music, USA*, pp. 445–456.

17. What I have said in earlier publications is much more true today: "The literature on Elvis Presley is vast and proliferating." The best accounts of those seminal Sun years are Greil Marcus, *Mystery Train: Images of America in Rock 'n' Roll*, 2d rev. ed. (New York: E. P. Dutton, 1982), and Guralnick, *Last Train to Memphis*.

18. W. J. Cash's famous *The Mind of the South* (New York: Alfred A. Knopf, 1941), is the source of this influential idea. A provocative testing of the idea is Ted Ownby, *Subduing Satan: Religion, Recreation, and Manhood in the Rural South, 1865–1920* (Chapel Hill: University of North Carolina Press, 1990).

19. This interchange supposedly came during one of Elvis's early appearances on *Louisiana Hayride*. I heard it on a bootleg tape.

20. Guralnick, *Last Train to Memphis*, p. 335.

21. For a discussion of Presley's powerful early influence in west Texas, see Joe Carr and Alan Munde, *Prairie Nights to Neon Lights: The Story of Country Music in West Texas* (Lubbock: Texas Tech University Press, 1995).

22. Bill Ivey, "Commercialization and Tradition in the Nashville Sound," in *Folk Music and Modern Sound*, ed. William Ferris and Mary Hart (Jackson: University Press of Mississippi, 1982), pp. 129–141.

23. Their story is told elsewhere in this volume by Steve Tucker, and by Nick Tosches, in "Rockabilly," *The Illustrated History of Country Music*, ed. Patrick Carr (New York: Country Music Magazine Press, 1979), pp. 217–237. See also Bill C. Malone, *Southern Music/American Music* (Lexington: University Press of Kentucky, 1979).

24. Robert Windeler, "Bio—Chet Atkins," *People Weekly*, December 16, 1974: 62; Bill Ivey, "Chet Atkins," *Stars of Country Music*, ed. Bill C. Malone and Judith McCulloh (Urbana: University of Illinois Press, 1976).

25. In October 1985, the "neotraditionalists" won most of the awards at the Country Music Association's annual convention. The next year the *Journal of Country Music* (11 [1] [1986]: 2–25) devoted special attention to the phenomenon in a section called "The Old Sound of New Country."

26. Karen Schoemer, "Marty Stuart Doesn't Need a Big Hat to Be Country," *New York Times*, July 12, 1992, p. 22.

27. In his fine study of southern industrialization in this century, James C. Cobb argued that "imperfect as it was, the story of Dixie's industrial growth was a success story for a great many southerners, especially those who remembered the futility of tilling worn-out soil and the pain of explaining to their children why the family could not afford a decent place to live or a respectable automobile." *Industrialization and Southern Society, 1877–1984* (Lexington: University Press of Kentucky, 1984), p. 143.

28. In reviewing the first edition of *Country Music, USA* (1968), I find that although I did recognize the mixed origins of Elvis's music (country, R&B, gospel), my assessment of his impact on country music was, at best, ambiguous and, at worst, hostile. See pp. 243–244. The reader might compare this treatment with that found in the 1985 revised edition of the book at pp. 248–250.

29. Clyde Julian "Red" Foley's original version of the song was recorded on Decca 5944 on March 4, 1941.

Chapter Two

1. "Visions of Elvis: Changing Perceptions in National Magazines, 1956–1965," *Southern Quarterly* 18 (Fall 1979): 39.

2. *Mystery Train: Images of America in Rock 'n' Roll Music* (New York: Dutton, 1975), p. 163

3. For detailed documentation of Lennon's debt to Elvis, see Philip Norman, *Shout! The Beatles in Their Generation* (New York: Fireside, 1981), pp. 12, 36, 38, 41, 63, and Ray Coleman, *Lennon* (New York: McGraw-Hill, 1984), pp. 54–55.

4. *White Boy Singin' the Blues: The Black Roots of White Rock* (New York: Penguin, 1982), p. 107.

5. "Rockabilly," in *Rolling Stone Illustrated History of Rock & Roll*, 2d ed., ed. Jim Miller (New York: Random House/Rolling Stone Press, 1980), p. 62.

6. A slightly different and more thorough definition is found in Craig Morrison, "Rockabilly: A Regional Music with a World-Wide Audience" (M.A. thesis, York University, Canada, 1983), pp. 11–17.

7. *The Early Days of Rock 'n' Roll*, documentary.

8. Quoted in Peter Guralnick, *Lost Highway: Journeys and Arrivals of American Musicians* (Boston: Godine, 1979), pp. 94–95.

9. Stanley Booth, "A Hound Dog, to the Manor Born," in *The Age of Rock: Sounds of the American Cultural Revolution,* ed. Jonathan Eisen (New York: Vintage, 1969), p. 49. Dewey Phillips is heard to great effect on *Red, Hot & Blue: Dewey Phillips' Live Radio Broadcasts from 1952–1964* (audio cassette), Memphis Archives MA 7016 (1995).

10. *The Early Days of Rock 'n' Roll.*

11. "Disc Jockey Urges Return to Spinning Only Country Music," *Downbeat*, January 26, 1955, unpaginated.

12. Phillip H. Ennis, *The Seventh Stream: The Emergence of Rocknroll in American Popular Music* (Hanover, NH: Wesleyan University/University of New Hampshire Press, 1992), p. 239.

13. "Rockabilly!" in *The Illustrated History of Country Music*, ed. Patrick Carr (Garden City, NY: Doubleday/Dolphin, 1980), p. 230.

14. W. J. Cash, *The Mind of the South* (New York: Knopf, 1941), pp. 32, 43, 44, 46, 47.

15. Cash, *The Mind of the South*, p. 51.

16. Ed.—Cash's description of the "drunkenness" of southern rhetoric invites comparison both with flamboyant rockabillies like Elvis and Jerry Lee Lewis and equally reckless southern poets and writers like Faulkner and James Dickey.

17. Cash, *The Mind of the South*, pp. 53, 296.

18. Ed.—Tucker's analogy may not be as far-fetched as it seems, at least not with regard to Faulkner's "rockabilly" reading of the Civil War *avant la lettre*. In *Flags in the Dust* (New York: Vintage/Random House, 1974 [1929]), for example, he describes, from the point of view of Aunt Jenny, a harsh critic of southern masculinity, the politics of the historical Jeb Stuart and fictional Bayard Sartoris, who risk their lives and the lives of their Confederate regiment on "a hair-brained prank of two heedless and reckless boys wild with their own youth" to steal coffee from General Pope's camp. The war was fought by such southern daredevils, says the narrator, "in a spirit of pure fun: neither Jeb Stuart nor Bayard Sartoris, as their actions clearly showed, had any political convictions involved at all" (pp. 14, 15 ff.). My comparison between canonized high-southern literature and low-down rockabilly has the added advantage of foregrounding the prankish quality of southern artistic invention, as the passage from *Flags* may suggest about Faulkner's own literary jokes.

19. Geoffrey Stokes, *The Beatles* (New York: Rolling Stone Press, 1980), p. 9.

Chapter Four

1. (London: Faber and Faber, 1990), p. 43.

2. (London: Bogle-L'Ouverture Press, 1992), p. 90.

3. See Peter Nazareth, ed., with the assistance of Joseph K. Henry, *Goan Literature: A Modern Reader*, issue of *Journal of South Asian Literature* 18 (1) (Winter-Spring 1983). See also Sasenarine Persaud, "The General and the Ghost. Telescoping Novels: The Indian African Diaspora Through the Indian Caribbean Diaspora," *Indo Caribbean Review*, 2 (1) 1995, ed. V. Chris Lakhan.

4. Elaine Dundy, *Elvis and Gladys* (New York: Macmillan, 1985), "Gladys' Roots," pp. 12–29. Ed.—Compare Nazareth's genealogy of Elvis with that offered by John

Shelton Reed in "Elvis as Southerner." Interestingly, each version accentuates aspects of the respective writer's own genealogy: Nazareth's Elvis is multiracial, multicultural, transcontinental, "conscious of having colonizer and colonized in him"; Reed's Elvis is "much the same as . . . hundreds of thousands of other southern white boys."

5. Alice Walker, "Nineteen Fifty-Five," in *You Can't Keep a Good Woman Down* (San Diego: Harcourt Brace Jovanovich, 1981), p. 4; also included in *Daughters of Africa*, subtitled "An International Anthology of Words and Writings by Women of African Descent: From the Ancient Egyptian to the Present," edited and with an introduction by Margaret Busby (New York: Pantheon Books, 1992), p. 643.

6. "Elvis really got into the role of Pacer Burton not only because he had some Cherokee blood in him (on the *Smith* side), but also because he no doubt remembered the way he was treated in grade school, at L. C. Humes, in Memphis, and the way his so-called neighbors treated him and Aunt Gladys on Audubon Drive, when all that Aunt Gladys had done was hang clothes on a line in her own yard," says Gene Smith in *Elvis's Man Friday* (Nashville: Light of Day Publications, 1994), p. 243.

Ed.—The reader should note, however, that Nazareth blurs the distinction between the historical Elvis and his multiple fictional personae and scripts, many of which the individual Elvis had no direct hand in shaping. Because he moves with ease, and often without warning, between these multiple levels, Nazareth's Elvis should best be regarded as always in quotation marks or, as Derrida would have it, under "erasure."

7. During my first year at Makerere University College I found that there was no dance band. I could play harmonica; when I went home for the long vacation in 1958, I persuaded my father to buy me a clarinet, which I spent the whole vacation learning. I knew I had succeeded when the dog stopped howling. I went back to Makerere and started a band and a Jazz Society, as a result of which I got to meet Herbie Mann in 1959 and Louis Armstrong in 1960 when they performed in Uganda. "You kick a tin can, that's not music," said Herbie Mann when he found out I liked Elvis. I asked Armstrong what he thought of Elvis. He shook his shoulders and said, "Yeah, I like Elvis!"

8. Ed.—With his suggestive use of the word "cover," a music-business term for when a singer or group rerecords an earlier song, sometimes so commandingly as to put into doubt the relationship between "original" and "secondary," Nazareth skillfully evokes important themes of deconstructive criticism: the myth of origins, alterity, supplementarity, *différance* (the play of differences), *mise en abîme* (infinite regression/progression) of the image-space between, say, two mirrors or what Nazareth calls "twinning" (Elvis's own twinship by birth establishing this semantic and semiotic doubling first congenitally, then performatively), and so forth. Peter, who likes to joke that the only deconstructive critics he has use for are Bugs Bunny and Elmer Fudd, would not be happy with this footnote.

9. Judith Valente, "Now All the Imitators of the King Will Start to Croon 'O Sole Mio,'" *Wall Street Journal*, January 8, 1992.

10. My novel, *In a Brown Mantle*, was launched with full publicity in Kampala in July 1972; a week later, Idi Amin announced the expulsion of Asians, that is, people of Indian origin, which was prophesied in the novel. My Ugandan citizenship was taken away, but I was exempted from leaving the country because of my job as Senior Finance Officer. However, I received the Seymour Lustman Fellowship to Yale University and left two months after the deadline of the expulsion.

11. Greil Marcus, *Mystery Train: Images of America in Rock 'n' Roll Music* (New York: Dutton, 1976), pp. 202–203. I had been on a hunt for a good book on rock 'n' roll, a book that had a literary, political, and musical consciousness reflected in a creative use of language, and found it at last in Marcus.

12. Peter Guralnick says on his liner notes to *Chuck Willis—My Story*, "Presley's version of 'I Feel So Bad' was virtually a note for note copy, even down to a fluffed line" (Columbia Records, New York, 1980). "Elvis recorded 'I Feel So Bad' on March 12, 1961, at RCA's Nashville studios," say Fred L. Worth and Steve D. Tamerius in *Elvis: His Life from A to Z* (Chicago: Contemporary Books, 1990), p. 401. "He copied Willis's version almost note for note, including a blown line. Both versions feature a piano and saxophone."

13. Andrew Salkey, *The Late Emancipation of Jerry Stover* (London: Longman, 1981). See my *In the Trickster Tradition: The Novels of Andrew Salkey, Francis Ebejer, and Ishmael Reed* (London: Bogle-L'Ouverture, 1994).

14. Ishmael Reed, *The Terrible Threes* (New York: Atheneum, 1989); the novel mentions Elvis and Colonel Tom Parker; Chuck Berry, *The Autobiography* (New York: Harmony, 1987).

15. Ed.—Nazareth's course, "Elvis as Anthology," was launched in the spring semester of 1992 at the University of Iowa. Unknown to him at the time, there were indeed others listening in America. I, too, in the spring of 1992, began teaching my first, full-fledged Elvis course, "Blue Hawaii: The Polynesian Novels and Hawaiian Movies of Melville and Elvis," at the University of Mississippi. Peter and I had been "twinned" by Elvis and we didn't even know it!

16. Bessie Head, *Maru* (London: Heinemann, 1972). In an essay written for my class on African literature, Julie Markussen showed that the sequence of pronouns in the novel was identical to that in "Heartbreak Hotel."

17. *The Rolling Stone Interviews* (New York: The Paperback Library, 1971), p. 371.

18. Tayeb Salih, *Season of Migration to the North*, trans. Denys Johnson-Davies (London: Heinemann, 1969). See my "The Narrator as Artist and the Reader as Critic in *Season of Migration to the North*," in Tayeb Salih's *Season of Migration to the North: A Casebook*, ed. Mona Takieddine Amyuni (Beirut: American University of Beirut, 1985).

19. See Dundy, *Elvis and Gladys*, ch. 5, pp. 64–79. Ed.—Meanwhile, see the first full-fledged study of the theme of twins and twinning in Elvis by clinical psychologist Peter Whitmer, *The Inner Elvis: A Psychological Biography of Elvis Aaron Presley* (New York: Hyperion, 1996).

20. Mark Childress, *Tender* (New York: Harmony, 1990). "Leroy" was the name of bluesman Robert Johnson and the second name of Jackie Wilson; Ivory Joe Hunter was born in Kirbyville, Texas. Twinning is becoming a favorite theme of Elvis fiction, a recent example being Gerald Duff, *That's All Right Mama: The Unauthorized Life of Elvis's Twin* (New York: Baskerville, 1995). Given the covers of the first two LPs, and the male-female balance Elvis sought in a great deal of his work, the question could be asked whether the dead twin could have been a girl. The name was spelled "Jessie," which is the spelling Childress uses for the male twin, and that was the way Elvis's paternal grandfather spelled his name. But while "Jessie" is the spelling of the twin's name on the commemorative marker and Gladys's and Vernon's tombstones at Graceland, on Vernon's tombstone the name of his father is spelled "Jesse." Larry Arnett told me that Elvis was very careful with words, so "Jessie" must have been retained for a purpose, more so as "Aron" in Elvis's name was spelled "Aaron" on his gravestone.

21. Ed.—What Nazareth terms "Elvis himself," despite the biographical references to his identity as a twin, is clearly a composite Elvis that includes the conscious and unconscious intentions and strategies of dozens of producers, directors, and screenplay writers who collectively shaped the image and persona of "Elvis" projected by Hollywood in the 1960s. With regard to Nazareth's speculation that Elvis's dead twin could

have been a girl, one now can better appreciate the intelligent parody of San Francisco–based female impersonator Elvis Herselvis.

22. Joachim-Ernst Berendt, *The Third Ear*, trans. Tim Nevill (New York: An Owl Book/Henry Holt, 1992), p. 44.

23. Berendt, *The Third Ear*, p. 119, my emphasis. Ed.—What Berendt and Nazareth think with these key concepts of Indian music—*anahata* and *ahata*, the unplayed and the played note—has affinities with the sign, the trace, the unthought, and the unspoken of poststructuralist thinkers like Heidegger and Derrida. In this context, also see Nazareth's discussion of the "engrams" of Elvis near the end of the essay.

24. Wilson Harris, *Palace of the Peacock* (London: Faber and Faber, 1960).

25. Ed.—Sam Phillips also had a hand in creating this striking echo effect. As Peter Guralnick explains, "For the first time [with the recording of 'Blue Moon'] Sam made extensive use of what he had come to call slapback, a kind of homemade echo device that was created by running the original recording signal through a second Ampex machine and thereby achieving an almost sibilant effect. This undoubtedly added not only to the presence but to the excitement of the recording." *Last Train to Memphis: The Rise of Elvis Presley* (Boston: Little, Brown, 1994), p. 103.

26. Berendt, *The Third Ear*, pp. 27–28.

27. Ed.—Interpretive flourishes like Nazareth's discussion of the peacock are often cited by conservative critics as proof of the degeneracy of cultural studies and its parallel discourses in poststructuralist and deconstructive criticism. But such attacks are usually based on unexamined norms of individual authorship, consciousness, and intentionality. As Nazareth brilliantly shows there are other texts to be read—collective texts formed by patterns of imagery and thematic motifs running through the universal history of the world.

28. Peter Guralnick, in the booklet included with the five-CD RCA/BMG set, *Elvis: The King of Rock 'n' Roll*, 1992, unpaginated but probably page 36.

29. In accordance with the notion that "One Night of Sin" is the version Elvis would have liked to release, it appears that RCA/BMG's five-CD set remastered the two versions so that "One Night" sounds "tinny" compared to "One Night of Sin." On the 1958 album I have, "One Night" sounds "heavier" and stronger than the first posthumous release of "One Night of Sin."

30. Walker, *You Can't Keep a Good Woman Down*, p. 4.

31. See Fred L. Worth and Steve D. Tamerius, *Elvis: His Life from A to Z* (Chicago: Contemporary Books, 1988), p. 230.

32. Liner notes by Peter Guralnick to *ELVIS: The Great Performances, Volume 2: The Man and the Music* (Burbank: Buena Vista, 1990). Of "Return to Sender" in the movie, Guralnick says: "Here we have the perfect homage to one of Elvis' true r&b heroes. There was no singer that Elvis admired more than Jackie Wilson, and no more unlikely place to display that admiration than this scene from the 1962 film *Girls! Girls! Girls!* It was prompted, evidently, by little more than a chance visit to The Trip in Hollywood to see Wilson perform a few days before filming, but Elvis gives back a witty, entertaining, almost flawless interpretation of Wilson's act with this r&b-flavored Otis Blackwell song. The hand gestures, the boxer's shuffle that stands in for The Twist, the self-amused little shoulder shrugs, even the facial expressions all suggest Wilson, one of the most dynamic performers of his, or any other, day. It was clearly a kind of inside joke made all the more ironic by the fact that Wilson was imitating Elvis when Elvis first saw him in Las Vegas in 1956." Guralnick describes it very well, except that I think the performance was prompted by more than just a chance visit to The Trip; the word "evidently" indicates his suspicion there may be more to the tribute than meets the eye.

For example, in an interview done circa 1973, released on *Jackie Wilson S. R. O.* (New Brunswick, NJ: Performance Records, 1987), Norm Nite asks Jackie whom he would play as a DJ if given an hour. Nite is taken aback when Jackie replies, "Elvis Presley," and he asks why Elvis. Jackie replies, "Elvis is a very good friend of mine."

33. Nelson George, *The Death of Rhythm & Blues* (New York: Plume/Penguin Group, 1988), p. 62.

34. Louis Cantor, *Wheelin' on Beale*, foreword by B. B. King (New York: Pharos Books, 1992), p. 191.

35. Childress, *Tender*, p. 559.

36. See Wilson Harris, "The Frontier on Which Heart of Darkness Stands," in *Joseph Conrad: Third World Perspectives*, ed. Robert Hamner (Washington, D.C.: Three Continents Press), pp. 165–166. Also my essay, "Out of Darkness: Conrad and Other Third World Writers," in the same volume.

37. Frantz Fanon, *Black Skin, White Masks*, trans. Charles Lam Markmann (New York: Grove Press, 1967).

38. Ishmael Reed, *Flight to Canada* (New York: Random House, 1976).

39. Ed.—More play between Elvis and Santa Claus (Colonel Parker in disguise) can be seen in the photo that Gene Smith provided for this volume (see Chapter 7).

40. How responsible was Elvis for this song and scene? Ernst Mikael Jørgensen, producer of the major box sets and other recent CD compilations of Elvis, said that the bosses wanted to reject "Can't Help Falling in Love" but Elvis chose to do it.

41. Alice Walker, *The Temple of My Familiar* (New York: Pocket Books, 1990), p. 188. On the next page, we read, "According to Ola, Elvis Presley and Johnny Cash are both Indians. A foreigner sees this immediately, he says; Americans do not. He says this explains Elvis's clothing style. His love of buckskin and fringe, of silver." I received a letter from Sean Waller of Wirral, England, who heard about my class from Radio One, in which he says that Elvis's "jump-suits were supposed to be Inca/Aztec warrior costume."

42. Carl Jung, quoted in Richard Lannoy, *The Speaking Tree* (London: Oxford, 1975), p. 172.

43. "You can hear the different characters in his voice," says Charlie Hodge, rhythm guitarist, backup singer, and aide to Elvis. "He would be Billy Eckstine, he would be Bill Kenny of the Ink Spots, he would be Hank Snow—all these people became Elvis Presley by the time he started touring. He had all these people inside of him." *Musician Magazine*, 168 (October 1992): 59.

44. Maxwell Maltz, *Psycho-Cybernetics* (New York: Pocket Books, 1960), pp. 241 and 242.

45. Ishmael Reed, *The Last Days of Louisiana Red* (New York: Random House, 1974).

46. F. Paul Wilson, "The Years the Music Died," from *WHISPERS* 6, ed. Stuart David Schiff (New York: Jove, 1989), pp. 131–144.

47. Joseph Conrad, *Heart of Darkness/The Secret Sharer* (New York: New American Library, 1983). "The drums pound incessantly, in a fierce, monotonous, emotional rhythm. A voice wails frantically, now and again reaching a falsetto shriek as it increases in frenzy. The dancers—young teenage boys and girls—leap and twist, now doing violent solo steps and now clutching each other in passionate dance duets. The sight and the sound merge into a mad maelstrom—furious, pagan, erotic. / Where do you think you are? Deep in the Belgian Congo? In the Australian bush? On some south sea island? / Nonsense—this is America, 1957." This is from an article by Blake Martin entitled, "Exposed: The Strange Cult of Rock-and-Roll," originally published in a magazine called *True Strange*. A yellow band divides the cover painting diagonally.

Below the line are African "tribal" dancers, above Bill Haley and a monster-like Elvis. Arguing that rock 'n' roll is "a linear descendant of African tribal music," the article ends ominously, "Rock-and-roll roars on—and it will probably crash with a bang like every other cult that has ever existed." See *Elvis Album* (Lincolnwood, Ill.: Publications International, Ltd., 1991), p. 79, where this article is reproduced.

48. "All of the publicity about Elvis having his hair cut off sounded like it was being announced to one and all that the army had the power to take something away from Elvis," says Gene Smith, "namely, his hair, or his individuality, so, in a sense, it was a kind of castration." Smith, *Elvis's Man Friday*, p. 202.

49. Ed.—This is one of the burning questions of critical cultural studies, the question of illusory versus real oppositional texts. "[Raymond] Williams suggests that much of the opposition to the dominant culture is still hegemonic and thus only illusory; it still takes place within the framework of what is allowed by the dominant culture. But not all opposition is illusory, and this leads to one of the most important theoretical problems of cultural analysis: Which analyses are truly oppositional and outside of hegemonic domination and which are only seemingly oppositional and dominated by hegemonic imperatives?" Arthur Asa Berger, *Cultural Criticism: A Primer of Key Concepts* (Thousand Oaks, Calif.: Sage Publications, 1995), p. 64.

50. Ngugi wa Thiong'o, *A Grain of Wheat* (London: Heinemann, 1967).

51. The volume by Joel Whitburn I have used is *Joel Whitburn's Pop Annual, 1955–1977* (Menomonee Falls, Wis.: Record Research Inc., 1978). "Two Hound Dogs" was the B-side; the A-side was "Razzle Dazzle," which reached No. 15 on the charts.

52. Arnold Shaw, *Honkers and Shouters*, subtitled *The Golden Years of Rhythm & Blues* (New York: Coller, 1978), p. 482. Peter Guralnick also does not seem to realize that Elvis changed the meaning of "Hound Dog." He says it "was a very odd choice for a male performer, since it was written from a female point of view" (Guralnick, *Last Train to Memphis*, p. 273).

53. Dan Cushman, *Stay Away, Joe* (New York: Bantam, 1953).

54. Berendt, *The Third Ear*, p. 21.

55. Berendt, *The Third Ear*, pp. 17 and 24. One of the verses in "Too Much Monkey Business" is about a blonde-haired woman who wants to marry the singer and get him to settle down and write a book. The book will not tell the full story of the outsider, the underclass, the colonials: The book is an ideological construct reflecting the attitudes and power of a certain class. In this piece on Elvis, I am giving voice to everyone I heard saying something important to me about Elvis: One can blow up or stretch the book so that it accommodates what can and must be heard. The book tends to go in a straight line: In dealing with Elvis, I have gone in a spiral.

56. Harris, *Palace of the Peacock*, pp. 150 and 152.

57. See Ishmael Reed, "I'm a Cowboy on the Boat of Ra," in his *New and Collected Poems* (New York: Atheneum, 1988), pp. 17–18.

Chapter Five

1. From UNCOVER (Denver: Carl, Inc.), an online table-of-contents database covering approximately 17,000 journals.

2. From *Newspaper Abstracts* (University Microfilm, Inc.), an online database with abstracts of articles and editorials in thirty U. S. newspapers.

3. Ed.—Elvis's "first-name basis with the world," however, conceals the elision of family and regional history in his rise to the status of celebrity icon, trademark, and corporate logo. One could chart the same global trajectory in such southern products as Coca-Cola, Holiday Inn, Federal Express, and of course rock 'n' roll.

4. The discussion below is drawn primarily from Elaine Dundy, *Elvis and Gladys* (New York: Macmillan, 1985). I have also made use of Peter Guralnick, *Last Train to Memphis: The Rise of Elvis Presley* (Boston: Little Brown, 1994).

5. Ed.—Compare Reed's portrait of Elvis's ancestry, "typical for a southern white boy," to the exotic multiracial, multicultural, transcontinental "anthology" given by Peter Nazareth in "Elvis as Anthology"; see Chapter 4. By now, after the careful research of Elaine Dundy, Vaughan Grisham, Peter Guralnick, and others, Albert Goldman's chapter "Redneck Roots" may be accepted for what it is: racist distortions and lies. See his *Elvis* (New York: McGraw-Hill, 1981), pp. 53–60.

6. Daniel R. Hundley, *Social Relations in Our Southern States* (Baton Rouge: Louisiana State University Press, 1979 [1860], pp. 192–216.

7. Frank L. Owsley, *Plain Folk of the Old South* (Baton Rouge: Louisiana State University Press, 1949).

8. Ed.—At Ole Miss, a bastion of traditional white southern self-consciousness, the Elvis conference was received with a mixture of skepticism and scorn from both faculty and students. But what are regarded as southern "traditions" worthy of pride and preservation, turn out, upon closer inspection by scholars such as Reed, to be the clichés and fictions of button-down suburbanites desperately clinging to racial symbols of authority and high-cultural status. For many southerners, Elvis is the pariah of the New Corporate South, his "redneck" image the antitype of both proper southern history and acceptable southern progress.

9. Ed.—"For Southerners, this fusion of 'Dixie,' 'All My Trials,' and 'The Battle Hymn of the Republic' has nothing to do with the rest of America, although its popularity around the country suggests that other Americans do relate it to their own history. The trilogy seems to capture Southern history through the changes of the civil rights movement and the awareness of black suffering which had hitherto largely been excluded from popular white images of Southern history. The piece could not have emerged before the seventies because only then had the 'marching' brought a glimmer of hope. Even Elvis could not have sung this trilogy in New York's Madison Square Garden before there was some reason for pride and appropriate musical history from one whose music moved always in the fused racial experiences of the region's oppressed." Linda Ray Pratt, "Elvis, or the Ironies of a Southern Identity" (1979), reprinted in Kevin Quain, ed., *The Elvis Reader* (New York: St. Martin's Press, 1992), p. 99.

10. Ed.—See Will Campbell's discussion in Chapter 6 of the coalition formed in the 1930s and 1940s by these poor southern whites and blacks—the Southern Tenant Farmers' Union.

11. Ed.—Performing at the Elvis conference's Gospel Revival Singing was Queen Elizabeth Weeden, whose mother worked with Gladys Presley at St. Joseph's Hospital in Memphis. She witnessed to this fact during a gutsy rendition of "Stand By Me."

12. James Agee, *Let Us Now Praise Famous Men* (Boston: Houghton Mifflin, 1941), with photographs by Walker Evans. These families were revisited in the 1980s by (among others) Dale Maharidge, in *And Their Children After Them* (New York: Pantheon, 1989).

13. National Emergency Council, *Report on Economic Conditions of the South* (Washington, D.C.: U.S. Government Printing Office, 1938).

14. Charles Angoff and H. L. Mencken, "The Worst American State," *American Mercury* 24 (September, October, November 1931): 1–16, 177–188, 355–371.

15. Unless otherwise indicated, information on Tupelo and Lee County comes from Federal Writers' Project of the Works Progress Administration, *Mississippi: A Guide to the Magnolia State* (New York: Viking Press, 1938), and Vaughan L. Grisham, *Tupelo,*

Mississippi: From Settlement to Industrial Community, 1860 to 1970 (M.A. thesis, Department of History, University of North Carolina at Chapel Hill, 1975).

16. Ed.—Scholars are today coming forth in recognition of the place of "Elvis" in southern history much like Faulkner's call to historians and poets to recognize the "mule": "Some Cincinnatus of the cotton fields should contemplate the lowly destiny, some Homer should sing the saga, of the mule and of his place in the South." *Flags in the Dust* (New York: Vintage Books, 1973), p. 313. Linda Ray Pratt, slicing through the silence, suppression, and kitsch that edits official representations of the South in literature, education, and tourism, was one of the first to place "Elvis's South" on the map of southern history and scholarship. See my introduction to the present volume.

17. W. J. Cash, *The Mind of the South* (New York: Alfred A. Knopf, 1941).

18. Ed.—In contrast to the overt racism, as cited here by Reed, of many of Tupelo's political, civic, and business leaders in the pre–civil rights era, the following statement by Vernon Presley is all the more remarkable: "There were times we had nothing to eat but corn bread and water, but we always had compassion for people. Poor we were, I'll never deny that. But trash we weren't.... We never had any prejudice. We never put anybody down. Neither did Elvis." Quoted in Guaralnick, *Last Train to Memphis*, p. 29.

19. Ed.—See Reverend Howard Finster's description of this Pentecostal and Holiness movement in the South, especially as it pertains to Elvis's religiously inspired music (Chapter 16).

20. "Elvis Defends Low-Down Style," *Charlotte Observer*, June 27, 1956. Cited in Guralnick, *Last Train to Memphis*, p. 289.

Chapter Six

1. *Elvis* (New York: McGraw-Hill, 1981), p. 77.

2. Ed.—The Center for the Study of Southern Culture was established at the University of Mississippi in 1977. A teaching, research, and service division of the university, the center is best known for its development of the comprehensive reference guide *The Encyclopedia of Southern Culture* as well as its cosponsorship of the annual Faulkner conference. Despite long-standing institutional and community support for its teaching and research (the center also cosponsors an annual *Conference for the Book* and underwrites *Living Blues: A Magazine of the African-American Experience*), the center's involvement in the Elvis conference sparked a controversy unprecedented in its eighteen-year existence.

3. Ed.—The Southern Christian Leadership Conference was founded in 1957 in Atlanta's Ebenezer Baptist Church, which was pastored by the Reverend Martin Luther King Sr., whose son, Martin Jr., became its first president. Its early membership consisted mostly of black ministers and northern activists.

4. Ed.—Orval Eugene Faubus, six-term governor of Arkansas (1955–1967). For his defiant stand in Little Rock, he became a symbol of southern resistance to desegregation.

5. Ed.—With twenty-one books currently in print, Jeff Foxworthy has made a cottage industry out of the "redneck." His titles include *Games Rednecks Play: A Postcard Book*; *Redneck Test Volume 43*; *You Might Be a Redneck If . . . : A Laugh-a-Day for 1996*; *Check Your Neck: More of "You Might Be a Redneck If . . . "*; *Red Ain't Dead: 150 More Ways to Tell if You're a Redneck*.

6. Howard Fineman, *Newsweek*, January 25, 1995.

7. Ed.—Theodore Bilbo (1877–1947), two-term governor of Mississippi, 1916–1920 and 1928–1932. Benjamin Ryan "Pitchfork Ben" Tillman, senator from South Carolina.

8. Racism, as I understand it, arose from the Stoic notion that power to rule inheres naturally in the best men. In later societies, that notion resulted in the divine right of kings and the belief that one *class* was better prepared to rule than another. Racialism is an extension of this notion.

9. Ed.—With "In the Ghetto," recorded in January 1969 at American Studios in Memphis, Elvis raised his voice with other powerful voices of protest in that historic year of American social history.

10. Ed.—The painter is Jean-François Millet, whose painting *The Man with the Hoe,* exhibited at the official Paris Salon in 1863, was bitterly criticized for its "low" subject matter. The poet is the American Edwin Markham, whose poem (1899) of the same title, "Written after seeing Millet's World-Famous Painting," is a spirited protest against exploitation of the working poor. See *A Little Treasury of Modern Poetry*, English and American rev. ed., edited and with an introduction by Oscar Williams (New York: Scribners, 1952), pp. 568–570. Line references refer to this edition.

11. Ed.—For example, in an interview that aired nationally on *ABC Nightly News* during the Elvis conference, John Leslie, mayor of Oxford, Mississippi, stated that Elvis was "beneath the dignity of the university and beneath the dignity of the city," a city that prides (and markets) itself on the high-cultural status of William Faulkner.

12. *Elvis's Man Friday* (Nashville: Light of Day, 1994).

13. Ed.—On July 29, 1967, President Lyndon B. Johnson appointed a National Advisory Commission on Civil Disorders, chaired by Otto Kerner, governor of Illinois, to study racial violence in America. The commission was convened in an atmosphere of crisis resulting from a series of explosive riots that rocked over twenty-three American cities that summer. These "urban disorders," as they were called, the worst of which occurred in Newark and Detroit, were national scenes of confrontation between poor inner-city blacks and white local police forces and the National Guard.

14. Ed.—Founded in Tyronza, Arkansas, in April 1934, the Southern Tenant Farmers' Union was an important biracial and interclass grassroots attempt to redress institutionalized biases of New Deal agricultural policy affecting southern sharecroppers, tenants, and small businessmen. Anticipating the modern civil rights movement in the South, the STFU changed gospel songs like "We Shall Not Be Moved" into protest songs. See Donald H. Grubbs, *Cry from the Cotton: The Southern Tenant Farmers' Union and the New Deal* (Chapel Hill: University of North Carolina Press, 1971).

15. Ed.—In 1994, after two previous mistrials, Byron de la Beckwith was found guilty in Jackson, Mississippi, of the 1964 slaying of black civil rights leader Medgar Evers.

16. Ross R. Barnett (1898–1988), governor of Mississippi (1960–1964). His defiance of a federal court order to integrate the University of Mississippi precipitated a riot between federal troops and an angry mob that left two dead and scores injured.

17. Ed.—A presidential statement issued in behalf of the American people on August 17, 1977.

Chapter Seven

1. Ed.—This essay is my edited transcription of Gene Smith's oral presentation delivered at the Elvis conference. It incorporates additional comments Gene made in response to questions from the floor. With Gene's permission, I have retained wherever desirable the original flavor of the spoken word. When academic work liberates itself from the misguided neutrality and abstraction of so-called objective professional speech, a whole world of essential life-meanings, usually hidden and suppressed, is unlocked. See Martin Heidegger, "Sprache und Heimat," *Hebbel-Jahrbuch* (1960): 27–50.

"The essence of language is rooted in dialect. The familiar and trusted things of home are also rooted in dialect, when one's native art of speaking is the mother of language. Such a native, regional art of speaking is not only the language of the mother but first and foremost the mother of language. Yet at this hour—I mean at this moment in our historical epoch—the received ancestral relations between language, mother tongue, the art of speaking, and home are out of joint. Man appears to have lost the language fatefully and historically assigned to him and in this sense has become speechless, although never in human history has so much talk been so incessantly broadcast around the globe" (my translation).

2. Ed.—On January 20, 1958, Elvis was inducted into the army, classified 1-A. Gene, who was by then married, did not accompany him to Germany, though he stood by his cousin during basic training at Fort Hood, Texas.

3. Ed.—Elvis's poor, insular childhood may have been further traumatized by his father's imprisonment in 1938, leaving the three-year-old at home with his protective mother. In literature one thinks of Blake's chimney sweeper and Dickens's Oliver Twist as examples of such troubled adolescent dreaming.

4. Ed.—Gene Smith, *Elvis's Man Friday* (Nashville: Light of Day Publishing, 1994).

5. Ed.—January 6, 1957, Elvis's third and last appearance. Elvis wore a gold lamé vest with black satin lining that belonged to an expensive gold-and-silver suit Elvis had had hand-tailored in Las Vegas. Later that year, Colonel Parker commissioned Nudie's of Hollywood to custom-make the famous $10,000 gold lamé tuxedo Elvis wore in 1959 for the cover of *50,000,000 Elvis Fans Can't Be Wrong*, the first of a long line of allusions to Liberace in Elvis's stage performance.

6. Ed.—This incident occurred around September 1956 during the filming of *Love Me Tender.*

7. Ed.—"Then when the service was well under way and all eyes were on Reverend Hamill [of the First Assembly of God in South Memphis], they would sneak out the door and drive down to the colored church at East Trigg, less than a mile away, where the Reverend Brewster delivered his stirring sermons and Queen C. Anderson and the Brewsteraires were the featured soloists. They reveled in the exotic atmosphere, the music was out of this world—but they could only stay a few minutes, they had to get back to First Assembly before they were missed." Peter Guralnick, *Last Train to Memphis: The Rise of Elvis Presley* (Boston: Little, Brown, 1994), p. 75. Did Elvis really need to "sneak" off to the black church, as Guralnick dramatizes the scene, given the thorough biracial nature of the Presleys' South Memphis neighborhood and experience?

8. Ed.—It would be a mistake to dismiss these antics as juvenile. Gene Smith's "paper" delivered to the Elvis conference can best be taken as a "folktale" and its mode of address that of "signifying" in the African-American sense of devious speech in the presence of the "boss man."

9. Ed.—"On the way to Vegas we all listened to music, nibbled on snacks, and drank Pepsis. In the front seat, Elvis and Gene joked in their own language. Elvis would say something and Gene would reply with a complete non sequitur." Priscilla Beaulieu Presley, with Sandra Harmon, *Elvis and Me* (New York: Berkley, 1986), p. 77.

Chapter Eight

1. "Elvis Defends Low-Down Style," *Charlotte Observer*, June 27, 1956. Cited in Peter Guralnick, *Last Train to Memphis: The Rise of Elvis Presley* (Boston: Little, Brown, 1994), p. 289.

2. *Tri-State Defender,* February 2, 1957. Cited in Guralnick, *Last Train to Memphis,* p. 369.

3. "Suddenly Singing Elvis Presley Zooms into Recording Stardom," *Memphis Press-Scimitar,* February 5, 1955. Cited in Guralnick, *Last Train to Memphis,* p. 162.

4. Guralnick, *Last Train to Memphis,* p. 47.

5. Leonard E. Barrett, *Soul-Force: African Heritage in Afro-American Religion* (Garden City, N.Y.: Anchor/Doubleday, 1974), pp. 83–84.

6. Ed.—For a contrasting view of American sacred musical traditions, white and black, see Don Cusic, *The Sound of Light: A History of Gospel Music* (Bowling Green, Ohio: Bowling Green State University Popular Pess, 1990), with its important chapter "Elvis and Gospel." Cusic traces the history of American church music from colonial psalms to the introduction of "hymns" during the Great Awakening (ca. 1734) to the creation of the distinctively American "gospel hymn" during the Great Revival of the late nineteenth century.

7. Ed.—Spencer implies that the sexual revolution of the 1960s, usually represented in American cultural histories by the antiwar and hippie movements, was really the outgrowth of at least a half-century of "sexual seduction of whites into blackness" taking place in various forms of black entertainment, chiefly music and dance. One can add to this scenario the perspective of D. H. Lawrence in *Studies in Classical American Literature* (1923), especially the essays on Melville and Whitman.

8. Cited in Guralnick, *Last Train to Memphis,* p. 285.

9. Ed.—Compare Spencer's account of the "blackness" of sexual expression in American popular music with Malone's discussion in Chapter 1.

10. Ed.—The term "rockabilly" applied to early southern rockers both appropriated this black-coded nomenclature and confused and complicated it with other racial and regional stereotypes. What did it mean? Gene Smith, who was helping to make this music with Elvis, had misgivings about the term. Referring to the early, mid-fifties characterization of Elvis's music in the media, Smith writes: "It was either 'hillbilly,' or '*rockabilly,*' a term that had suddenly come into frequent use, but neither Elvis nor I nor anyone in our family knew what that was supposed to mean, exactly. Not liking the term 'hillbilly' any more than he liked the term 'redneck,' Elvis found the term '*rockabilly*' to be an instant turnoff. So did I and Carroll Junior, and everyone else connected with Elvis, as far as I know. Elvis knew the term was a put-down, like 'poor white,' or 'white trash,' but neither he nor I understood how the term originated or how it could have gained popularity." Gene Smith, *Elvis's Man Friday* (Nashville: Light of Day Publishing, 1994), p. 113.

11. Camille Paglia, *Sex, Art, and American Culture* (New York: Vintage, 1992), p. 211.

12. C. G. Jung, "Your Negroid and Indian Behavior," *The Forum* (April 1930): 193, 196.

13. "Negroid America," *New York Amsterdam News,* April 16, 1930, p. 24.

14. Ralph Ellison, "What America Would Be Like Without Blacks," *Time,* April 6, 1970, pp. 54–55.

15. Jung, "Your Negroid and Indian Behavior," p. 196.

16. Alan W. Watts, *Nature, Man, and Woman* (New York: Vintage, 1991 [1958]), p. 204.

17. James H. Cone, *The Spirituals and the Blues: An Interpretation* (New York: Seabury, 1972), pp. 128, 132.

18. Ed.—Deconstructive criticism, to name one relevant perspective here below, from my editorial space, teaches caution with regard to the "reconciliation" of binary oppositions. As Derrida argues, a two-step strategy of inversion and displacement may

be required: "On the one hand, we must traverse a phase of *overturning*. To do justice to this necessity is to recognize that in a classical philosophical opposition we are not dealing with the peaceful coexistence of a *vis-à-vis*, but rather with a violent hierarchy. One of the two terms governs the other (axiologically, logically, etc.), or has the upper hand. To deconstruct the opposition, first of all, is to overturn the hierarchy at a given moment. To overlook this phase of overturning is to forget the conflictual and subordinating structure of the opposition. Therefore one might proceed too quickly to a *neutralization* that *in practice* would leave the field untouched, leaving one no hold on the previous opposition, thereby preventing any means of intervening in the field effectively. Jacques Derrida, *Positions*, trans. Alan Bass (Chicago: University of Chicago Press, 1972), p. 41.

19. Cone, *The Spirtuals and the Blues*, p. 131.

20. Ed.—Spencer's thesis, which was echoed by other scholars at the conference, was not lost on Ron Rosenbaum, who reviewed the conference for the *New York Times Magazine*, September 24, 1995: "The scholars' Elvis has more in common with the one the fans cry out to: the Healing Elvis. This is Elvis as racial integrator, as gender-liberating sexual healer. The Multicultural Elvis is an even grander figure than the one the fans conceive of—an Elvis who heals not just personal pain in individual souls but painful rifts in the nation's soul, rifts not only between black and white but between sex and spirituality in America" (p. 54).

21. Richard Middleton, "All Shook Up? Innovation and Continuity in Elvis's Vocal Style," in *The Elvis Reader: Texts and Sources on the King of Rock n Roll*, ed. Kevin Quain (New York: St. Martin's Press, 1992), pp. 4–5.

22. Camille Paglia, *Sexual Personae: Art and Decadence from Nefertiti to Emily Dickinson* (New York: Vintage, 1991), p. 361.

23. Paglia, *Sex, Art, and American Culture*, p. 91.

Chapter Nine

1. Reynolds Price, "A Single Meaning," in *A Common Room: Essays, 1954–1987* (New York: Atheneum, 1987), pp. 243, 249.

2. Ed.—The fairy-tale-like theme of the stolen hog may be apocryphal. It was advanced by Elaine Dundy in *Elvis and Gladys* (New York: St. Martin's Press, 1985): "So why would a delivery boy, that low-but-essential man on the totem pole, suddenly have the whistle blown on him? There seemed to have been an accumulation of things. Vernon was involved in selling a hog here and there whose original ownership was in doubt, and there is one recorded instance in which a horse he sold turned out to be dead on delivery. For whatever reason or reasons, Vernon was certainly let go by L. P. McCarty. And one day either in late September or early October (accounts vary), the Presleys headed for Memphis and a new start" (pp. 131–132).

3. *Outsider Art* (London: Studio Vista/New York: Praeger Publishers, 1972). See also Michael D. Hall and Eugene W. Metcalf Jr., eds., *The Artist Outsider: Creativity and the Boundaries of Culture* (Washington, D.C.: Smithsonian Institution Press, 1994).

4. Ed.—Since his pioneering study, Cardinal's concept of an anticultural, alternative art has expanded in America beyond its initial identification with the institutionalized insane (Dubuffet's Adolf Wölfli, for example). The term "outsider" is today variously applied to "naive," "visionary," "self-taught," and "primitive" artists working outside mainstream traditions as well as to certain canonized figures of academic and popular culture (like Elvis) whose work nonetheless defies orthodox interpretation. See my review essay, "A Portrait of the Young King as Outsider Artist," *New York Observer*, October 31, 1994.

5. For a more extensive treatment of this subject, see my *Signs and Wonders: Outsider Art Inside North Carolina* (Raleigh: North Carolina Museum of Art, 1989).

6. Ed.—The other two early-warning signs of outsider artists are whirligigs and strange roadside mailboxes.

7. Ed.—The image of Elvis in Howard Finster's art functions in a manner remarkably similar to what marketing theorists call "branded identity." Finster has brilliantly figured out on his own what corporate executives are paid six-figure salaries to know: In order to compete in a global marketplace in which products and services of big organizations are increasingly similar, "identity is going to make the difference between successful companies and failures." See Wally Olins, *Corporate Identity: Making Business Strategy Visible Through Design* (Cambridge: Harvard Business School Press, 1989), p. 35. Likewise, in the crowded marketplace of ideas Finster appropriates the iconography of famous American presidents and inventors like Washington, Lincoln, Edison, and Ford, world-renowned celebrities like Elvis Presley and Marilyn Monroe, or global commercial products like Coca-Cola as the vehicles of a second-order discourse conveying Finster's own spiritual messages. In Chapter 16, "Sermon on Alvis," Finster explains how he discovered this strategy of folk-art sermonizing in the parables of Jesus. Here again we discover how southerners, like the proverbial tortoise and hare, are slowly colonizing the world from their own backyards. See Kinky Friedman, *Elvis, Jesus, and Coca-Cola* (New York: Bantam Books, 1994).

8. Ed.—Manley's moving testimony to the inherent dignity and worth of self-taught artists and their outsider art—irrespective of academies, museums, and markets—was powerful confirmation, from one of the leading experts in the field, of the educational outreach symbolized by "Elvis" and actualized by the Elvis conference. His talk laid the intellectual and humane groundwork for the appreciation of such "outsiders" to the university as Howard Finster, Paul and Elvis MacLeod, Black Elvis, and El Vez.

Chapter Ten

1. Ed.—A collection of such votive graffiti addressed to Elvis, 1989–1996, has recently appeared. See Daniel Wright, with a foreword by Vernon Chadwick, *Dear Elvis: Graffiti from Graceland* (Memphis: Mustang Press, 1996).

2. Ed.—Andy Warhol's variously silkscreened Elvises, as early as 1963 with *Single Elvis* and *Triple Elvis* (synthetic polymer paint and silkscreen on canvas), mark the beginning of the appropriation of the Elvis image for contemporary art.

3. Ed.—The best book documenting the impact of the image of Elvis on contemporary art is Geri DePaoli, ed., *Elvis + Marilyn: 2 x Immortal* (New York: Rizzoli, 1995).

Chapter Eleven

1. Ed.—This chapter is my edited transcription of Joni Mabe's lecture and slide presentation delivered at the Elvis conference. It incorporates additional comments Joni made in response to questions from the floor. With her permission, I have retained wherever desirable the original flavor of the spoken word. See my more expansive footnote concerning dialect, spoken communication, and home at the beginning of Chapter 7.

2. Ed.—Joni Mabe is an interesting test case of the dismissive attitudes of an all-too-gullible public, precisely the one P. T. Barnum loved to fool. With such sideshow wonders as the *Elvis Wart* and the *Maybe Elvis Toenail* she slyly aligns her art parodically with a grand tradition of fetishism ranging from the medieval veneration of saints to the nineteenth-century American museum of curiosities to Ripley's "Believe It Or Not."

See Philip B. Kunhardt, *P. T. Barnum: America's Greatest Showman* (New York: Knopf, 1995).

3. Ed.—I am convinced that Joni Mabe's *Elvis Prayer Rug* will become one of the enduring images of the twentieth century.

4. Ed.—Mabe's "production by rejection" follows a logic as devious as Hegel's *Aufhebung*. For his part, Nazareth attempts to formulate it as the peculiar "Hound Dog" logic of the underdog: "In other words, Elvis did not have absolute power: he had to acquire power the way the underdog did by 'signifying' (to use the black American term)." See Chapter 4.

5. Ed.—Surrealism is indeed a powerful precursor to the Elvis art movement. In fact, I would go so far as to say that Elvis art is the only authentic, homegrown surrealist art being produced in America today. Oddly enough, it is the American South that has excelled in American surrealism in the more precise sense of an attitude and sensibility of wonder toward everyday life and everyday objects. In other words, Mabe and other southern surrealists are inspired by Elvis to answer the challenge André Breton made to all "mad" artists of the everyday: "In [the object found] alone can we recognize the marvelous precipitate of desire. It alone can enlarge the universe, causing it to relinquish some of its opacity, letting us discover its extraordinary capacities for reserve, proportionate to the innumerable needs of the spirit. Daily life abounds, moreover, in just this sort of small discovery, where there is frequently an element of apparent gratuitousness, very probably a function of our provisional incomprehension, discoveries that seem to me not in the least unimportant." *Mad Love*, trans. Mary Ann Caws (Lincoln, Neb.: University of Nebraska Press, 1987 [1937]), pp. 13–15.

Chapter Twelve

1. Ed.—This chapter is my edited transcription of Paul MacLeod's oral presentation delivered at the Elvis conference. It incorporates additional comments Paul made in response to questions from the floor. With his permission, I have retained wherever desirable the original flavor of the spoken word. As in all the transcriptions of oral speech made for this book, I have been guided by the hermeneutic principles of Elvis Country. Above all, hermeneutics seeks to understand another person's language with respect to the speaker's life-process, his or her internal or mental history. Judging a speaker's language only according to the rules of formal grammar and usage disregards its all-important "linguistic disposition," the character of the speaker as revealed by the world held open by his speech. See F.D.E. Schleiermacher, "Hermeneutics: Outline of the 1819 Lectures," trans. Jan Wojcik and Roland Hass, *New Literary History* 10 (1) (1978): 1–16.

2. Ed.—Similar to variant spellings of Shakespeare in Elizabethan documents, confusion abounds in the spelling of proper names in the Elvis canon. Depending on which certificate, memorial, or marker you read, the name of Elvis's twin is spelled "Jessie" or "Jesse," while Elvis's middle name is variously "Aron" and "Aaron." Even the doctor who delivered Elvis and his stillborn brother on that bitterly cold night of January 7–8, 1935, compounded the polysemy by spelling the surviving baby's name "Evis Aaron" on the birth certificate. Though during his lifetime Elvis spelled his middle name "Aron," his father, Vernon, seems to have been responsible for "correcting" it to "Aaron" on his son's tombstone at Graceland. Many fans like Paul have henceforth followed the latter spelling fixed in death.

3. Ed.—Again notice the precise terminology. An important existential distinction obtains between a Graceland *Two*, which only wants to be a replica, an imitation of the one in Memphis, and a Graceland *Too*, which proves that anyone's home, if approached

in the right spirit, can be a Graceland also. In this sense Graceland Too is an act of appropriation every bit as creative and self-reliant as Faulkner's nearby Rowan Oak, whose name, by the way, is Scottish for, you guessed it, "graceland."

4. Ed.—The printed program read "Guitarist—Elvis Prestly."

5. Ed.—The theme of "sacrifice for Elvis" runs through the testimonials of many die-hard Elvis fans, but note here the quintessentially American appeal to material sacrifice, especially with regard to that greatest of all tropes of American consumption, the Cadillac. See John Brooks, *Showing Off in America: From Conspicuous Consumption to Parody Display* (Boston: Little, Brown, 1981), and Jay Hirsch, *Great American Dream Machines: Classic Cars of the 50s and 60s* (New York: Macmillan, 1985).

6. Ed.—Like Graceland in Memphis or, for that matter, the Vietnam Memorial Wall in Washington, D.C., Graceland Too in Holly Springs, Mississippi, is a magnet for what medieval scholar Gary Vikan calls the "impromptu votive communication." Comparing Graceland tourists to pilgrims and Elvis to a canonized saint, Vikan writes: "The second type of Graceland votive is the graffito message, the counterpart to the fourth-century sketch in the Chapel of St. Vartan. (Recall that the Piacenza pilgrim wrote the names of his parents on the couch at Cana.) In the early Christian *locus sanctus* such impromptu votive communications were common. Some called for or acknowledged help from the 'friend,' and some simply recorded a name, either of the pilgrim himself, or else of a relative or friend who could not make the journey. In either case the intention was the same: to perpetuate the pilgrim's 'presence' at the holy place, and more specifically, to actualize his communication with the saint commemorated there, as later pilgrims would read his words, and perhaps even recite them aloud." "Graceland as *Locus Sanctus*," in *Elvis + Marilyn: 2 x Immortal* (New York: Rizzoli, 1994), p. 163.

7. Ed.—As postmodern commentators point out, the American experience is increasingly a pastiche of heterogeneous reference. Here Elvis sightings, The Second Coming, and *Walpurgisnacht* coalesce in the "mystery" of Houdini. See Raymund Fitzsimons, *Death and the Magician: The Mystery of Houdini* (New York: Atheneum, 1981).

8. Ed.—See chapter frontispiece for a photograph of Paul with his lamp. As a response to the trauma of Elvis's death, the birth of the idea to create this artwork conforms nicely to Roger Manley's thesis concerning outsider and self-taught art (Chapter 9). Paul's auctioneer-like itemization of his lamp's special features, however, could also be fruitfully approached in the context of the African-American "toast." See Jackson Bruce, *Get Your Ass in the Water and Swim Like Me: Narrative Poetry from Black Oral Tradition* (Cambridge: Harvard University Press, 1974).

9. Ed.—Strengthening the connection between Elvis and self-taught art is the song that Elvis made his signature ballad in the last, tragic years of his life: "My Way." Ironically, this song, which testifies to what Heidegger calls *Jemeinigkeit* or "my-ownness," was cowritten by Paul Anka and trademarked by Frank Sinatra before Elvis made it definitively his own in 1973.

10. Ed.—It makes sense that the "The Greatest" and "The King of Rock 'n' Roll" would be friends. No stranger to Las Vegas, Muhammed Ali was a frequent backstage visitor at Elvis's concerts in the early 70s. Ali wore the purple robe Elvis gave him to his first Norton fight. See Muhammad Ali, with Richard Durham, *The Greatest: My Own Story* (New York: Random House, 1975).

11. Ed.—Paul's "secret sharing" in the history of Elvis finds its place in that venerable American tradition of Whitmanian empathy: "I am the man, I suffer'd, I was there." In a charming itinerary reminiscent of Marvel's *Fantastic Four*, Paul MacLeod enjoys the role of the "third man" invisibly present in Elvis's meetings with Muhammad Ali, James Brown, and Jackie Wilson.

12. Ed.—See Peter Nazareth's parallel discussion of the tête-à-tête between Elvis and Jackie Wilson in Chapter 4.

13. Ed.—Paul MacLeod's "true story" provides the perfect opportunity for examining a fundamental insight of personalist hermeneutics: "Language can be learned only by understanding what is spoken, and the inner make-up of a person, as well as the way in which external objects affect him, can only be understood from his speaking." Friedrich Schleiermacher, "General Theory and Art of Interpretation," in *The Hermeneutics Reader*, ed. Kurt Mueller-Vollmer (New York: Continuum, 1988), p. 76. In this sense "what is spoken" resides less in the literal statement than in the relationship *between* speaker and statement, which for Paul MacLeod is always a matter of defiant faith—"believe it or not."

14. Ed.—As Ted Harrison points out, numerology, wordplay, allegory, and other ingenious, aleatory techniques of midrash all play a prominent role in the increasingly religious character of the Elvis following. See *Elvis People: The Cult of the King* (London: HarperCollins/Fount, 1992). After nearly a dozen visits to Graceland Too and careful attention to what I heard there, it is clear to me that Paul MacLeod suffered a powerful conversion experience. Though the details are sketchy, it appears his vision to found Graceland Too came to him when he was accidentally locked up in the mausoleum at Forest Hill Cemetery together with James Brown, Ann-Margret, and, yes, Elvis's corpse. A photograph on display at Graceland Too shows Paul leaving the mausoleum "glowing red like a Cherokee Indian." "And you know what?" Paul quickly adds. "Elvis had Cherokee blood in him."

15. Ed.—From the spoken text of "Are You Lonesome Tonight." Given Paul's hermeneutic vigilance, it seems appropriate that he ends his talk quoting Elvis on the subject of the noble lie.

Chapter Thirteen

1. Ed.—In his own words Elvis MacLeod restates, with the help of "Walk a Mile in My Shoes," Wilhelm Dilthey's "highest form of understanding in which the totality of mental life is active." "It rests with two factors; envisaging an environment or situation vividly always stimulates re-experiencing; imagination can strengthen or diminish the emphasis on attitudes, powers, feelings, aspirations and ideas contained in our own lives and this enables us to re-produce the mental life of another person." "The Understanding of Other Persons and Their Life-Expressions," in *The Hermeneutics Reader*, ed. Kurt Mueller-Vollmer (New York: Continuum, 1988), p. 160.

2. Ed.—Since this essay is concerned with genealogies of reception, it is worth noting that father-and-son teams like Paul and Elvis MacLeod are a frequent theme in both Elvis impersonation and a type of theater it sometimes resembles, the world of championship wrestling. See the portrait of Julian "Elvis" Campo and Angelo "Elvis" Campo in *I Am Elvis: A Guide to Elvis Impersonators*, ed. Marie Cahill (New York: Simon and Schuster/Pocket Books, 1991), pp. 23–25; Ray F. Carson, *Counter Control for Championship Wrestling* (South Brunswick, NJ: A. S. Barnes, 1976); Roberta Morgan, *Main Event* (New York: Dial Press, 1979).

3. Ed.—In an interesting transvaluation of values, Elvis Presley, who began his career as the epitome of that fifties-style "rebel without a cause" known as the juvenile delinquent, ends up offering to a later, similarly disaffiliated generation its raison d'être. Elvis MacLeod's concept of "Generation E"—only the latest in genealogies of twentieth-century American culture that include the lost, angry, beat, boomer, Vietnam, Woodstock, new, and last generations—reminds us of the generational character of his-

tory and the indispensable need for generational theory in cultural studies. Robert Wohl's *The Generation of 1914* (Cambridge: Harvard University Press, 1979) is a classic of generational analysis. But also see such diverse studies as Maxine Davis, *The Lost Generation: A Portrait of American Youth Today* (New York: Macmillan, 1936); Samuel Putnam, *Paris Was Our Mistress: Memoirs of a Lost and Found Generation* (New York: Viking, 1947); Steven Watson, *The Birth of the Beat Generation: Visionaries, Rebels, and Hipsters* (New York: Pantheon Books, 1995); Charles Kaiser, *1968 in America: Music, Politics, Chaos, Counterculture, and the Shaping of a Generation* (New York: Weidenfeld and Nicolson, 1988); Elliott Landy, *Woodstock Vision: The Spirit of a Generation* (New York: Continuum, 1994). For recent attempts to "define" Generation X, see Karen Ritchie, *Marketing to Generation X* (New York: Lexington Books, 1995) and Geoffrey Holtz, *Welcome to the Jungle* (New York: St. Martin's Press, 1995).

4. Ed.—For an interesting analysis of the Clinton-Elvis connection, see Sebastian Mallaby, "Bill Presley and Elvis Clinton," *The Economist*, August 10, 1996.

5. Ed.—Ger Rijff has documented the unprecedented *Kulturkampf* incited by Elvis in the fifties. See his *Long Lonely Highway* (Amsterdam: Tutti Frutti Productions, 1985). Lest we forget, Elvis's "stage antics" on the Dorsey brothers, Milton Berle, Steve Allen, and Ed Sullivan shows occurred against the sentimental and moralistic backdrop of fifties TV. See Nina C. Leibman, *Living Room Lectures: The Fifties Family in Film and Television* (Austin: University of Texas Press, 1995).

6. Ed.—Graceland Too, the MacLeod's home, museum, and shrine devoted exclusively to Elvis, opened to the public on August 10, 1991.

7. Ed.—On the distinction between "fans" and "friends," see "We're Not Elvis Fans, We're Elvis Friends," *Commerical Appeal*, August 16, 1992.

8. Ed.—Recorded in February 1976 and released as a single in March with "For the Heart," "Hurt" is especially revered by Elvis fans. Describing an impersonator concert he attended during Death Week in Memphis, Ron Rosenbaum put it this way: "'*Hurt! Hurt! Hurt!*' It was a demand, a song request, yes, but in a sense it was more than that: it was a self-diagnosis. It was Elvis fans expressing what they, commoners, shared most deeply with the King: hurt. The pain of their lives, of life itself, a pain that was acute and unappeasable, whether experienced in Graceland or a trailer park; the kind of pain that pills and religions seek to minister to, the kind of pain that is the true source of the growing reach of the Elvis faith." "Among the Believers," *New York Times Magazine*, September 24, 1995, p. 53.

9. Ed.—Elvis MacLeod's dad, Paul, claims to have videotaped Elvis on his last motorcycle ride in front of the gates of Graceland. In the Graceland Too canon, this video (much discussed but never shown to the public) occupies the same place as the Zapruder film in the JFK assassination mythos.

10. Ed.—Elaine Dundy was one of the first to point out the connection between the lightning bolt insignia of the 1940s comic-book hero Captain Marvel Jr., "the most powerful boy in the world," and Elvis's own TCB logo, "Taking Care of Business" in a flash. See *Elvis and Gladys* (New York: St. Martin's Press, 1985), pp. 3–6 (and illustrations). Since the 1970s, rejection of modernism's hierarchical notions of the aesthetic has opened up the field of mass culture to analysis of popular constructions of identity and experience. For the history of comic books in the United States, see Les Daniels, *Marvel: Five Fabulous Decades of the World's Greatest Comics* (New York: H. N. Abrams, 1991) and *DC Comics: Sixty Years of the World's Favorite Comic Book Heroes* (Boston: Little, Brown, 1995). Specialized studies relevant to the superhero role played by Elvis in popular American culture include: Wiley Lee Umphlett, *Mythmakers of the*

American Dream: The Nostalgic Vision in Popular Culture (Lewisburg, Pa.: Bucknell University Press, 1983); Mike Benton, *Superhero Comics of the Golden Age: The Illustrated History* (Dallas: Taylor, 1992); Richard Reynolds, *Super Heroes: A Modern Mythology* (Jackson: University Press of Mississippi, 1994).

11. Ed.—Gary Vikan points out structural similarities between the fans' account of the life and death of Elvis and the typical *vita* of the medieval saint: "The *vitae*, most of which constitute an extended *apologia* responding to Albert Goldman's damning portrait of Elvis, speak instead of a dirt-poor southern boy who rose to fame and glory, of the love of a son for his mother, of humility and generosity, and of superhuman achievement in the face of adversity. They emphasize Elvis' profound spiritualism and his painful, premature death—a death described as coming at the hands of his own fans, whose merciless demands for Elvis entertainment exhausted and ultimately killed Elvis the entertainer. . . . In their eyes, he had died for them, and any further revelations of his seeming debauchery would, ironically, only reconfirm and intensify their image of his suffering." "Graceland as *Locus Sanctus*," in *Elvis + Marilyn: 2 x Immortal* (New York: Rizzoli, 1994), p. 150.

12. Ed.—Albert Goldman describes the same occurrence this way: "As they were carrying the coffin through the house door, there was a loud cracking overhead and a dead limb fell from one of the oak trees. Lamar [Fike] recalled Elvis saying many times: 'Wherever I am, if there is a way to communicate with you—I'll find it!'" *Elvis* (New York: McGraw-Hill, 1981), p. 578.

13. Ed.—The ancient Greeks experienced this "eternal gift" as "charisma," a divine quality with the power to bind communities. The sociologist Max Weber pioneered the application of this concept to the dynamics of group formation. The charismatic possesses "a certain quality of an individual personality by virtue of which he is set apart from ordinary men and treated as endowed with supernatural, superhuman, or at least specifically exceptional powers or qualities." *Economy and Society I-III* (New York: Bedminster Press, 1968), I, p. 241, quoted in Vikan, "Graceland as *Locus Sanctus*," p. 150. See also *Max Weber on Charisma and Institution Building: Selected Papers*, ed. S. N. Eisenstadt (Chicago: University of Chicago Press, 1968), and Edward Shils, *The Constitution of Society* (Chicago: University of Chicago Press, 1982).

14. Ed.—With its extreme density of Elvis memorabilia and décor, Graceland Too can be fruitfully appreciated in the context of outsider "home art." As Roger Manley explains, "The kind of *horror vacui* that accounts for much of the obsessive allover patterning of work and environment that characterizes much outsider art" may be motivated by the need to shut out social isolation and personal loss felt by marginalized individuals. Seen in this light, a roadside attraction like Graceland Too, in which the all-important guest book records not only names but social acceptance, uses Elvis to create a stage for social interaction otherwise impossible to the "outsider." See *Signs and Wonders: Outsider Art Inside North Carolina* (Raleigh: North Carolina Museum of Art, 1989), p. 18 ff.

Chapter Fourteen

1. Ed.—It is remarkable how much "serious" history can be recounted using popular culture and everyday life as springboards. Rijff's "Elvis" names both the political history of postwar Holland and the personal history of his postwar upbringing. For landmark scholarship in this area, see Phillippe Aries and Georges Duby, eds., *A History of Private Life* (Cambridge: Belknap/Harvard University Press, 1987–), five volumes to date. For phenomenology's contribution to theories of "history and private

life," see Rudolf A. Makkreel, "Husserl, Dilthey, and the Relation of the Life-World to History," in *Husserl and Contemporary Thought*, ed. John Sallis (Atlantic Highlands, N.J.: Humanities Press, 1983). Finally, see Benita Eisler's interesting case studies, *Private Lives: Men and Women of the Fifties* (New York: Franklin Watts, 1986).

2. Ed.—In the wake of Euro-Disney much has been written about the cultural colonization or "Americanization" of Europe—and ultimately the globe—since World War II. An early example is John Ney's *The European Surrender: A Descriptive Study of the American Social and Economic Conquest* (Boston: Little, Brown, 1970). Yet, as Rijff's personal account suggests, the dynamics of cultural change and exchange require a much more nuanced approach. See the excellent essays collected in John Dean and Jean-Paul Gabilliet, eds., *European Readings of American Popular Culture* (Westport, Conn.: Greenwood Press, 1996), especially Mel van Elteren, "Rocking and Rapping in the Dutch Welfare State."

3. Ed.—Elvis Presley's displacement of the cowboy as the symbol of America is one of the least researched histories of American cultural influence abroad. Among other international relations, Elvis as symbol of America helps to explain the enormous popularity of Elvis impersonation both among U.S. immigrant populations and worldwide: The Elvis impersonator is a kind of Statue of Liberty in full swivel. For the role of Roy Rogers in this story, see Robert W. Phillips, *Roy Rogers: A Biography* (Jefferson, N.C.: McFarland, 1995).

4. Ed.—It is worth noting the history of the term "G.I.," since it plays a major role in both the postwar European and postarmy American receptions of Elvis: "Originally abbreviation for *galvanized iron*, army clerks' term for items such as trash cans, but later taken to be abbreviation for *general issue* or *government issue*, and extended to include all articles and finally soldiers themselves" (*American Heritage Dictionary*). Given the European war experience, Elvis's postarmy movie roles in *G.I. Blues* and *Blue Hawaii* were caught up in a vastly different climate of reception than that in the United States. Similarly, the story of Elvis's military service and problematic postarmy career (John Lennon: "Elvis died in the army.") has attracted a sizable Elvis following among Vietnam veterans. For background to this fascinating subcultural mosaic, see Richard R. Moser, *The New Winter Soldiers: GI and Veteran Dissent During the Vietnam Era* (New Brunswick, N.J.: Rutgers University Press, 1996).

5. Ed.—Between 1969 and 1976 the Las Vegas Hilton (originally the International) was the site of the Elvis Summer Festival. A precursor of today's Elvis Week in Memphis, this annual August extravaganza attracted fans from around the world.

6. Ed.—Elvis has inspired not only folk or self-taught artists but also a special breed of bright, curious, knowledgeable people I call "self-taught scholars." Clearly, Ger Rijff's research at the Library of Congress and Memphis Public Library should be regarded not only as scholarship but as scholarship of a kind that other scholars, either out of prejudice, ignorance, or the socializations of formal education, have neglected to pursue. Elvis MacLeod is another example in this book of the self-taught Elvis scholar. Though he failed to graduate from high school, he has taught himself writing, computer, and archival skills manifestly more advanced and enterprising than those of many of the Ole Miss students I teach.

7. *Memphis Press-Scimitar*, July 21, 1954.

8. *Long Lonely Highway* (Amsterdam: Tutti Frutti Productions, 1985). See Peter Guralnick, *Lost Highway* (Boston: Godine, 1979) and *Last Train to Memphis: The Rise of Elvis Presley* (New York: Little, Brown, 1994).

9. The U.S. title was *Elvis Close-Up: Rare, Intimate, Unpublished Photographs of Elvis Presley in 1956*, by Jay B. Leviton and Ger J. Rijff, with an introduction by Kurt

Loder (New York: Fireside/Simon and Schuster, 1988). My other U.S. publication was *The Cool King* (Wilmington, Del.: Atomium Books, 1990).

10. *60 Million TV Viewers Can't Be Wrong! Elvis' Legendary Performances on the Ed Sullivan Show*, texts by Andrew Solf and Gordon Minto (Amsterdam: Tutti Frutti Productions, 1994); *Inside Jailhouse Rock* (Amsterdam: Tutti Frutti Productions, 1994); *Growing Up with the Memphis Flash*, texts by W. A. Harbinson and Kay Wheeler (Amsterdam: Tutti Frutti Productions, 1994); *Songs of Innocence* (Amsterdam: Tutti Frutti Productions, 1995).

Chapter Fifteen

1. Greil Marcus, *Dead Elvis: A Chronicle of a Cultural Obsession* (New York: Doubleday, 1991).

2. Ed.—Critical social theory utilizes a precise concept of the "articulation" between cultural production and social organization. "Cultural studies delineates how cultural artifacts articulate social ideologies, values, and representations of gender, race, and class, and how these phenomena are related to each other. Situating cultural texts in their social context thus involves tracing the articulations through which societies produce culture and how culture in turn shapes society through its influence on individuals and groups." Douglas Kellner, *Media Culture: Cultural Studies, Identity, and Politics Between the Modern and the Postmodern* (New York: Routledge, 1995), p. 25.

3. Ed.—In the first instance "commodification" refers to the manufacture of material goods, especially consumer items. But in critical social theory the term also connotes Marxist themes of alienation, mystification, and sexual displacement generated by capitalist exchange relations. Such "commodities," as opposed to mere physical products of labor and their material contexts, articulate "a definite social relation between men, that assumes, in their eyes, the fantastic form of a relation between things." Karl Marx, *Capital*, in *The Marx-Engels Reader*, ed. R. C. Tucker (New York: Norton, 1972), p. 217.

4. Ed.—In fact, one of the most influential works of the Middle Ages, Thomas à Kempis's *Imitatio Christi* (1426), was a guidebook to Jesus impersonation. See Johan Huizinga, *The Waning of the Middle Ages: A Study of the Forms of Life, Thought, and Art in France and the Netherlands in the XIVth and XVth Centuries* (Garden City, N.Y.: Doubleday/Anchor, 1954). Both literate and bodily religious experiences also intersect in the meditative practices of seventeenth-century English poets. See Louis Martz, *The Poetry of Meditation: A Study in English Religious Literature of the Seventeenth Century* (New Haven: Yale University Press, 1954).

5. Ed.—The renewed emphasis on the importance of experiencing pain, loss, grief, and anxiety in twentieth-century existentialism, for example, may be viewed as a reaction against the quest to eliminate pain in modern life and religious experience. See Elaine Scarry, *The Body in Pain: The Making and Unmaking of the World* (New York: Oxford University Press, 1985), especially against the vast backdrop cast by Roselyne Rey, *The History of Pain*, trans. Louise Elliott Wallace, J. A. Cadden, and S. W. Cadden (Cambridge: Harvard University Press, 1995). For a more contemporary treatment of the problem relevant to Elvis, see David B. Morris, "Postmodern Pain," in *Heterotopia: Postmodern Utopia and the Body Politic*, ed. Tobin Siebers (Ann Arbor: University of Michigan Press, 1994).

6. Ed.—For the classic essay introducing the concept of "aura" in relation to the mass manufacture of material objects, see Walter Benjamin, "The Work of Art in an Age of Mechanical Reproduction," in *Illuminations*, trans. Harry Zohn (New York: Schocken Books, 1986).

7. Ed.—The relationship between the body of Elvis, both alive and dead, and its corporate commodification raises, among other things, interesting questions about the role of copyright, trademark, and intellectual property law in a postmodern era. See David Wall, *Policing the Soul of Elvis* (forthcoming).

8. Ed.—Though striking exceptions exist. As any tourist to Rome will attest, every imaginable souvenir of Jesus and the Pope—from Day Glo buttons to holographic key chains—is hawked in the shadows of the Vatican. Or closer to home, in Mexico images of Elvis on velvet coexist happily with those ever popular standards, Jesus and the Virgin of Guadalupe.

9. Marcus, *Dead Elvis*, p. 122.

10. Ed.—While the body plays an equally important role in both systems, Elvis as "other Jesus" is present not in sacred bread and wine but in secular commodities like bubble-gum cards and vials of sweat. One should not conclude, however, that Elvis's "otherness" can be reduced to a simple contrast between the sacred of organized religions and the secular of popular culture. For a toolkit of usable discourses of otherness in contemporary cultural analysis, see *Encountering the Other(s): Studies in Literature, History, and Culture*, ed. Gisela Brinker-Gabler (Albany: State University of New York Press, 1995), especially Angelika Bammer, "Xenophobia, Xenophilia, and No Place to Rest."

11. Ed.—John Strausbaugh makes a similar point: "Elvism is part of a larger move from *populist religions* like Santeria or Mediterranean Catholicism to *popular-culture religions*. The degree to which popular culture impinges on all facets of modern life and influences the formation of belief systems cannot be overstated. If Western civilization, with its mass media and all-pervasive transmission of commerical culture, 'killed God' in the first half of the twentieth century, in the latter half of the century this same popular culture busied itself refilling the void it had created, providing the masses with new myths, new legends, a new pantheon of pop-star gods." John Strausbaugh, *E: Reflections on the Birth of the Elvis Faith* (New York: Blast Books, 1995), p. 13.

12. Ed.—The theory of "commodity fetishism" has been dominated by feminist appropriations of Freud in an attempt to construct a unified theory of phallocentric society. See Jane Gaines, "Women and Representation: Can We Enjoy Alternative Pleasure?" in *American Media and Mass Culture: New Left Perspectives*, ed. D. Lazere (Berkeley: University of California Press). One wonders, however, whether the commodity fetishism inspired by Elvis conforms to such a model. For fascinating discussions relevant to the prehistory of Elvis's notorious preference for pink, see Penny Sparke, *As Long as It's Pink: The Sexual Politics of Taste* (San Francisco: Pandora, 1995).

13. Ed.—Elvis's "multiple manifestations" are not only metaphysical but multicultural, a condition for which the Santeria experience of blacks in the Diaspora provides a highly suggestive figure. See George Brandon, *Santeria from Africa to the New World: The Dead Sell Memories* (Bloomington: Indiana University Press, 1993).

14. Marcus, *Dead Elvis*, p. 121.

15. Ed.—See Stuart Ewen and Elizabeth Ewen, *Channels of Desire: Mass Images and the Shaping of American Consciousness* (New York: McGraw-Hill, 1982) and Arthur Asa Berger, *Manufacturing Desire: Media, Popular Culture, and Everyday Life* (New Brunswick, N.J.: Transaction, 1996).

16. Ed.—Elvis impersonation is one of the most maligned and misunderstood features of the Elvis world. And for good reason: It blurs not only the boundaries of the sacred and secular but also the boundaries between gender and sexuality. Thus the simulation generated by the sign system of Elvis can also be seen to include elements of camp, transvestism, and cross-dressing—in other words, all the repressed features of

the history of Western drama. For an entertaining overview, see Michael F. Moore, *Drag! Male and Female Impersonators on Stage, Screen, and Television: An Illustrated World History* (Jefferson, N.C.: McFarland, 1994). Contemporary gender analysis hasn't yet discovered Elvis impersonation, but the critical issues are canvassed in *Crossing the Stage: Controversies on Cross-Dressing*, ed. Leslie Ferris (New York: Routledge, 1993). Pamela Robertson's study of Mae West impersonation is a model for future Elvis research: *Guilty Pleasures: Feminist Camp from Mae West to Madonna* (Durham: Duke University Press, 1996). For a brilliant analysis of constructions of sexual identity in pop art and glitter rock (Iggy Pop, David Bowie, Alice Cooper, et al.) parallel to Elvis's Vegas performances, see Van M. Cagle, *Reconstructing Pop/Subculture: Art, Rock, and Andy Warhol* (Thousand Oaks, Calif.: Sage, 1995). Less attention has been devoted to "male impersonation" in popular music, but see Lucy O' Brien, *She Bop: The Definitive History of Women in Rock, Pop, and Soul* (New York: Penguin Books, 1996), especially ch. 8: "She Wears the Trousers: Artistry, Androgyny, and the Lesbian Question."

17. Ed.—More specifically, even the joy of being American. As the international character of Elvis impersonation suggests, Kauffman's liberation of the "foreign guy" to become "Elvis" is facilitated by a further sign system signifying "America, the land of the free."

18. See Umberto Eco, *A Theory of Semiotics* (Bloomington: Indiana University Press, 1976), and my own *Postmodern Semiotics: Material Culture and the Forms of Postmodern Life* (Oxford: Blackwell, 1995).

19. Umberto Eco, "Social Life as a Sign System," in *Structuralism: An Introduction*, ed. D. Robey (Oxford: Clarendon Press), pp. 57–72.

20. Ed.—Granted that the Las Vegas Elvis sign system is the most developed for impersonation, why is the "image" of the young Elvis still *consciously* preferred? This is a question perhaps for the psychoanalysis of American Elvis culture. My preliminary suspicion is that it has to do with a collective national complex of nostalgia and despair in which "Elvis" provides a screen for both the confession of American social decline (fat Elvis) and its denial (thin Elvis).

21. Roland Barthes, *Mythologies*, trans. A. Lavers (New York: Hill and Wang, 1972).

22. Ed.—In fact, one of Elvis's most characteristic expressions to his family and friends was the question: "Are ya havin' fun?"

23. Ed.—The more general code of Elvis is available for appropriation by other generations too. See Chapter 13, "Generation E."

Chapter Sixteen

1. Ed.—This is my edited transcription of a sermon preached without text or notes by Reverend Howard Finster at the Elvis conference. With his permission, I have retained wherever desirable the original flavor of the spoken word. As in all the transcriptions of oral speech made for this book, I have been guided by the hermeneutics of Elvis Country outlined in my introduction. For further discussions of language and method, see my introductory footnotes to Chapters 7, 11, 12, and 13. Finster's speech bears all the regional, religious, and rural traits of his north Alabama–Georgia upbringing in the early half of this century. Most scholars take the position that such "nonstandard" speech should be regularized for publication. They naturally assume that their own professional standards of grammatical correctness are superior to colloquial speech and that "improving it" shows respect for the "weak." On the contrary, throughout the transcriptions made for this book I have been guided by the understanding that language is not only an instrument for information but a space of inti-

macy through which human beings inhabit their worlds and share those worlds with others. Language, like music, establishes these worlds, beyond technical-logical rules, in such things as tone, accent, rhythm, melody, and the multitudinous regional, familial, generational, and idiosyncratic variants to which speech is prone. In the hermeneutics of Elvis Country, every human being is endowed with a basic linguistic disposition shaped by his or her unique moment in history. Above all, it is this unique linguistic disposition, in all the fullness of the speaker's personal history, that I have respected in Howard Finster's sermon.

2. Ed.—Compare Finster's opening account of his trip to Mississippi to the opening paragraph of Faulkner's *Light in August*: "Sitting beside the road, watching the wagon mount the hill toward her, Lena thinks, 'I have come from Alabama: a fur piece. All the way from Alabama a-walking. A fur piece.' Thinking *although I have not been quite a month on the road I am already in Mississippi, further from home than I have ever been before. I am now further from Doane's Mill than I have been since I was twelve years old.*" Faulkner sought to reproduce in idiosyncrasies of speech and thought the phenomenology of space and time experienced by his characters. For Howard, as for Faulkner's Lena, the trip to Mississippi is a "fur piece" full of border crossings.

3. Ed.—Like Elvis, Finster too has a fondness for Cadillacs. See Chapter 9 and the photo of Howard's Cadillac at Paradise Garden. Meditating on this Presley icon, Finster prepared himself mentally for his "Sermon on Alvis" as well as produced mnemonic keepsakes of his journey to Mississippi.

4. Ed.—Titled *Happy 200th Anniversary Tennessee*, this piece (reproduced at the beginning of this chapter and on the cover) is one of Finster's most ambitious works of the past five years.

5. Ed.—Sometime in the winter or summer of 1976, after nearly forty years as a country preacher in Alabama and Georgia, Finster, at the age of sixty, received a vision from God that challenged him to rededicate his life to "sacred art." As the story goes, he took out a dollar bill and painted George Washington, the first of many American folk heroes, including Elvis, he would enshrine on plywood, sheet metal, aluminum foil, and other found materials. In addition to themes in American history, Finster uses art as "sermons in paint" that communicate his religious messages and visions to the masses. See Norman Girardot, *The World's Folk Art Church: Reverend Howard Finster and Family* (Bethlehem, Penn.: Lehigh University Art Galleries, 1986); James Smith Pierce, *Howard Finster: Painter of Sermons* (Lexington: Folk Art Society of Kentucky, 1988); Howard Finster and Tom Patterson, *Howard Finster, Stranger from Another World: Man of Visions Now on This Earth* (New York: Abbeville Press, 1989); Howard Finster, *Howard Finster: Man of Visions* (Atlanta: Peachtree, 1989); and J. F. Turner, *Howard Finster: Man of Visions* (New York: Knopf, 1989). See also the excellent documentary by Dave Carr, Julie Desroberts, and Randy Paskal, *Howard Finster: Man of Visions*, First Run Icarus Films, 1988.

6. Ed.—This spelling preserves Finster's distinctive pronunciation of Elvis, which is characteristic of a whole subculture of rural southerners with similar backgrounds and experiences. Their Elvis—as "Alvis"—is not a mainstream pop icon, a commodity fetish. Rather, he is a miracle of native soil, the righteous vindication of an oppressed region and people, a folk hero and popular saint, an angel loved by God.

7. Ed.—Actually, Finster was nineteen years old when Elvis was born in 1935.

8. Ed.—Like many philosophers before him, Finster has a "great man" theory of history. What Finster calls "blocks" are steps and stages, often "filled in" by outstanding individuals (American presidents, inventors, cultural icons like Elvis and Marilyn), in the providential unfolding of God's plan not only on earth but throughout all cre-

ation. The majority of Finster's art and writing is based on hermetic interpretations of the Bible as prophecy, with emphasis on the special role of America in the divine plan. For Finster's most elaborate vision of the future to date, see his *Vision of 1982, Vision of 200 Light Years Away, Space Born of Three Generations, from Earth to the Heaven of Heavens* (Summerville, Ga.: privately published, 1982).

9. Ed.—The theme of creativity and invention abounds in Finster's oeuvre. Like William Blake, that other painter-poet visionary whom he rivals, Finster is obsessed with the conception of divinity as awesome creative power—poetic, artistic, scientific, technological, and (especially) sexual. In addition to a very active career as a minister, which by his count included 4,625 sermons, 400 funerals, and 200 weddings, Finster has practiced some twenty-two trades, including repairing TVs, lawnmowers, and bicycles. Although he began his artistic career at the age of sixty, in just twenty years Finster has managed to create over 30,000 works of sacred art, including several elaborate garden environments, paintings, prints, sculptures, albums of his own musical compositions and sermons, and new techniques of architectural design and construction. In fact, Finster has invented new techniques in almost every area in which he has been active: engraving, the grafting of plants, and casting cement. Back at home in his repair shop in Pennville, Georgia, Finster is still at work on that ultimate expression of God's creative power—perpetual motion. Given all this productivity, it is not surprising that Finster would be drawn to Elvis Presley, the most prolific recording artist of all time, and would interpret Elvis's unpecedented record sales (which, in some estimates, have reached 2 billion) as nothing short of divine.

10. Ed.—Like Andy Warhol in the sixties, Finster has figured out a way to appropriate "the media"—whether traditional visual arts, mass manufacture, entertainment, or news—for preaching his message. Hence his readiness to use national symbols like Washington and Lincoln, folk heroes like Edison and Ford, branded identities like Coca-Cola, and global icons like Elvis and Marilyn as vehicles for his visions. In this regard, Finster's work implies a pedagogy open to entertainment and popular culture similar to that advocated by some educational reformers, myself included. After forty years as a minister, Finster became disillusioned with conventional preaching when a survey he conducted at his church indicated that very few could remember what he said in his sermons. Clearly, Finster's turn to popular modes of expression is exemplified by his fascination with Elvis Presley as far more than a great entertainer. As he said in a 1978 interview, "I had a deep feeling about Elvis Presley, a real deep feeling about Elvis. I felt that, in the last years of his life, he was meant to be a minister of the gospel. That was the feeling that come to me. Because with his publicity, he could have won more souls than anybody in the world. I said to myself that if I ever had the publicity of Elvis Presley, I would use it for the Lord." Interview with Susie Mee in *Howard Finster: Man of Visions* (Atlanta: Peachtree, 1989), n.p.

11. Ed.—There has been much speculation, pro and con, on the influence of Pentecostalism on Elvis Presley's musical style. Most of the critics, however, have been many degrees removed from the actual culture and practice of Pentecostal worship. Finster gives a credible, first-person account of the evangelical affinities between rock 'n' roll and holy rollin'. Sadly, this ecstatic common spirit—"pure and alive" as Finster says—has been buried in pedantic tomes of religious history. Yet see Harvey Cox, *Fire from Heaven: The Rise of Pentecostal Spirituality and the Reshaping of Religion in the Twenty-First Century* (Reading, Mass.: Addison-Wesley Publishers, 1995).

12. Ed.—Finster plays the banjo and writes his own songs. In the documentary *Howard Finster: Man of Visions,* he indulges in a few of his own Elvisian moves, strumming his banjo while sliding across the floor on his knees.

13. Ed.—Finster's essentially democratic definition of the folk artist as "the man who does his own thing" may be more appropriate to the self-taught or outsider artist. Since the 1960s, folklorists have sought to limit the term "folk art" by emphasizing its roots in traditional, communal values usually handed down from parent to child. See Charles G. Zug III, "Folk Art and Outsider Art: A Folklorist's Perspective," in *The Artist Outsider: Creativity and the Boundaries of Culture*, ed. Michael D. Hall and Eugene W. Metcalf Jr. (Washington, D.C.: Smithsonian Institution Press, 1994), pp. 145–160.

14. Ed.—Finster used the occasion of his invitation to speak at the University of Mississippi to draw attention to his outsider status vis-à-vis formal education. His affirmations of artistic and intellectual independence notwithstanding, the sting of disenfranchisement is unmistakable in his remarks. Here another meaning of "Alvis" arises from the world of poor southern whites represented by Howard Finster: "Alvis" means overcoming the stigma of limited formal education through tenacious personal achievement. Consider the irony in Finster's words—"I couldn't get inside of a schoolhouse door"—in that in 1962 the University of Mississippi attempted to deny admission to its first black student, James Meredith, and then again in 1995 and 1996 repeated the same gesture against another historically excluded group—"Alvis." See Thomas G. Dyer, "Higher Education in the South Since the Civil War: Historiographical Issues and Trends," in *The Web of Southern Social Relations: Women, Family and Education*, ed. Walter J. Fraser Jr., R. Frank Saunders Jr., and Jon L. Wakelyn (Athens: University of Georgia Press, 1985), pp. 127–145; David G. Sansing, *Making Haste Slowly: The Troubled History of Higher Education in Mississippi* (Jackson: University Press of Mississippi, 1990); and my introduction to this volume.

15. Ed.—Note how Finster's memory of his educational impoverishment is followed by an even stronger memory of the religious hope and compensation offered by his childhood schoolhouse. To the generation of "Alvis," more compelling than the roll call in the classroom is the roll call in heaven.

16. Ed.—As figures employed in the spiritual narrative known as the "parable," the difference between the mustard or wheat seed and Elvis Presley is important. Whereas the universal meaning of the former is rooted in natural experience, Elvis is an image created by mass media. In a fascinating appropriation whose significance has not been fully appreciated, Finster updates the parables of Jesus using the materials of popular media culture. For the history of figuration in spiritual narrative, see Eric Auerbach's classic essay "Figura," in *Scenes from the Drama of European Literature: Six Essays* (New York: Meridian Books, 1959). For the history of American folk preaching, with valuable insights into gospel culture, see Bruce A. Rosenberg, *Can These Bones Live? The Art of the American Folk Preacher*, rev. ed. (Urbana: University of Illinois Press, 1988).

17. Ed.—At this point in his sermon Finster began displaying various Elvis artworks he has created, especially the famous winged *Elvis at 3 Is a Angel to Me.*

18. Ed.—As Roger Manley points out, "There is something about the notion of potential, rather than Elvis's realized adulthood, that appeals to Finster." See Chapter 9 and the famous photograph of Elvis at three years old reproduced in Chapter 5.

19. Ed.—This is a good formulation of Finster's personalist theory of creativity that stresses the heartfelt involvement of the artist in every work of art. Though Finster also stresses productivity (he's up to 37,163 works of sacred art and counting), he rejects mass reproduction on spiritual not aesthetic grounds.

20. Ed.—It's worth noting that the three most recognizable names in the history of the world all have special claims to being *southern* products—Elvis, Jesus, and Coca-Cola. As a kind of folk Andy Warhol, Finster has given the art world his own powerful

treatment of these global icons. See Kinky Friedman, *Elvis, Jesus, and Coca-Cola* (New York: Bantam Books, 1994).

21. Ed.—Like William Blake's "bounding line," Finster's "two faces with one line" could be taken as a key definition of his approach to drawing. With this plywood cutout portrait, Finster gives his own ingenious definition to Gottdiener's proposition of Elvis as "other Jesus." See Chapter 15.

22. Ed.—Originally named the Plant Farm Museum, Paradise Garden is a rambling two-acre sculpture and art-object park Finster has created out of the swampy land behind his home in Pennville, Georgia. A walk-in Bible, a museum of history and technology, a repository of surrealist found objects, Paradise Garden has been called "Finster's own spiritual self-portrait, portraying his longing to improve the world through invention and to lead mankind to a better way of life." Pierce, *Howard Finster: Painter of Sermons*," p. 15. Finster's description of the hanging portrait—always moving, kept alive by the wind—identifies Alvis as the *genius loci* of Paradise Garden.

23. Ed.—This remarkable series of meditations on dogs—"Hound Dog," the dog of the New Testament parables, and Finster's own poodle dog—is an excellent example of his anagogical method grounded in scriptural exegesis. But Pierce has also pointed out the similarities with surrealism: "A surrealist *après la lettre*, Finster has independently invented the processes and formal principles introduced by the pioneers of modernism. He follows the flow of his visions in a continuous stream of the conscious and the subconscious, employing automatic writing, neologisms, the automatism of scribbling, doodling, dripping, decalcomania, finger painting, and transparent overlay. He appropriates and transforms found images as well as ready-mades and *objets-trouvés*, reassembling them in surprising juxtapositions, double and triple images, sudden scale shifts, and fusions of painting and sculpture, word and image, images evoking words, words releasing images, uncovering the surreal, the real world behind the real—in Finster's case, the anagogical sphere of 'simultions' rather than the Freudian realm of the sexual subconscious explored by the surrealists in the twenties and thirties." *Howard Finster: Painter of Sermons*, pp. 16–17. See also Peter Nazareth on "dogs" in Chapter 4.

24. Ed.—Here begins the long-awaited account of Finster's encounter with the angel of Alvis in Paradise Garden. It is a highly stylized set piece with interesting analogues in the Christian folk tradition of spiritual visitation. It is also an impressive prose poem, reminiscent of James Dickey in its mixture of intense dramatic experience and folksy verve. Finster's deflation of the high point of revelation with a joke—"Howard, I'm on a tight schedule"—draws upon deep wells of proverbial insight into the human-divine relationship. As the old Jewish adage would have it, "Man thinks, God laughs."

25. Ed.—Like William Blake, whose intense vision of his dead brother Robert converted him to art and religion, Howard Finster has placed equal emphasis on a childhood vision he had of his dead sister Abbie. See his moving account in *Howard Finster: Man of Visions*, n.p.

26. Ed.—Ron Rosenbaum, discussing the conflicting theories of Elvis's sexuality (or what, with appropriate humor, he calls the "Leg Wiggle Controversy"), reported Finster's views this way: "For Finster, a self-proclaimed 'man of visions' who says he's been visited himself by an angelic vision of Elvis, the Leg Wiggle was on a Mission for God: 'Elvis was sent by God to revive sex,' he told me, to 'stimulate sex and nature' at a time America needed to raise its reproduction rate. Elvis was, although the reverend didn't put it this way, a fertility totem, the baby maker of the baby boom. (Presumably that's why, when God saw the population rising too rapidly, He sent us the Captain and Tennille.)" "Among the Believers," *New York Times Magazine*, September 24, 1995, p. 56.

27. Ed.—Finster has also preached his "rules of sex" in a magnificent work of art entitled *Cow Woman: The Rules of Sex.*

28. Ed.—A bomb-size sculpture at Paradise Garden bearing various warnings against war and nuclear holocaust.

Chapter Seventeen

1. Ed.—The allusion here is to a perceived class difference between Tupelo and Oxford, Elvis and Ole Miss, that made it "embarrassing" for a proper Ole Miss coed to show public interest in Elvis. Historians of the fifties are beginning to recognize, however, that Elvis contributed to the women's movement by encouraging greater freedom of sexual expression, especially in straitjacketed patriarchal societies like the South.

2. Ed.—The combination of personal public display and private shyness is often found in outsider artists who seek social acceptance without social conformity. Unusual modes of dress are what Roger Manley calls "mobile signposts of outsider work": "Distinctive canes and hats offer outsiders opportunities to attract attention and make public statements, but at the same time they are traditional opportunities for personal adornment." Roger Manley, *Signs and Wonders: Outsider Art Inside North Carolina* (Raleigh: North Carolina Museum of Art, 1989), p. 66. See Chapter 9.

3. Ed.—It is probably true that the 1995 Ole Miss Elvis conference is the most publicized Elvis event, second only to his death. I have documented 325 articles (of an estimated 500–600) published or broadcast worldwide between April and December 1995. Unlike the death of Elvis, however, the Elvis conference was an *academic* event that raised new critical questions about how scholars and the mass media communicate. For a good collection of essays on this theme, see Marjorie Garber, Jann Matlock, and Rebecca L. Walkowitz, eds., *Media Spectacles* (New York: Routledge, 1993).

4. *Television News Index and Abstracts*, August 1977 (Nashville: Vanderbilt Television News Archive).

5. Interviews with William Behanna, director of press relations, A. C. Nielsen Companies, and Connie Anthes, manager of communications, the Arbitron Company.

6. Interview with David Brinkley.

7. *Elvis.* NBC Television news special, August 16, 1977.

8. Ed.—Notice how in the age of political correctness "redneck" has become an acceptable term in the media since Elvis's death. See Chapter 6. Neal Gregory points out how Elvis's death provoked a controversy among the nation's media powers—a controversy that reveals not just issues of corporate management but the dissemination of fundamental, socially influential attitudes toward class and cultural values. Eighteen years later, the controversy surrounding the Elvis conference exposed the same prejudices in the media and at our universities. The U.S. media did not report on the Elvis conference so much as participate in its frivolous, condescending reception. Although dozens of journalists editorialized over the Rodney King affair, few were capable of critically assessing the same issues of racism and classism raised by the Elvis Presley conference. A study of the "redneck" in the national media has yet to appear, but see Christopher P. Campbell, *Race, Myth, and the News* (Thousand Oaks, Calif.: Sage Publications, 1995).

9. Interview with David Brinkley.

10. Interview with Burton Benjamin Jr.

11. Ed.—See, for example, Robin Ridless, *Ideology and Art: Theories of Mass Culture from Walter Benjamin to Umberto Eco* (New York: P. Lang, 1984); James Lull, *Media, Communication, Culture: A Global Approach* (New York: Columbia Univer-

sity Press, 1995); James M. Fallows, *Breaking the News: How the Media Undermine American Democracy* (New York: Pantheon Books, 1996).

12. Interview with Harry Rosenthal.

13. Interview with Molly Ivins. Ed.—Note the interesting reverse rhetorical connotations here. Just as America was slow to accord black people the legitimacy and dignity conveyed by the title "Mr.," so too a similar uneasy reluctance (concealed by humor) with respect to Elvis the "redneck." See Will Campbell's conscious usage of "Mr. Presley" in Chapter 6.

14. Interview with Jerry Doolittle.

15. Interview with Hendrik Hertzberg.

16. White House press release, August 17, 1977. See also *Public Papers of the Presidents of the United States: Jimmy Carter, 1977* (Washington, D.C.: Government Printing Office, 1978), p. 1478.

17. PElvis homepage at http://www.princeton.edu/~pelvis/.

18. Ed.—See Bill Malone's discussion of Elvis's impact on modern country music at the end of Chapter 1.

19. Ed.—1967, "Best Sacred Performance," *How Great Thou Art* (album); 1974, "Best Inspirational Performance," *How Great Thou Art* (live version).

20. Ed.—Elvis's movie career is probably the least analyzed and appreciated aspect of his history. See my "Camp Elvis: Totem and Taboo, Hawaiian Style," *Southern Reader* 6 (1991). The Elvis Movie is the subject of the Third Annual International Conference on Elvis Presley: "The King's Reign: Elvis in Hollywood, 1956–1969," August 4–9, 1997.

21. Interview with George David Weiss. Ed.—See Nazareth's parallel discussion of this episode in Chapter 4.

22. Mike Royko, "Here's to King Elvis—He Fooled a Generation," *Chicago Daily News*, August 17, 1977.

23. Steve Allen, "TV Is Junk Food for the Mind," *U.S. News & World Report*, March 13, 1978.

24. Letters to the editor, *U.S. News & World Report*, April 24, 1978. Interview with Robert Ames, associate editor.

25. David Halberstam, *The Fifties* (New York: Villard Books, 1993), p. 456.

26. Ed.—Little did Janice Gregory know that university officials were meeting even as she spoke to discuss the cancellation of any future Elvis conferences at the University of Mississippi.

27. Ed.—See Greil Marcus's superb deconstruction of an anonymous Memphian's statement, "[Elvis] stuck to his roots and I think that was part of his downfall." "1986: Good Book on Elvis Published—Shocking Truth Revealed," in *Dead Elvis: A Chronicle of a Cultural Obsession* (New York: Anchor/Doubleday, 1991), p. 112.

28. *Elvis Monthly,* December 1977.

29. Eudora Welty, *Place in Fiction* (New York: House of Books, 1957), n.p.

30. Ed.—The best general discussion of subcultural fans and the media can be found in Dick Hebdige, *Subculture: The Meaning of Style* (London: Methuen, 1979). See also Lawrence Grossberg, "Is There a Fan in the House?" in *The Adoring Audience*, ed. Lisa A. Lewis (New York: Routledge, 1992), pp. 9–29.

31. Raymond A. Moody Jr., *Elvis After Death* (Atlanta: Peachtree Publishers, 1987).

32. Ed.—See Ted Harrison, *Elvis People: The Cult of the King* (London: Harper-Collins/Fount, 1992), John Strausbaugh, *E: Reflections on the Birth of the Elvis Faith* (New York: Blast Books, 1995), and Gary Vikan's forthcoming study, *Saint Elvis*. See also Chapters 15 and 16 in this volume.

33. Interview with Janelle McComb.

34. Ed.—The Elvis Presley Memorial Chapel, dedicated August 17, 1979, stands close by the birthplace in Tupelo, Mississippi.

35. "Amazing Graceland," editorial, *Washington Post,* January 30, 1994.

36. "Dylan Thomas: A Sobering View," *Economist*, January 14, 1995.

37. Lee Hockstader, "Elvis Scene in Moscow!" *Washington Post,* August 17, 1993.

38. Ed.—Modern academia is notorious for lacking a sense of humor or even seeing the relationship between humor and intellect. The Russian literary theorist Mikhail Bakhtin is perhaps the best guide to this repressed theme in the history of Western culture and education. Elvis inspires what Bakhtin calls the "carnivalesque symposium." See Mikhail Bakhtin, *Rabelais and His World,* trans. Hèléne Iswolsky (Bloomington: Indiana University Press, 1984 [1965]), p. 224, especially ch. 1, "Rabelais in the History of Laughter," pp. 59–144.

39. *The Ed Sullivan Show*, CBS Televsion, September 9, 1956.

40. *Elvis*. CBS Television news special, August 18, 1977.

41. Bob Greene, "He Would Have Laughed," *Chicago Sun-Times*, August 19, 1977.

42. David Landis, "Elvis Stamp of Approval: Post Offices Mobbed," *USA Today*, January 11, 1993.

43. *Neue Züricker Zeitung*, Zürich, Switzerland, August 18, 1977.

About the Editor
and Contributors

Vernon Chadwick, a native Mississippian, is founder and director of the International Conference on Elvis Presley, the most publicized academic conference on record. The *New York Times Magazine* calls him "perhaps academia's foremost Elvis scholar." He teaches literature and cultural studies at the University of Mississippi, where he has offered courses on Elvis Presley, James Brown, Howard Finster, and other southern folk geniuses. He holds degrees from Dartmouth, Oxford, and Yale, where he received his Ph.D. in comparative literature. For part-time employment while a student in Europe, he fed dairy cattle in Norway, trimmed trees in the Black Forest, and led bicycle tours for students from Vienna to London. In 1979–1981 he studied philosophy at the University of Freiburg as a Fulbright scholar. His diverse publications include works for television and cyberspace as well as English translations of German philosophy; he is the author of noted essays on Elvis, James Brown, and the material and musical cultures of the American South. Currently he is writer and creative consultant for the groundbreaking DigIcon CyberElvis project in Hollywood.

Will Campbell is the award-winning author of ten books, including *Brother to a Dragonfly*, *Forty Acres and a Goat*, *Providence*, and most recently *The Stem of Jesse: The Costs of Community at a 1960s Southern School*. A director of the Committee of Southern Churchmen in the 1960s, he spoke courageously from the pulpit against racism and resistance to social change in the segregated South. He lives with his wife of forty-six years on a farm near Mount Juliet, Tennessee.

Howard Finster, the self-described "Man of Visions," is one of America's best-known folk artists. Creator of over 30,000 works of sacred art, he credits the ghost of Elvis Presley for the inspiration of some of his masterpieces. He lives in Pennville, Georgia, where his outdoor sculpture park, Paradise Garden, is a unique tourist attraction.

Mark Gottdiener is professor and chair of sociology at the State University of New York in Buffalo. He is the author or editor of ten books, including *The Social Production of Urban Space*, *Postmodern Semiotics: Material Culture and the Forms of Postmodern Life*, and *The Theming of America: Dreams, Visions, and Commercial Spaces* (Westview, 1997). He is currently completing a book on Las Vegas.

Neal and Janice Gregory are authors of *When Elvis Died*, a critically acclaimed study of Elvis, the media, and popular culture. They live and work in Washington, D.C., where Janice Gregory is vice president of a trade association and Neal Gregory heads a public relations firm.

Katherine Herndon is curator of Delta Axis Contemporary Arts Center, Memphis, Tennessee.

Ernst Jørgensen is a compilation producer and researcher for RCA Records in New York. He is the producer of the prestigious box sets of Elvis's music of the 1950s, *The King of Rock 'n' Roll*; the 1960s, *From Nashville to Memphis;* and the 1970s, *Walk a Mile in My Shoes*. He is also coauthor of *Reconsider Baby*, the first sessionography of Elvis Presley's music. He lives in Markov, Denmark.

Joni Mabe, one of the South's most celebrated contemporary artists, is the creator of *The Traveling Panoramic Encyclopedia of Everything Elvis*, a roving museum of Elvis art, souvenirs, relics, and fashion that explores the magical, fetishistic world of Elvis Culture. Her Elvis installation was featured at the 1996 Summer Olympics. She lives in Athens, Georgia.

Paul and Elvis MacLeod, the self-styled "World's Number One Elvis Fans," are the creators of Graceland Too, their antebellum home that features an extensive collection of Elvis memorabilia. Located halfway between Tupelo and Memphis in Holly Springs, Mississippi, Graceland Too is open to the public twenty-fours hours a day, seven days a week, three hundred sixty-five days a year.

Bill Malone is professor of history at Tulane University. He is one of America's foremost authorities on country music, with such classic publications as *Country Music, USA: A Fifty-Year History, Southern Music/American Music*, and *Singing Cowboys, Musical Mountaineers: Southern Culture and the Roots of Country Music*. He has also compiled and annotated *The Smithsonian Collection of Classic Country Music*, a box set of original recordings from the 1920s to the 1980s.

Roger Manley is a photographer, folklorist, curator, and writer who lives in Durham, North Carolina. His photographs and essays on southern vernacular culture and outsider art have appeared in *Aperture Magazine, Art Papers, New Art Examiner, Raw Vision*, and many other publications. He has written or contributed to over thirty books, including *Home Made* (with Reynolds Price), *Howard Finster: Stranger from Another World* (with Howard Finster, Tom Patterson, and Victor Faccinto), *Plankhouse* (with Shelby Stephenson), and *Signs and Wonders: Outsider Art Inside North Carolina*.

Peter Nazareth is professor of English and African-American World Studies at the University of Iowa. In the spring of 1992 he received national attention for his course "Elvis as Anthology." He is the author of *In the Trickster Tradition: The Novels of Andrew Salkey, Francis Ebejer, and Ishmael Reed*.

John Shelton Reed is William Rand Kenan Jr. Professor of Sociology and director of the Institute for Research in Social Science at the University of North Carolina at Chapel Hill. One of the best-known commentators on southern culture, he is the author or editor of twelve books, including *My Tears Spoiled My Aim, and Other Reflections on Southern Culture* and *Kicking Back: Further Dispatches from the South*.

Ger Rijff is an Elvis Presley archivist and publisher. His volumes of Presleyana include *Faces and Stages: An Elvis Presley Time-Frame, 60 Million TV Viewers Can't Be Wrong!: Elvis' Legendary Performances on the Ed Sullivan Show*, and *Growing Up With the Memphis Flash*. He lives in Amsterdam, Holland.

Gene Smith, Elvis Presley's first cousin, was the young rock 'n' roller's right-hand man during the madcap first decade of Elvis's career. Born just a few weeks before Elvis, he in a way became the twin brother Elvis lost at birth. *Elvis's Man Friday*, his recently published memoirs of the Presley-Smith family saga in Tupelo and Memphis, is "an important treatment of American family values beyond political rhetoric," states one critic. He lives in Memphis.

Jon Michael Spencer is Tyler and Alice Haynes Professor of American Studies and professor of music at the University of Richmond. He is the author of numerous books on African-American music and musical culture, including *Blues and Evil*, *Sing a New Song: Liberating Black Hymnody*, and *The Rhythms of Black Folk: Race, Religion, and Pan-Africanism*.

Stephen Tucker is a music critic and historian who specializes in rockabilly and country-western music. His essay "Visions of Elvis: Changing Perceptions in National Magazines, 1956–1965" appeared in *Elvis: Images and Fancies*. He lives in New Orleans.

Index